THE BIRD WITH A BROKEN WING

To Carol ~
with Joy!
May all your
days be bright with
hope ~ your friend

DeeAnn Brandon

DeeAnn Brandon
2-12-03

𝒲ᵒ𝒲

Words on Wings, Ltd.
Bozeman, Montana

Published by:
Words on Wings, Ltd.
P.O. Box 1604
Bozeman, Montana 59771
U.S.A.
(406) 586-3808
Internet: www.wordsonwings.net
E-Mail: dab@wordsonwings.net

Manufactured in the United States of America
First Edition

ISBN: 0-9720123-0-3
LCCN: 2002105854

Cover artwork: Copyright © 2002 Rocky Hawkins
Back cover photograph: Copyright © 2002 Bruce Pitcher
Western Cafe photograph: Copyright © 2002 Curt Brandon

Cover, interior, and logo design by Kenneth and Talita Paolini
Paolini International, LLC
P.O. Box 32
Pray, Montana 59065
(406) 333-4475
Internet: www.factsource.com
E-Mail: paolini@factsource.com

In memory of
my beloved Calli

Contents

Prologue

The soul can crack without making a sound, crack like a bone. Mine was leaking terrifying thoughts and images late summer 1991 when I began to write my story. Stuffing words in the fracture like Super Glue, I hoped they'd hold until I could find out what was wrong with me. In the four-and-a-half years I'd sought help from professionals, no one could come up with a reason why I went insane at times. Prescription drugs made me worse and were addictive. I thought I'd been healing without the experts' help until one hot night in August of '91. I went crazy in the mall parking lot.

The next morning I began writing my story. I didn't ask myself the questions that were on the psychologist's diagnostic test, the personality test, and in his eyes when he said prescription drugs would put my thoughts in order. Since I'd celebrated President George Washington's birthday in Mrs. Watson's first grade class, I thought I knew truth just like the boy who never told a lie. And I did know truth. But growing up, I lost it among the lies. I wrote to find my way back to the little girl I once knew and an identity I could count on.

It was the identity that a child's prayer wouldn't let me forget: "Thy Kingdom come, Thy will be done, on earth as it is in heaven."

Thousands of pages later—some bound, some unbound—I don't see myself as a leaky vessel, but as a woman who knows that a broken soul can sing one song, if you listen closely.

> There are songs which can only be learned in the valley.
> No art can teach them; no rules of voice can make them
>   perfectly sung.
> Their music is in the heart.

They are songs of memory, of personal experience. They bring out their burden from the shadow of the past; they mount on the wings of yesterday.
George Matheson

The Bird with a Broken Wing is my song.

We stood on the threshold of paradise,
but the gates were slammed in our faces.
Ferdinand Freiligrath, 1848

1

It Could Be Paradise

The furnace in my home office vents hot air on my cold skin, making it tingle. My feet are numb from a morning walk, and my heart's beating fast, but not because I hurried. The discoveries I made on the nature trail make me feel like a child.

Silence sharpens my senses like nothing else. It was so quiet I could hear snow falling off branches. I didn't feel human and had to look at my own footprints to make sure I wasn't just a thought on God's mind. When a bird the size of an aspen leaf stood on a rock in the middle of the river and bathed while I watched, I felt as if we were speaking the same language. Wild mallards were swimming on the pond where it hasn't frozen over yet this winter. They seemed as content as I am to swim in the small lake east of town, long before the summer crowds start to come. The drakes were more interested in diving for food on the bottom than they were in the hens that swam nearby, which told me spring's a long way off yet. Just thinking about the scent of rose hips in bloom made me dizzy, but the woolly cattails took my mind off them. I never noticed how much like sheep's wool their down is until last year around March when I started walking in the mornings to let my imagination wander wherever it wanted to before I returned home to write.

All I have to do is see my own breath and I feel as if I've awakened in another Kingdom. One where a woman can accomplish anything she's able to imagine, even a woman who's passed her prime and fears there's not enough time left to live the dreams she squandered when she was younger. The angry world I live in hasn't really changed since I was a stubborn little girl who insisted it paid to fight back. No wonder my walks have become so important to nurturing my hard-won freedom from the dark side.

Walking in the cold quiet, my breathing is not all I hear. I hear voices not of this earth, and none of them are crying like we do here. God's voice is one of them. This morning He said, *I love you,*

DeeAnn, and my fears fell away like snow falls off frozen branches.

Immersed as I was in two worlds at the same time, I could have walked for miles on the way home from the Western Cafe where I join my husband Curt for coffee most mornings. I could have walked right passed my turnoff and kept going for a couple of miles until I crossed the snowy fields and pastures that used to belong to the Roths before they sold them to developers, which ironically is where the trail ends. Too often nature ends where man begins, around Bozeman, Montana. I needed to get home to write while my breath was still forming clouds in what could have been Paradise.

Sitting at the computer, I pick up the book that's been lying open on my desk for a couple of days. I read parts of it from time to time. This morning I sense there's a message in it for me. In this story, a man's about to commit suicide when he has a dream that changes his life. He says, "I suddenly found myself standing on that other earth, wallowing in the bright, gorgeous sunlight of a day in Paradise."

I don't think the guy's just dreaming in Fyodor Dostoyevsky's short story "The Dream of a Ridiculous Man." [1] On the brink of death, his spirit wakes him to the Truth of the real world he can live in, for a price: He has to give up the lies.

With all my heart, I want to live there too: ". . . they didn't need science to tell them how to live," he says. ". . . they'd found the language of the plants, and I'm sure they could understand them. The animals lived in peace with them, never attacked them, loved them; they were subdued . . . by love."

Sounds to me like God showed him heaven.

I remember another story told by a Lakota holy man who had a vision: The fish in the salty sea told him man was going to kill them and poison the waters, long before the atom bomb was tested in the ocean. The chill of truth makes me shiver. For most of my life, I've been told God only talks to Christians if we are saints. We'll go to heaven if we believe in Jesus Christ, but to hell if we don't. My friend Gloria Wells Norlin is Pembina Chippewa and Czechoslovakian. She talks with God, and she believes in Jesus. Gloria also believes the buffalo is sacred and goes to the slaughter fields outside

[1] Fyodor Dostoyevsky, *Dostoyevsky: Notes From the Underground*, trans. Andrew R. MacAndrew (New York: Penguin Group, 1961), 204-226.

Yellowstone Park to carve and package their meat before it rots. She personally delivers it to hungry people, many of them on reservations. Gloria told me once there are two forces at work within us, good and evil. The one that is fed the most rules the soul. My friend's true name is Life's Hard She Said. She's spent time in prison for a crime she didn't commit. Being Native American was crime enough for those who falsely accused her. Now she talks to whomever and does whatever she must to stop the Native American children from doing drugs and drinking alcohol and killing themselves. Because they have the highest rate of suicide in the nation, Gloria tries to help them have an identity they can be proud of as God's children.

Nine years ago I learned I have an identity to be proud of. "Thank you, God, for thinking of me." Imagine Him thinking the universe into existence, a galaxy at a time.

The other world is so real to me at times, I wonder if this world is the illusion. Until this moment, I had forgotten what happened to me in Glacier National Park several years ago. It was my first time to drive through the magnificent forest, but Curt had traveled the Going-to-the-Sun Highway on his motorcycle years before. It was summertime and I was feeling homeless, realizing a second marriage wasn't going to give me the sense of permanence I thought it would. Having no doubt Curt was the man I loved, I wanted to start an album of our lives together and fill it with pictures that would give me the security I thought I needed. Just before noon, the sun was sparkling on the river, looking like diamonds spilled from the sky. We were taking pictures of each other as we stood on the banks of the diamond river when the film ran out. Once we were on the road again, all I could think about was how my eyes hurt from the splendor around me.

That's when it happened. Through the naked eye, I saw the river. Yet, in my spirit, I saw a range of rugged red cliffs and jagged peaks aglow in the setting sun. It was noon, but twilight was upon the mountains within.

Leaving the river behind us, we climbed the Going-to-the-Sun Highway until the earth seemed to fall off on the other side of the rail—when there was one. I forgot about the splendor I thought I'd imagined until the sun began to set on the mountains ahead. Like ghosts of nature, the glowing red peaks I had seen in my spirit were actually looming above us.

Breathless over the mystery, I tried to let the truth sink in. Is this earth the mirror of eternity, and eternity the earth's uncorrupt twin? I felt as if I'd brought my new husband home for a vacation.

Dostoyevky's dreamer and I may share the same reality. Inspired, I read on, ". . . somehow everything inside me knew that this sun was exactly the same as the other, its copy, its double . . . light kindred to that which had given me birth warmed my heart and brought it back to life. And, for the first time since the grave, I felt alive."

Tears blur my vision. In the fight for my life, all eternity stood on my side. Truly, I know the light the dreamer's talking about. Yesterday I put the story of how I rose from the grave of my mind on the shelf, but I wanted to throw it in the fire where it could smolder with other dreams as the winter of my life grows colder and colder. It was just a feeling.

I don't feel cold now. He's here.

Remember Jacob, God says.

Jacob? What I remember is Tenny DeWitt's bronze of Jacob's legendary fight with God for his identity. When I was writing about my friend's sculptures, close to forty of them, he told me that he had to wrestle his own angel to create the monument he called *The Eternal Struggle*. I saw only the bronzed piece but can picture the sculptor forming the armature from steel and wire. I can imagine him adding clay to the wire skeleton in layers. His hands are the primary tool of his craft, instruments of revelation. Using every part of them, he smoothes, shapes, scrapes, and refines. It's taken years for him to complete some of his monuments.

I think of the unpublished book I almost burned, my story of healing, and another on freedom. Maybe they're like Mr. DeWitt's sculptures, and this memoir I'm writing now is another layer. Maybe the struggle of life shapes my eternal identity, one page at a time.

But what about Jacob's struggle with the angel?

As the story goes, he is a wealthy rancher who sends his wives, children, hired hands, and fat animals across the river to Canaan, ahead of him. Alone on this side of paradise, he's approached by a stranger. They're in a fight before Jacob knows how it started. Crippled by a brutal blow to his thigh, he recognizes his opponent.

Clinging to the angel of God, he says, "I want you to bless me." The angel says, "Your name shall no longer be Jacob, but Israel, for you have striven with God and with men and prevailed." Israel means soldier of God.

Both Gloria and Jacob have special names. I remember times God called me "warrior." He also called me a "bird with a broken wing." My soul was broken.

After nine years I can still remember how shocked I was when the psychologist Dr. D diagnosed my battle with flashbacks of rape: "You have an addiction to the dark side. You didn't choose it, but an addiction that's been forced on you from the outside is harder to break than one a person chooses." Lies made me crazy.

Years later I can smell them on a person's breath, spy them on billboards, see them over television, and catch their scent on the wind before I hear them spoken. I'm a hound on their heels. Lies are the illegal drug that has run right in front of our eyes, and if a woman's not careful, she's in bondage before she knows it. Depression, anxiety, and low self-worth form a suffocating circle around pain that has no center and begs for relief. Addictions are the lies your body and mind tell you, the need that never gets filled. The stranger that approaches just before you cross the river to Paradise is you, and the struggle for identity seems to be eternal.

When the truth sets you free, for a while you're like an angry dog with a bone, shaking it and growling. Stretching out on the rug of ownership, you gnaw until its juices slide down your throat.

Now what? you think, feeling ready to take on the world, if you have to.

There is a bigger picture that I want you to see.

Yes, just like that the Spirit speaks, proving you chose the winning team to fight on.

A bigger picture? Instantly I imagine the splash that a rock makes when you throw it in the water. Circles multiply outward. Curt and my love works like that. Now that our children are adults, the ripples come back to us in waves.

Maybe God's talking about a bigger picture yet. I think of my paintings. Until lately they've been a beginner's efforts to speak a language she's never spoken before. Now there's a place that won't let go of me. Is it Paradise that demands huge canvases—huge for me anyway—and tubes of oils that I can't afford? My son Ryan says it's hard to tell where this setting is, if there is any place in this world that has such color. He and his fiancé Jen have traveled to some spectacular locations—surfed and dived off Australia's coast—so they've seen sunsets on the ocean horizon I can only imagine.

Curt loves the story the brilliant colors tell and can't wait to see the next painting and the next. Aching to go there, I tell him these paintings aren't dreams. Each scene is real to me. Is it Montana? Israel? I saw a documentary recently on the Holy Land that had the same rugged slopes, the high plateaus, halos of clouds.

On canvas the mountains are as alive as the people who live in the village covered by their shadow. Below the sun-licked peaks, the land flows like a sea, a prism of color reflecting the sky. If there were no land or sky, just forms and colors, I'd still recognize the truth of this place. Matter is frozen light, I've heard. When nature is broken down into its smallest component, maybe matter and spirit are one.

With my paintbrush in hand, I feel like a friend to scientists who measure the immeasurable with quarks and superstrings and believe they'll find the Law of Everything. For them, faith is also the substance of research and revelation, the seed of invention. Perhaps the search for truth makes children of all of us. When we are abandoned to our passion, anything seems possible. At least this place I paint makes me think so. Is it heaven? Earth?

I need to know. It could be Paradise.

Suddenly I have to find a mirror. Above the sink in the bathroom, I look for a warrior in the glass, but all I see is a woman who has a tear trail on her upper right cheek just under the eye. It's deep. I wanted more laugh lines. If the mirror showed inside me, there would be a scar for every battle. I've lost many, but the fact I'm alive says I won a couple that mattered. All warriors don't fight with guns and missiles, I guess. Some just stand their ground. It's all they can do, and hope it's the high ground, like I'm hoping now. . . .

What if I paint this mysterious place in words and take you into the village to meet the people who live there? Will shades of trust and betrayal, innocence and evil reveal truths that reach beyond memories and the things I know? If I listen to my heart, will I find Paradise on this angry earth where man has learned how to lie, has come to love it, and has grown "to appreciate the beauty of untruth?" Or is that Kingdom where birds and children are safe only in dreams and paintings? I hope this story will tell.

2

Martin's Cafe

The coach is at the door at last;
The eager children, mounting fast
And kissing hands, in chorus sing:
Good-bye, good-bye, to everything!
    Robert Louis Stevenson
    "Farewell to the Farm"
    A *Child's Garden of Verses*, 1916

When that light within is shining strong and there's a bare canvas in front of you, it doesn't matter where you begin. Load your brush with a blazing blend, warm as a stoked fire in winter, and paint a shape you like off-center.

On a cold night in January, the old depot café in Livingston, Montana, feels as warm to me as that first brush stroke on canvas. The year 2000 seems to mean nothing more than another chance to gather with friends when Curt and I walk through the door of Martin's family diner. "Millennial madness" or Y2K is last year's headlines, and photos of early calves are on the cover of *Agri-News*, but ranchers must take time out from chores to eat like the rest of us.

The rich smell of fresh coffee wafts by me as the waitress leads us to a table. Looking around the room, I notice how Martin's Cafe wears its years without pride or the need to apologize for its humble appearance. Framed in barn wood and centered on dark paneling above the ice cream freezer is the fishing report. Across the top of the slick white board, "Hatch Finder" is written in tall bold letters. Scribbled beneath with a black felt pen is this sentence, "The best place to catch fish is in the water." Winter has laid its cold blanket on the land as if it plans to stay awhile. As soon as the Yellowstone thaws, this place will be packed with fishermen who've come here for years to see which kinds of flies the fish are rising for in the blue ribbon rivers of Montana.

Tonight mostly locals stand in line at the special Sunday buffet with Curt and me. I feel like a local even though we live in Bozeman. Bozeman was still a cow town when I moved there from Southern California twenty-six years ago. If you're escaping death threats like I was or digging deep as you can into this earth for roots to hold onto, one cow town feels as good as another in Montana, especially when you eat at old cafés like Martin's.

The line at the buffet moves slowly, but I don't mind. Soon it will be my turn to sample food I can almost taste by its smell. The slow flow gives me more time to enjoy the familiar banter I hear going on between friends and families. It reminds me of why Curt and I meet for coffee at the Western Cafe in Bozeman most mornings. From what the old timers have told us, strangers started becoming neighbors there long before the Second World War. It's a priceless capsule in time that I don't want to lose sight of. It's where I go to taste the salt of the earth among ranchers, veterans, and retired wise men and their faithful wives who've loved them through the good times and the bad. Some of the older cowboys have broken bones that have healed crooked, but they know truth when they hear it, and I respect them for that. The Western's a place where waitresses seem like family and where artists, attorneys, stockbrokers, and mechanics discover what they have in common and become friends. Now and then a movie star will show up wearing Levi's, boots, and dark glasses, trying to fit in. Or a freelance writer will snap pictures and do a story on the place, which eventually ends up framed and hung on the pitted wood paneling after the article's featured in some travel, food, or wine magazine.

Several times a year local and state politicians stop to eat a bite and find out what's going on at America's grassroots. Cultivating support for the next election, most know that old timers look for two things right off: a strong handshake and a man or woman who looks them straight in the eye.

Regulars like Curt and I don't care what the rest of the world thinks about the café. We go there to start the day, whether I revise a chapter while he reads the paper, or friends join us to visit. First thing most mornings, I walk a mile down the nature trail to join my husband and the others. I can hardly wait to catch the scents of hash browns, pancakes, and fried bacon that hang around the café just off the corner of Church and Main.

Martin's is bigger, but it feels the same, a place where people can come together to learn what loving your neighbor means. Today Curt and I swam and soaked in the steaming water at Chico Hot Springs until our stomachs started to growl; then he said, "Let's go to Martin's now." The springs are halfway between Livingston and Yellowstone Park, so he drove the back route I love, through Pine Creek to town. He was probably hoping I'd forget how hungry I was, oohing and aahing over the spectacular ranch country in Paradise Valley, acting as if I was seeing it for the very first time. Joined at the seam by the fluid silver thread called the Yellowstone, guarded by the sheer cliffs of the Absaroka Range above, the moody valley puts me in a trance every time we drive through it. Caught in the silent language between light and shadows, a yearning grips me so deep inside it makes me want to stop and listen to the east wind as it blows through trees, over rocks, off the obsidian river, and works like a soft velvet cloth polishing granite peaks. Here I feel as if I was born to talk with birds instead of people. And Curt knows it; that's why he drove the back way along the bench below the mountains for the hundredth time.

Still feeling cozy and warm from the steaming water and the drive that rocked me like a baby in the cradle of the Rockies, I listen to the friendly hum at the tables while I scoop salads on my plate. Merry notes to happy songs make me smile the way I used to as a child when Mom sang me to sleep after I said my prayers at night.

Low as the roll of thunder in the wild Montana sky, a woman's voice calls out, "You want my horses, Hal?"

I turn around. She's about my age, mid-fifties, a short woman who walks tall. Dressed in Levi's and a suede western jacket, she strides across the big crowded room toward an old guy in coveralls who's sitting by himself.

"Sure, Sandy. I'll take your horses, not to buy, but I'll board them until you get back on your feet."

"Could be awhile." She laughs.

I don't think she's laughing inside, as I wait my turn for barbequed ribs.

At his table, they lower their voices, and I remember back nine years when I came to this café in the mornings to count my blessings and recover from a decade of severe losses. Not once, but several times a week, from January through late April 1991, I sat at one of these tables. Formica and chrome, I notice now, just like the one where my family ate meals when I was a girl. Divorce and depression were behind me that January; I had two great kids, a job I loved, and a man who loved me. Then my daughter died. Spring didn't end the long, severe winter of my life in '91.

This woman hasn't said she's lost nearly everything that matters to her, like I did, but she looks distraught. Too many friends struggle to keep their farm and ranch operations going for me to miss the meaning of the catch in her voice. Husbands and wives work two jobs to survive on their farms. Their bodies break down at the same rate the equipment does. That doesn't stop them from working hard all day after they've sat up all night to ease their pain, long after doctors have given up on them, or vice versa. When their enemy is drought or hail, it's tragic enough, but at least a person can hope next year's weather will be kinder, to make up for the losses. When their enemy's big money, the rules by which good people live set them up for the fall.

I've lost my appetite, so I pass up ribs and walk to our table.

You're not eating much for being so hungry." Curt sits down with a plateful. His skin glows from the combination of hot water and the winter chill. Silver streaks shimmer in his thick hair, and his honest blue eyes are asking me questions.

"That woman can't afford to keep her horses," I tell him.

"I heard."

Did he hear what I heard? I wonder. "She's in danger of losing her identity, what she stands for. What I feel I stand for too." I want to talk about it.

"It's becoming a common story, isn't it?" Curt glances over at the woman.

"But it's so wrong. How long can the ordinary farmer survive? What's going to happen to the Hams?"

Cliff Ham, one of our rancher friends, isn't the only person who's told us there are four big packing companies and four grain companies that control the market prices, forcing farmers and ranchers to either go bankrupt or work for the corporations.

"Maybe pig cities are fine for some countries, but not mine." Why can't life be as simple as I used to think it was when old western movies made sure the good guys ran the crooked banker Bad Bart and his gang out of town?

"Pig cities?" Curt looks lost.

"Remember the program we watched on corporate farms a few months ago that showed where farming and ranching are going? Remember the huge pig farms the big corporations are building in South America? The reporter said they're in America too."

Curt thinks a minute. "Yeah. They showed complexes of sick or dead chickens that the corporation had poisoned because the farmers didn't follow the rules."

Nowadays Bad Bart hires lobbyists to pay politicians to change the rules. Independent ranchers don't have the time or money to pay lawyers to fight for them. They don't trust lawyers anyway.

"What stuck in my mind was how the big corporations built the pig cities in valleys that looked a lot like Paradise Valley, the Gallatin Valley, and the Shields."

"And you're seeing pig cities in Paradise?" Curt asks.

Irritated, I say, "No, I'm thinking about the food we're eating and how good it is. Cliff said their meat's no good. Documentaries seem to support his opinions. Corporations don't always use organic farming and crop rotation, which nourish the land and animals. They poison them both with chemicals, anything to stimulate production and ensure big profits. What do you think?"

Curt just looks at me. "You've been doing your homework, haven't you? Are you going to write a book on the family farm or something?"

He hasn't asked for a heavy discussion tonight. We are supposed to be having fun, first swimming at Chico, then eating dinner at Martin's. I try to smile and take a deep breath. Curt's my party, and the big room's shrinking to the color of his eyes. Where is my faith?

"Can you imagine going to the Western and not seeing cowboy hats that dirt and sweat hold together?" I haven't thought about Dad's hat for years, but I can see it clearly now: It was tan felt, the old style, and he wore it everywhere, even to the outhouse.

"Okay." Curt cuts a big bite of roast beef and rolls it in gravy. "Get it all out, so you can eat."

"We've talked about this before." I take a sip of hot tea. "We talked about it before we heard that five hundred farms and ranches were going under every week in this country. We talked about it five or six years ago when we first drove all over Montana to meet your real estate clients. Some of them were fighting crooked bankers, judges, attorneys, and the IRS to save their ranches and farms. Remember the man the IRS robbed of everything he'd worked his whole life for who ended up in a mental institution?"

Curt nods. "That wasn't long before we started hearing about the revolt of the Freemen and Militia."

The last time we drove through Roundup, clerks and waitresses were on the alert for FBI agents who grilled them with questions. Freemen were locked up in the local jail, and a quiet was on the town that seemed unnatural. The sleepy cow town we had always enjoyed so much that we made reservations to stay over at a cozy motel was on the front lines of a deadly standoff. The tension didn't go away when we turned the lights off to go to sleep at night.

"It seems so long ago." The years don't seem friendly. "Now some of those men are in prison."

"Where they probably belong," Curt says. "Meanwhile, the ones who follow the rules and respect the law work their butts off trying to survive."

"Like John Ham, you mean?"

"Yes, like John."

Cliff's dad was born on the old homestead. Curt and I think the tall, lean man looks like he's been chiseled out of the cliff above their place instead of born of woman like the rest of us. If the Rockies ever shook to the ground, John looks like he'd still be standing, probably figuring out a way to put the mountains back where they belong.

Now I have a question. "Did you hear Cliff say that a farmer can't use the seeds Monsanto sells them more than once, instead of year after year? They've manipulated the genetics to make more money."

"No. But I heard them say that, as much as they need computerized tractors, they don't like having to depend on greedy mechanics instead of working on their own equipment like they used to." Curt looks beyond me. "All four of us kids worked on the ranch when I was growing up. My older brother was the mechanic who helped Dad work on our equipment when it broke down. Ranching was in his blood, I guess. I wanted to move on."

"Have you ever been sorry?"

"I miss the ranch, fishing on the Milk River with my dog Betsy, and I miss the picnics Mom fixed for us to eat after the work was done. If I'd never learned I could play baseball better than the other boys when I was ten years old, maybe I would have learned to like repairing machinery in temperatures so cold they froze skin to steel."

I nod. Curt's trophies and medals tell me he listened to his heart when he was ten years old and it treated him good in the years that followed. In sports and business, he was a champion, but his first marriage was not a ranch kid's dream. Right after she divorced him, he had a near fatal motorcycle accident that changed the only identity he'd known for thirty-four years.

Stripped of our youthful dreams, our hearts were about all we had to follow when we married on 30 April, during that long cold spring of 1991. A win-win combination, Curt said. Neither of us wants our life to look like the rusted old parts I've seen piled up in ranchers' shops and yards, icons to the rugged independence their owners stood for. Sometimes I feel like one of those old parts, especially when someone tries to tell me how to think, like thinking for yourself is outdated and doesn't work anymore.

This isn't the first time I've thought of Masada, the high mountain fortress overlooking the Dead Sea, where the Romans wiped out the line of Judah in A.D. 73. Rather than give up their freedom to worship God, as they had for centuries, five thousand zealots resisted Roman legions from the mountain top for two years until a mammoth weapon broke through stone walls. Rather than surrender their identity, they all committed suicide in their last stand for freedom. I wonder if America's last stand for freedom is being made on her fields and pastures.

Some experts believe the Roman Empire began to crumble when it abandoned its farmers, the ones who knew the language of the earth before science showed them how to reap a harvest. Perhaps when a society ignores its roots in the earth, it severs its roots in heaven. And a woman suddenly finds herself desperate to restore the connection. She paints places she doesn't recognize and writes about people and places she does. I don't know for sure, but it's possible.

3

The Open Range Is Gone

Like Dad's worn felt hat, the old cafés feel permanent, but I know they're not. The Western's for sale. Tonight I'm feeling the connection between this land and myself, strong as blood. The bond is close to what I felt on the nature trail the other morning.

I inhale the smell of the food on my plate and taste every dish. Although my back's turned to the ranch woman, I know when she's getting up from her chair. Her friend pats her shoulder, his big thick hand, a grizzly paw, gentle as a sow with her cub.

"Listening to that woman took me back." I'm thinking out loud rather than asking for conversation.

"And?" Curt's eyes turn into steel doors for a moment.

"She sounds like she's losing everything. . . ."

"We both know how that feels," Curt says. Emotion darkens the scars around his left eye and cheek. We don't talk about the past as much as we used to. A phone call in the night would make us break out in a sweat. Experts on torture and brainwashing list startling victims in their sleep as an effective tactic. If an armed police squad had broken down our front door those nights, we wouldn't have felt more tormented and helpless. Sounding like a siren in the night, his ex-wife would call. I saw her as a crisis looking for a place to happen, a grudge counting the days between paybacks. If their kids weren't in the line of fire, we could have left the phone off the hook.

"Don't you love them anymore? Don't you care about us?" Whatever it took, Vera held on to the man she'd thrown away.

Now that the kids are grown, and the nightmare over, I try to replace the painful memories with gentler ones. I picture the soft smile on her face as she watched her oldest daughter dance with the handsome groom at their wedding reception a few years ago. Curt, she, and I were almost like old friends that night. If only we could have been.

A wave of loneliness crashes down on me as I watch the ranch woman hug one friend after another on her way out of the café. Most of them offer to help her if she needs anything. There are times when no one can do anything for you. Strength has to come from within. No matter how hard I try to shake off a helpless feeling, it clings. It seems like yesterday I found out I didn't have as much control as I thought I did over my life or anyone else's, not even my own kids', the one responsibility God had trusted me with.

"You lost much more than horses." Curt knows my thoughts.

The woman nervously fingers strands of her hair. She's probably already survived more than she'll ever tell anyone. Now she has to farm out her horses and whatever else she can't afford to take care of, until fragments of her soul are scattered everywhere. It could force her to the edge of sanity.

"Everyone has a breaking point," I tell him. "Remember the suicide letter written by that Iowa farmer to his family?"

He nods. "The man had wanted to farm from the time he was a kid and had tried to survive as long as he could, but was tired out and couldn't fight 'them' anymore." Curt pauses. "We've both been there."

In the back of my head, I can hear the Surgeon General giving his special New Year Report on mental illness to the nation on television. Apparently, we still don't know what causes mental illness or how to prevent it, but we do know that drugs can cure it.

Talking back to the television, I challenged him, "So you think Prozac is getting to the root of our problems?" I was sick of TV commercials that suggested drugs could cure anything. Too many Americans are on "meds." Teenagers and young children are taking antidepressants and other drugs for neuroses. Not even pets are exempt from the "cure."

My experience with prescription drugs has no doubt colored my thinking. The three weeks I threw up withdrawing from a "non-addictive" antidepressant isn't the only reason I'm suspicious of the pill cure and those who prescribe and sell it.

Thinking out loud, I say, "The dark side doesn't take over all at once; it moves in a little at a time on the back of despair, pain, anger, and loss of vision."

Curt keeps eating and lets me think.

That's how depression moved in on me when I was in my prime. I didn't realize what was happening at the time. I didn't know a woman can crack like a coffee cup and drain her core dry. How could I have known antidepressants can cause more problems than they solve when the psychologist said I needed to take them to order my thoughts and get some sleep at night? Doctors didn't seem to know any more about side effects than their patients did. They didn't have any better grip on reality either, most of the time.

"Why so quiet now?" Curt looks at me like he knows why I'm quiet. His eyes have the same look mine did when my son—who was about four years old—knelt on his baby rabbit's tail and accidentally pulled it off. The tiny creature screamed a scream that still draws goose bumps to the surface of my skin, even on a hot day.

Curt's shivers are in his eyes.

Looking at my cold white mashed potatoes, I feel shame drain the blood from the surface of my skin. After all these years. I thought I'd dealt with it.

He reaches for my hand. "It wasn't your fault."

"Blame doesn't matter when you're the one who's given yourself a black eye." I want to slam my fist on the table.

Curt gets up to go back to the buffet. I stay and remember. It was midsummer 1993. For the first time since I remembered the rapes two years before, I was writing about them in my story of healing. It was like walking on land mines and daring them to blow up—a survival exercise. The more I resisted triggers, the stronger I grew, but that summer Curt and I were both vulnerable. He said something that triggered a flashback for me. Engulfed in emotional pain, I staggered into the bedroom where I doubled up my fists and beat my head and face. Desperate to stop myself, I cried out, "It's a lie. It's a lie." I was too late.

Less than twenty minutes later, I sat on the office floor and cut out pictures from magazines. Laying them out in front of me like a mirror to look into, I chose to believe this was my identity. One photograph was of a tall oak tree rising out of heavy mist. Another showed a herd of Clydesdale horses running so fast over an open range their hooves didn't touch the ground. The picture of a lake was as serene and deep as God's love. Crying, I said, "This is who I am. This is who I am! Strong, free, loved. I didn't deserve what Dad did or what I'm doing to myself."

Curt came in about then and asked what I was doing. He helped me up, and we walked into the living room where he sat down, pulled me onto his lap, and into his arms. "It's okay, little warrior," he said. "It's going to be okay. I'm sorry."

When I called our psychologist Dr. D and told him what I'd done, he said the more healed I was, the harder I'd fall, and asked if I could have my story done by 1 September. He used words like best–seller. He said it could help people who also suffered from problems caused by rejection, abandonment, and sexual abuse. The next morning I covered my bruises with makeup, put on the scarlet western hat that Curt had recently bought me on a trip to Southern California, then drove to the Western Cafe to work on what I called "the book."

"What are you smiling about?" Curt asks.

"Scarlet."

"You mean your 'give 'em hell' hat?" He looks proud of me.

Even though I had to go to the emergency room twice with severe stomach and chest pains before the book was done, I didn't abuse my own body again. On the morning of 1 September, I handed the manuscript to Dr. D and then went to my writers group where good friends celebrated my victory. It wasn't the last celebration I've had in nine years, but it was the only one I've ever had for the hardest job I've done in my whole life.

"Have some olives." Curt puts a few on my plate before he sits.

"Thanks, honey," but I'm not hungry. Dr. D never told me that after I healed, I'd still feel like a stranger in this world that revolves around man's approval. Writing has given me the distance I've needed to separate my thinking from everyone else's.

"Our battles have made us both stronger," Curt says.

I give him a look.

"The village is an angry one, Curt, and we live right in the middle of it."

"What village?" he asks.

"It's something in my book." He probably isn't sure which book I'm talking about. He listened to me read every chapter of the first one, my story of healing. I don't have the heart to read to him now.

"When are you going to read to me again?"

"I don't know."

A middle-aged woman walks across the room carrying a plate piled with sweet potatoes and green beans. Her ankles are so swollen they hang over the edge of her shoes. "Will we see you at church Wednesday night, Grace?" she says to the ranch woman.

I look at Curt. "I'm glad to hear that her name's Grace. She needs it."

"We've survived, DeeAnn."

I know it's true.

"Eat. Your food's getting cold." He starts to eat his dinner.

"Is surviving what's important?" I don't care if he's shaking his head. I want more than survival. "I want to run with abandon like wild horses run across the open range."

Curt puts his fork down and looks at me. "The open range is almost gone. If my real estate seminar was accurate, property rights are a thing of the past."

This fire building inside me is meant for good, not destruction.

Curt takes a bite out of the soft center of his roll. I know he cares. Long before President Clinton was impeached by the House of Representatives for lying under oath, my husband worried about a leader who was involved in scandal after scandal. The documentary we saw before he was elected for a second term exposed a list of crimes he had never been tried for. Neither of us needed to hear the testimony of Arkansas' former Supreme Court Justice to know the president made a mockery of the law. Truth and justice aren't always two sides of the same coin any more.

A memory stops time for a minute. I can hear the poet Maya Angelou delivering her poem "On the Pulse of Morning" at the president's inauguration eight years ago:

> The Rock cries out to us today, you may stand upon me, . . .

> Lift up your eyes upon
> This day breaking for you.
> Give birth again
> To the dream.

I thought the Rock was God, and He was Truth. I thought the poet was speaking to me, and I was listening.

"Do you remember what the reporter said about the National Farm Bureau on *60 Minutes* the other night?" Curt asks.

"Not exactly."

"The National Farm Bureau uses the ranchers' and farmers' money to lobby for big business and corporate farms. They lobby for their political agenda regardless of what the family farmers really need to survive. Money goes to fatten the Bureau's stock while families starve and farmers lose their land."

I take a small bite of Curt's turkey with gravy, but anticipation and conflict have curbed my appetite.

"Sometimes choices are taken out of a person's hands." Curt stands up and heads for the buffet. He's probably going to get a second helping of the juicy roast beef. You can tell he's been raised on a ranch, whereas I lived on the farm just long enough to make me think I belonged there.

"I think I'll get some turkey and gravy." I follow him across the room. It's the first time I notice that country music is on the radio, which on any other day would make me tap my feet, move my hips, and wish I had a guitar to strum. Tonight it makes me sad.

It's been a long time since I've thought of Dad, thought about what could have been if he'd chosen to change, even at the last minute, before he died. Growing up didn't change my little girl dream that our family could be one of those miracles Jesus worked in the Bible.

Dad's dad, Grandpa Jones, used to play the spoons to "country." He tried to teach me, but I never learned how. I don't like sweet pickles but drop one on my plate. Grandma Jones always served hers homemade, so I take a couple the way I used to whenever I went to her and Grandpa's house for dinner. Grandma's thick noodles and gravy was a blue ribbon plate.

I move down the line, looking under lids to find some. They're under the second one, so I scoop a few next to green salad, along with a whole lot of memories.

In my mind's eye, I can see Dad wiping tears from his eyes with his grease-stained fingers whenever Eddie Arnold sang "Amazing Grace" on the radio. When the "Tennessee Waltz" came over the air, he used to stop in the middle of whatever he was doing and call Mom to come dance with him on the hardwood floor in the living room. Those two put the stars in the sky when they square danced at the park near our house. We'd all go down to- gether once in a while. They danced and twirled while my older brother, Rod, little sister, Connie, and I sat on the grass and watched. Country music brought out the best in Dad the way I like to think farming made him the man I loved. It's been hard to think about the way I saw him as a child since I saw who he really was, nine years ago.

I've opened a window in Annie's world. That's what my fam- ily called me when I was a little girl. She would never have let a few disappointments get her down. Feeling her innocence and the trust she had in Dad, I imagine reaching for his hand and tell my- self it's safe to hold it for a little while, now that he's gone. If I hadn't smelled the potato cellar and felt its cool quiet, hadn't watched barn swallows dip and dive from the rafters, or wakened before dawn to ride next to Dad in the truck and watch fields turn pink when the sun came up, I might have missed my chance to learn the language of trust before he made trust dangerous. I spent my early years on the farm; the past nine have made me wonder if they weren't the most important years of my life.

Back at our table, I realize my deep roots in this earth may be the reason I've survived. Except for my daughter, Calli, they may be my strongest link with heaven, where truth's light never fades. On this special night, as the year 2000 unfolds, I'm holding onto that link with all my heart because the shaking's going to come. It always does.

In my mind, country music is playing to the same crowd, but Martin's is flooded with a different light that's transforming every face, including mine. I can feel the wrinkles disappear as a burden is lifted from my heart. And the woman who's farming out her horses is back at her table, laughing with friends, looking like a girl with a halo of flaming red hair.

"What are you smiling about?" Curt asks. The scene disap- pears from my mind. But in my heart it's still there, as if I lit a match in paradise and it burned bright for a little while.

"Paradise," I tell him, feeling stronger than ever that it's time to plant again, even if I'm the only one who ever sees the harvest in the privacy of my own office where the smell of the potato cellar is never forgotten.

"Let's go home, DeeAnnie," he says, and my knees buckle. Sometimes I think he knows me better than I know myself. My heart cries a little as I look at this man who gave it a reason to beat again. We shared a vision once.

I can't let go of another dream, not this dream. It's who I am.

4

Green So Deep

The next morning, Curt's body feels warm next to mine. The bedroom is too cold and dark to get out of bed, but I need to. My heart wants to spill itself on paper. I can't miss this chance to listen. Time's my keeper, although I wish it wasn't. I'm not that free yet.

On the way to my office, I glance out my studio window. Morning sun glistens on frosty branches, reminding me of the light that changed Martin's Cafe into Paradise last night. I wonder if that light would shine all the time if reason didn't argue, "It's just your imagination." The light shines in these paintings, I think, as I look at several where they stand on easels, like windows of my soul.

A yearning twists my heart like a mother's gentle hands, urging me to see something I don't want to see, to listen to something I don't want to hear for fear of losing it again. But I can't resist these colors, sounds, and scents that pull me into them. I can't resist green so deep it makes me feel like I can swim on the bottom of the ocean, makes me close my eyes and imagine that I am. I can't resist colors that make me want to get lost in them. Wonder so big it swallows my fears for the moment, makes me feel like a child running barefoot on shifting sand. Oh, God, is that what my paintings are—Annie, running barefoot on my heart again?

My excitement tells me to let her run wherever she wants to. Walking across the hall to my office, I sink into my soft chair and read the chapters I've written. Maybe the child who listened to the song of the meadowlark wants to paint this story now. Maybe she wants to hear the language of the streams and mountains, hear those voices from the other Kingdom where colors are alive and have the power to reach right down inside of a woman and massage her soul if she lets them. I've listened to the language of the seasons for a long time now. No one ever had to tell me that there's a reason the forest bursts into gold, crimson, and scarlet in the fall, a reason the air flutters like wings against your face just before it freezes for the longest season of all. It isn't just a scientific thing either, but a mystery to behold in solitude, with praise and awe.

Awe is what I feel as I look at the words on the page again. They've become a canvas of colors. I've never seen a word that doesn't suggest a color, feeling, or movement. Put to music, each one marks time. And without it, you'd know a beat was missing. These word-colors begin to talk to me like a playground of children, all calling my name at the same time, "Watch me, Annie. See how high I can swing, how long I can hang from the bars, how fast I can slide!" Some come up close enough to smell my breath while others hide and beg me to come find them. Like secrets waiting to be told, images flow from liquid, promising to reveal the story, if I will only listen.

In my excitement, I laugh out loud and feel like playing. My work is play. The painting is there. I can see it. You can't miss what the colors are saying if you imagine the Rockies on a winter's day, smell fresh coffee in a warm café. Imagine a woman who's trying to survive in a strange land, a couple who is not sure the hard times are behind them, and a mountain of old tractor, truck, and wagon parts that remind you dreams can rust if you don't take care of them, and you'll be here with me. Now imagine a brave slash of yellow, trying to hide in a field of stubble, and you'll know why I can't ignore that little girl who grew up fast on the farm in Colorado.

Annie's voice interrupts my thoughts. She's scolding me, *Have you forgotten already? Have you grown so old that you've forgotten me again after you promised that you wouldn't?*

I can't swallow for the tears that block my throat. *I haven't forgotten you, but I've never found a way to keep you close to me. It's not safe to be a child for long in this world.*

My excuse is pathetic. I can't believe I'm hearing her voice now, clear as if it was on the outside instead of the inside of my head. Mostly, I feel as if I failed myself when I let her go a second time, as if she was an orphan destined to wander the streets alone.

If she hadn't appeared when I needed her before, I could have lost my mind for good. When I told Dr. D I had found Annie, I was afraid he would tell me I had a split personality or something worse, but he didn't. He smiled and said, "Everyone has a child within, and I hope you never lose her again. She's the creative part of you, the one who could run naked in the field and not be ashamed. I hope she never grows past sixteen."

If you've ever tried to glue something back together that's been broken, you'll understand how every part is a whole piece in itself as well as a piece of the whole, like my glass hummingbird when it shattered on the kitchen floor. Healing from flashbacks of rape, I could see and feel each fragment of my soul until the jagged edges finally softened and blended into one identity. When Dr. D was talking to me, I could feel Annie warm up to him. He wasn't going to label her like the others had. He didn't require regular appointments and prescribe pills that would make me sink deeper into darkness like the first therapist had almost five years before.

Dr. D said something I've never forgotten: "Annie's the perfect match to the boy in Curt." A match made in heaven, he called us. Sometimes the doctor was as inspired as any poet I've ever heard.

Nevertheless, my husband was the first to see Annie, the first to love her enough when it was critical to saving my life and mind. Fragile as a bird with a broken wing, Annie came out of the shadows for this man. It seems like yesterday now. From the green velour chair where I was sitting, I could see storm clouds gathering outside the living room window in the fall of 1991 when a memory swallowed me into another time and place. A shade snapped up. I was on a bed, drugged. There was a camera and bright lights. "Oh, God, not this," I said, burdened with shame and an identity I didn't want, a past I thought I couldn't live with. The Holy Spirit had been revealing the truth to me for several days.

"Curt, I don't want anyone to know." How could I endure another memory? I had to. My freedom depended upon it.

My husband made me look him in the eyes. "To know what, DeeAnn? That you are one tough lady. That Annie was a strong, brave little girl? You have nothing to be ashamed of. You fought and survived. Look who you've become and what you've accomplished in spite of the pain." He shook his head. "I don't know how to say this, but I feel as if I'm talking to Annie. You have to let her have her say, to get it out. I want the child in you, DeeAnn. I want to love and protect her. You need to accept what you went through and accept the kid that was raped and broken. Annie deserves to be loved, to be free now. So see what you have to see. You won't heal or write until that part of you is free. You have to know the truth. Then you have to write your story."

I couldn't speak. Life was stirring within me. A child peeked out of a slightly open door, watched Curt, and listened timidly. What he was saying was true. If I didn't want to abandon myself again, I had to make the most important decision I'd ever made—right then. As if watching someone else, I took Annie's hand in mine and hugged her close. I wasn't ready for Curt to touch me. I could break too easily.

Once I took Annie's hand, I promised her I would never let go of it again.

Now she interrupts my thoughts. *I'm not a slash of yellow hiding in a field of stubble anymore. I haven't been hiding for a long time now and can take care of myself. Have you forgotten that too?*

She's so blunt. Fearless. It feels good to hear a voice that talks straight at you. Is it really my own? She's right, I have forgotten. I see her in the mirror sometimes, see her through the wrinkles in my skin. I hear her laugh the way she did when the meadowlarks used to wake her in the mornings and the stars twinkled in the sky over the outhouse at night. I probably learned to listen to the language of flowers and streams before I learned to talk. No wonder I love the nature trail; it reminds me to listen with my heart.

Curt walks into my office, holding a cup of coffee. "Would you like a cup?" He leans over to give me a coffee-flavored kiss as he sets my mug on the hot-pad by my computer.

"Thanks, Darlin'." I nuzzle his unshaven cheek.

He returns to the family room to drink his own coffee, and I return to thoughts of Annie.

Did memories of the farm bring you back? It seems natural to talk with her. *Or do you like having a paintbrush in your hand, loaded with colors that you can smear anywhere you like?*

She doesn't answer right away, but moments later the opaque wall next door becomes a movie screen, a screen for memories. Colors appear, colors too beautiful for a wall with yellow stains running from the windows that look like someone peed out of them. Stained-glass windows come to mind, vivid, as if I could touch them. California sun is shining through them. I'm still young enough to believe that Jesus lives in those transparent colors, yet old enough to know that Mom cries too much. My parents argue a lot. No matter how hard Dad works at his construction job, we never have enough money. Dad doesn't care about a nice house though. He moved us from Colorado to California to make money so he could buy his own ranch. Their arguments make my heart beat against my chest like the hammer inside the steel bell that rings from the steeple of that church with the stained-glass Jesus.

Maybe I should have prayed to be rich so that both Mom and Dad would have been happy, but I didn't. Almost every night I prayed to the Man I'd seen in those windows of heaven and asked him to heal our family. The stained-glass pictures showed that he loved kids, healed the crippled, the blind, and brought dead people back to life.

I haven't thought of that prayer since I was a child. Was it so important Annie's reminding me of it now?

There was more to that prayer. There was a painting. It was a vision of healing to me. Mom had talked Dad into buying a huge Bible from the salesman who came to our door. Painted in colors that made me feel like I could walk right into them was a lion sprawling under a huge umbrella of a tree with a lamb, a wolf, a calf, and a leopard. A child walked safely among them. I imagined her to be me. To have that many animals, a family would have to have a ranch, I thought. Most importantly though, everyone was safe. I didn't have to be able to read the message to know what the painting meant:

> And the wolf will dwell with the lamb.
> And the leopard will lie down with the kid,
> And the calf and the young lion and the fatling together;
> And a child will lead them.
>   Isaiah 11:7-9 NAS

It was like the prayer Mom and I prayed together at night: "Our Father who art in heaven, hallowed be Thy name, Thy kingdom come, Thy will be done on earth as it is in heaven."

Now I realize I've been looking for heaven on earth ever since.

I've been looking for Paradise, capitalized, like the one Dostoyevsky's dreamer found.

"What's our life if it isn't a dream?" the great writer asked those who accused him of hallucinating. Spared execution, Dostoyevsky was sentenced to Siberia for four years by his government. He hadn't been free long when he wrote about the dreamer, a man who'd seen Truth that wouldn't let go of him: "Love others as you love yourself."

The Truth that he saw won't let go of me either, but it's a child's prayer that's tugging hard on my heart now.

The shower's running in the bathroom, which means it's time for me to leave for my walk if I'm going to get to the Western about the same time Curt does. My long wool coat will feel good today. I button it up to my neck and wrap my electric blue scarf snugly.

Curt's soaped up when I open the shower curtain to get a wet good-bye kiss. "I'm leaving now."

"Are you taking the trail or Willson?" He'll pick me up if I take the main street to town.

"The nature trail."

I grab my hat and gloves from the basket on the way to the front door.

5

Annie's Prayer

The first breath I take after I walk outside forms a cloud close to my face. I feel sorry for all those Bozemanites who go to warm climates for the winter. Like a kid, I puff a few more clouds.

Ten minutes from home, I'm on the trail, listening for the ducks I hope to see swimming on the pond a little way ahead.

Gathered like feather pillows on the small patch of water that isn't iced over, drakes and hens float together. I can't remember when I've ever felt comfortable in groups, and I don't think it's because Dad stood me on a bar in front of strangers when I was little, either. Just because people are the same species doesn't make us alike. Educated masses would make it sound like we are or should be, but we aren't. The thought of working in one of those corporations that requires employees to go through group sensitivity training turns me cold as ice. No employer could give me enough money to fall off a ladder into anyone's arms. I think both of my great-grandmothers on Mom's side who pioneered Colorado would understand how I feel about group mania in our society. It's taken me most of my adult life to realize that not everyone thinks rugged individualism and privacy are what make a person strong. No wonder the village is an angry one. People need space, even if it means closing the bathroom door for longer than necessary.

Those drakes and hens can spread their wings and fly away anytime.

Looking around me as I always do, I see trees, the stream, and the sky. Nature's taught me more about the way I'm made than man has. An old tree grows at an angle from the bank of the stream, and it looks like it's going to fall, but it hasn't. Thick branches reach both up toward the sky and down to the ground on the other side of the water. Nature adapts to the circumstances it's given. I think that's what Annie did; my awake side prayed for the side that suffered and slept. The girl some adults called Sunshine was stubborn and independent. I was broken inside and growing up at an angle. Yet the sun burned into my bark a passion for justice, freedom, and healing.

Saplings grow along the stream that meanders near the trail. No matter how heavy the snowfall has been this year and last, their small branches carry their share. I guess I did too, the only way I could. Most people do, regardless of what terms the experts use to describe that load. The term mental illness is just another one of man's terms, one he uses to label a war he doesn't understand.

The saplings' branches reach toward the sun even though it's moved behind a dark cloud. Annie was like that, never doubting that the sun would come out. After I got my teaching credential in Southern California, I figured I'd been born to teach those thirty-six children in a bungalow that didn't have running water. I couldn't have felt more called if God had written "Go into the ghetto" on my bedroom wall.

Rivulets run like fingers from the pond. One prayer, but it had fingers.

Up ahead flocks of geese crowd a small melted patch on the pond at the condominiums where Curt and I were neighbors before we got married. I didn't realize that there is a stand of aspen among all the pines in the yard of the condo complex. I love the way I see when I walk here.

It's snowing now, light as flour.

Did a child's simple prayer work like a tablespoon of yeast in the warm water of my life, foaming through the years the way I've watched yeast foam before I've poured it into wheat flour to make my bread rise? Grinding my own wheat into a fine powder has always been healing for me. My two children, Calli and Ryan, used to love to eat bread fresh out of the oven, with honey butter. They gave me the only childhood I could remember until Annie came back. I thought my children would never know how it felt to be abandoned by their parents if God was in the center of our lives. He was my healer, all right.

If pink wasn't flowing from the Bridger Mountains like lava right now, the rugged cliffs would look like death traps, easy suicide. Life was pink for the kids and me. What could go wrong in Paradise?

A crash in the trees startles me. Wild ducks fly out of someone's yard. A man is outside in his housecoat feeding a flock of them. I think of Pastor Stone Harmon. He didn't have the heart to feed his flock. I wonder why he thought he'd been called. Did he need a retirement plan?

Too late warnings traveled around the nation. Six years had taken their toll on an entire congregation. We found out we were not as alone as we felt when a couple came to Bozeman to tell us that pastors all over the nation had used their authority to destroy the sheep instead of to protect them. Stone was one of them. Armies of wounded Christian soldiers were scattered across the battlefield. An epidemic of divorce, depression, and midlife crisis was raging through the ranks. Our family had suffered casualties, but I thought our love was strong enough to survive anything.

A tree that grows at an angle still leafs out in the spring and surrenders its seeds to the wind in the fall just like the ones that grow straight and tall.

A gust of wind makes my eyes water, blurring the trees that turn into skeletons this time of year. No one would know there's life and activity in their deep roots. When all I could see were the skeletons of my dreams, I wrote my first novel. In it, an old rancher takes in a boy who feels responsible for his little brother's drowning. In time, living on the ranch with the gentle rancher heals him.

"Keep writing, Mumzie," Calli and Ryan would say after I read another chapter to them or when they saw me working long periods at the typewriter. Writing was the tool that drew sap from my roots and gave me the strength to believe dreams come true. Without my pen, I don't know how I would have survived the depression, the divorce, and my daughter's death. On paper, I could safely approach God without fear of the church and how it would use Him against me. Today I wonder if writing wasn't my link with Annie before she emerged from the shadows she'd been hiding in.

Underneath my Levi's, my legs are tingling from the cold. The indifferent cold.

The regrets still make me swallow hard sometimes. It's the missing that makes me ache all over. I had one prayer for healing that I wanted God to answer with a miracle. Instead he took my daughter to be with him.

Now the tears fall.

It's winter, yet I find myself looking for the rose hips in bloom like I did the summer after Calli died. In my mind I thumb through the catalog pages to find all the wildflowers we picked together and pressed through the years. Calli ran up the mountainside and hurried from one tiny bloom to another, telling me stories about each flower, "This is the kind the bears eat," she'd say. "Pick some of these, Ryan," she told her brother when they were both still little enough to get lost in the tall grass. "Cal," he'd call, "come over here. You've never seen one like this before."

I feel so close to her this morning, just like I did when Curt and I walked this trail for the first time after she died and I spotted the pink rose hips in bloom. Bending down close enough to inhale their fragrance, I said, *Oh, Calli, look*, and wished she could hear me.

Wait until you see the purple ones ahead, Mom, she said. There was laughter in her voice. She always loved to surprise me.

I held my breath for the next twenty feet, the way you would if someone said that heaven was right around the corner. Hidden behind thick bushes was a garden of wild purple flowers. They were tall and cone-shaped. *Oh, Cal.* I cried silently, while Curt talked to me about something he thought I was paying attention to.

She laughed. *Wait until you see the yellow ones on down the trail, Mom.*

Dull yellow wildflowers, a mustard seed variety, covered the field, but she sounded as if there was something really yellow to look forward to. At the end of the path, which I'd never walked that time of year, was a huge rose bush, and it was on fire with yellow. The bush burned just for me. I gasped, and Calli giggled as if to say we'd play this game again sometime.

After Curt and I got home from our walk, I told him she'd talked to me. "That doesn't surprise me. She isn't gone, you know," he said.

Slowing my pace, now, I remember other times she spoke to me, bringing heaven to earth in a way I would never have prayed if I'd known the cost was my child. *You'll be healed now, Mom*, she said that fall nine years ago.

Suddenly I have a thought that makes me want to fall on my

face and cry my heart out. *Oh, Cal. What did you pray when you were little? What did you pray when you were in the hospital? What did God say to you when you were paralyzed with medicine for those nine days before you died?*

The cold wind's burning my face, burning like a child's prayer that's consumed my life. Is it still raging, turning up the heat on my soul, raw metal in a big vat, until every illusion rises to the top—so all that's left when I die is that prayer, challenging me to believe in the coming of a Kingdom on earth I won't live to see except in oils?

I'm at the end of the nature trail. The café is several blocks down the road. Directly on my left, at the edge of a yard, is a spiny little plant. This is all that's left of the burning rose bush that the owners pruned last year.

Vision breaks you like bread and throws you on the water. God is speaking to my heart.

Like debris caught in the boiling river of life, the beginning of the last decade rushes before my eyes.

6

Back to Martin's Cafe
January 1991

The floor begins to vibrate seconds before I see the engine of the train appear through the glass entryway. A massive mountain of steel rumbling like a waterfall over boulders the size of planets, the train speeds down the tracks that run not more than twenty feet from the outside wall of the old train station café. I clutch the table and wait for the huge photographs of dated locomotives, powerful enough to pull the Rockies off their foundations it seems, to shake off the walls and shatter glass on the linoleum floor. Completely unrattled, waitresses take orders and deliver food to customers without looking up. Like the western music that plays over the radio, the sound of the train is just another song to them.

Feeling stupid, I release my hold on the Formica table and move Terence Hogan's file away from my full cup of coffee. I write down his assignment for our class next week. After I finish meeting with my students at the Livingston Employment Office, I'll drop it off at the truck stop where he's a cook, on my way home to Bozeman. According to my watch, that's three hours from now. Hopefully, I'll catch him before the noon rush.

As I write his assignment in my notebook, I picture Terence with his jet-black hair, cut and combed like the rock singers in the sixties; black eyebrows arched over baby-blue eyes; black eyelashes longer than most girls'; and square jaw stubborn as two feet planted in concrete. At the top of the list are three pages in his second-grade math workbook and a chapter in his first-grade reader. In a composition notebook, I list five new vocabulary words and their meanings for him to use in sentences. At thirty-two years old, Terence has a wife and a year-old daughter he's trying to prove he's worthy of so they'll come home where they belong. He's the only student I have, among the dozen who were laid off when the lumber mill shut down before Christmas, who is illiterate. Most of the others are high school graduates and skilled laborers, several in their prime. They need to brush up on basic math and language skills as part of their retraining and employment program.

In Bozeman, I have twenty more clients who've been jolted out of their jobs by modern technology and global shifts in the economy. All of them have two things in common: The jobs that gave them their identities are gone, and they're not needed anymore. My clients need to believe they still have a reason to get up in the morning. That's why Montana's Director of Project Opportunity, Ron Sturgis, said he hired me to be the literacy teacher for Bozeman's office last September. He questioned whether my background in math was as strong as it should be to teach algebra, geometry, and accounting, but Ron believed I could give my disheartened clients a reason to live.

Ron Sturgis hired me to be an inspiration. It's ironic that the tragedies in my life made me good for something. Suffering has turned my heroes into saints; yet in the mirror, it sticks out like a scarlet letter on me. I'm not any different from my clients. We all need to believe in ourselves.

Hank's file is next. A hard worker like the rest, his trials never seem to end. Tall and lean, he's shy about taking credit for how good he was at training horses before his back went out on him. For his English assignment, he writes about ranching: "Ranching is a big business and a lot of hard work, and it is very costly. It depends on the weather and God. But most people who ranch think it is the only way of life." Hank writes about horses. "Horses are a lot like people. Some are easy to train and some take more time. . . . The only thing that makes a good horse is the person working the animal."

Hank writes about feelings that a proud man would hide otherwise. He was twelve years old when childhood was over and "the work began." A Vietnam vet, Hank was eighteen when he enlisted in the Air Force. For years, he "was so happy with his family. Then he [Hank wrote in third person] got hurt and was down with back trouble . . . things made a turn and things started going backwards."

Hank carries trouble like most men carry a wallet in their hip pocket—out of sight except for the slight bulge and worn spot that shows it's there. "After twenty-four years of married life and five kids, his wife up and left him without a word. And this woman was the only person he ever cared for. He loved her more than words could ever say."

Mascara smudges stand out on my white napkin. I've read Hank's story before, many times. Why a judge would keep this gentle man from seeing his kids, I can't imagine. Without the spirit of truth, the law is an instrument of destruction. Pain gradually breaks Hank's sentences into phrases, jagged pieces of his heart. "I still love and care for her and the kids. But don't know if I will ever see them again. After this all came down I was down and out. And now I'm trying to bring myself up. And work for myself and no one else. As time goes by, I will show all that put me down. I'm now forty-five years old and trying to learn a new way of life. I've been hurt in the body and mind. I've lost everything I've worked for in the last twenty-four years. But there is hope for the future."

His hope is that I can help him as he helps himself. God, help us both.

Other files are faces to me. Frank, Stuart, and Phil are Vietnam vets who are trying to get their degrees at Montana State University in Bozeman. It's not easy for any of them, but Frank's dyslexic and has to work harder than the others academically. Divorce, depression, and flashbacks haunt them all. PTSD (post-traumatic stress disorder) isn't the kind of credential these men need for the jobs they dream of having someday. Their future hangs on this program. And we all know that Project Opportunity depends on special funding that can go as quickly as it's come. I can't bear the thought of the government letting these men down again—not while I'm part of the system.

One of the Livingston crew is the petite woman who has mental blocks on tests. She grew up across from the old schoolhouse near Yellowstone Park, and she blocked back then too. Her dad did things to her in their old house, things she still can't remember clearly. By the time she got to the country school each day, she'd blanked out math, spelling, and English, along with the other lessons that her dad had taught her.

There's also Vince. He came to class last week with one side of his hair cut above his ear and the other down to his shoulder—said he cut it himself because he felt like it. He's taking pills the doctor prescribed for his illness, although he doesn't see them as a cure. Education is his hope. I wonder if Vince's doctor has ever seen how clear his eyes get when he talks about the swimming hole on the farm when he was a kid.

Alberto Juarez is different from my other clients, not because his roots are in Mexico, though. I suspect that, wherever Alberto lives, he's in a world of his own. I'm trying to motivate him to speak English instead of Spanish at home so he can compete for a technical job. He's in his early fifties and has saved enough money from his job driving farm equipment in Salinas, California, to buy a house for his wife and six children in Bozeman. Every week he tells me about businessmen who are trying to help him spend his savings. If Alberto doesn't learn that he has to be careful, I'm afraid he'll lose everything he's worked so hard for.

He's a romantic, the kind of dreamer that growing up on a ranch and riding the mesa nourished. Alberto loves to stop me in the middle of an English lesson to tell me stories about his home in Mexico and the mesa where his father and his great-grandfather raised cattle. Both of them carved legends on leather saddles. I'll admit it; I could listen to Alberto for hours as he sits across the table from me, looking tall and at home in that small straight-backed chair, his wavy black hair graying at the temples, his dark eyes fearless and too innocent for a man his age. Many of my clients worry me, but Alberto is the one who really scares me. He's the first one who noticed the rose on my desk and inhaled its fragrance so deeply I thought he'd pass out from pleasure. He's been betrayed and has wolves at his door, but you wouldn't know it. Sometimes he smiles at me like he has a secret he wants to tell, a secret I need to hear. Until I met his beautiful wife and saw how her black eyes snap at him and almost bark at his heels, I thought her love kept him in a trance.

Alberto doesn't seem to be afraid of anything. Maybe some day when I've been healed for a long time, I'll be in another world, too. I think I used to be when I was younger.

The clock high on the wall of Martin's is all face and hands. No eyes. No soul to be broken.

Lou Kramer, Bozeman's coordinator of Project Opportunity, should be here by now. He's a Vietnam vet who loves his job, and I suspect Ron Sturgis knew that when he hired him. I grab another file out of the pile on the table and remember when I felt as if a label on an empty file was all I was—dry bones without a story to tell. My clients will never feel like that when they're with me. I won't let them.

7

Dry Bones

I felt as if I'd failed at everything that had ever mattered to me the summer that over a third of Yellowstone Park burned. In August 1988, my television station's on-site news coverage took me to the front lines as high winds ignited hot embers and fanned raging flames that threatened to reduce Silver Gate and Cooke City to ashes, leaving nothing but memories and smoldering corpses of wildlife on the floor of God's country. From the safe distance of my upstairs family room, I watched people risk their lives to save their homes. With an experienced twist of the lens, cameramen diminished the human drama until it looked like colonies of ants driven from their nests. I felt like one of them—the ants, I mean. By that summer, my world was underground. To a woman who was called Sunshine as a girl, the dark side of the soul was a side only other people had, people who were too weak to fight addictions, insanity, and weak genes, those who didn't have the faith to overcome evil and endure suffering. Summer '88, I didn't recognize who I'd become.

Separating himself from the family he shattered, my first husband walked out on our two teenagers and me on Easter Day. It was early April. Not wanting to appear too eager to abandon his family when we needed him the most, Gabriel took us to church in Bozeman, as usual, then took us to lunch at our favorite restaurant, as usual. That afternoon he nailed down the shingles the wind was tearing from the roof before he packed his clothes and drove down the gravel driveway in his rig with the camp trailer, borrowed from friends, bumping along behind him. He never looked back to see his angry sixteen-year-old daughter, his bewildered fifteen-year-old son, and his relieved wife watching from the upstairs dormer window.

Maybe now his parents will stop punishing him for marrying me, I thought. I hadn't depended on them the way they wanted me to after we married. For twenty years, I'd hoped and prayed that Gabe would cut them loose and save us both from the endless roller coaster ride of their approval and rejection. But they finally won. In his luggage, I tried to pack all the guilt I'd worn like a ball and chain.

"Detach, or you won't survive!" Lars Mitchell, the psychotherapist, had told me. As my life drove away, I hoped my relief meant I'd cut the tie and tried not to think about the hole in my heart that was bleeding.

Somewhere—probably at the trailer park where he'd hook up for a while—a young blonde waited for him in a hot red sports car. Her husband was not yet history. As Gabe drove away, I thought I hadn't ever been physically raped by anyone, but I'd been lied to, and that day it had seemed like the same thing.

How disappointed had he been when I survived in spite of everything?

Standing there at the window, I watched clouds the color of a tidal wave gather above us—a reflection of the darkness that had gathered in my soul. It had socked in thick when I started seeing Lars Mitchell. At our first appointment just over a year before, Mitchell's compassion shrouded his professional jargon. It meant nothing to me: victim, spiritual rape. It may have started with your dad's emotional abuse. Drug therapy and a diagnostic test will help. Hadn't he heard me at all? We'd had a vision, my husband and I. We'd survived a war in the church to hold onto it. But now something in our marriage was sucking the life out of me. In the psychotherapist's misty powder-blue eyes, I thought I saw a little boy who'd just realized that pain is real.

Why had I gone back a second time? Because I knew I suffered from depression and my friend Tina had tried to commit suicide? Well, I'd never tried to commit suicide, never thought of hurting myself until I took prescription drugs for a year. After that, my will seemed like someone else's.

After our second appointment, I found myself wearing Lars's labels like they were the only pair of shoes in my closet. In the two weeks I'd been taking them, the drugs that were supposed to order my thoughts had made my body a stranger to me. The shoes hurt; they wore blisters on my soul. I knew from the beginning they were the wrong size, but I thought they were better than walking bare-foot through dark alleys. I was wrong.

After my appointment, I drove through a January blizzard to our home in the country, about four miles from town. I felt as if I was hovering over my own pathetic body, a zombie locked in cruise control. Desperate to have someone hear me, I fell on the bed next to Gabe soon after I walked in the door and sobbed. "The test showed twenty-three psychotic tendencies. I'm not crazy. I've been wounded and need time to heal."

Lars, the therapist, didn't believe me, didn't trust my think-ing. "You let me listen to God. You listen to me," he'd said.

"Don't tell me not to listen to God." Since we'd left Stone's church, I couldn't speak the name Jesus without sobbing, but I listened to God's voice the best I could. He was my sanity most of the time. Now I felt as if Lars had stripped me of my defenses, stripped me of confidence in my own thinking. I knew how a deadbolt sounded when you want to turn and run.

"Just be patient," Gabe had said while I sobbed in his arms. "Maybe he can help you sleep."

Sleep? If being knocked out for days, moving from the couch in the day to the bed at night was sleep, I'd slept. If being nearly unconscious for several days and being startled awake in the nights by emotions and memories that erupted from the depths of me was sleep, I'd slept.

If the ordered thoughts Lars promised me were those foggy names and faces that seemed to be bound like prisoners in the closet of my mind, I was a chemical wonder. If clear thinking was crying out in terror in the middle of the night, "Don't let him get me. Don't let him hurt Rod and Connie [my brother and sister]," until Gabe's voice brought me back to the present, then I was a shining example of what drugs could do to heal the soul.

Locked together in the closet inside me were fragmented memories of Pastor Harmon and the father whose violence wouldn't let me go. Yet when I told Mitchell about the flash-backs and symbolic images at our second appointment, he said I was hallucinating.

"The drugs will help you sleep," he said. If taking the blame for all that was wrong with not only myself but also Gabe was the kind of sleep I needed, then those little pills I took with a glass of milk daily were the cure for me.

For as long as I could remember, I was the one who read self-help books, sought counseling with pastors, and repented until there was not a tear left to cry. Hook, line, and pill, I owned my problems, and Gabe's problems, his folks' problems, my folks' problems, and the problems of the world. And Lars Mitchell was worse at seeing through the pile of garbage I was buried under than I was. His credentials didn't give him the wisdom to see through my husband's lies until it was too late, and then we both looked like fools. After Gabe was gone, he told the kids that Lars didn't have a clue what was really wrong with me. Had he known and let me run the course of insanity anyway? Was he trying to escape the burden of truth he would have had to carry if he'd stayed?

Not a hint of sunlight penetrated those dark clouds that gathered above the scene of abandonment on Easter, no matter how hard I looked. In the seven years I'd been writing, Gabe never read anything I wrote. An English professor at Montana State University recently said my first novel would sell if I made revisions. In the story, a family that's almost torn apart by a tragedy protects their bond. It was fiction, but I based it on how I saw our lives when I wrote it.

I had poems to market and research completed for another novel. In spite of the drugs that had made my body feel like it was someone else's, I wrote, researched, and drafted.

Until three months before Gabe left, I thought I proved I could endure anything. In a chemical daze, the razor seemed like the best way to move the pain from the inside to the outside. Before we made love one morning, the husband who seemed like a stranger demanded that I trust him, but I couldn't. Feeling close to insanity, I had to know what he was hiding. He withdrew completely, loading the unbearable burden of guilt on me again. Sinking into the pit of hell, I cut myself, careful to avoid the purple trails under the skin. Gabe said his patience had run out and drove off for the day—as if the burden of shame and guilt I carried wasn't punishment enough.

Switched from one chemical concoction to another by Dr. Reed, the psychiatrist Lars asked me to see, I was confined to the couch for weeks with flu-like symptoms. To walk across the room without swaying, falling, and blacking out was impossible. Instead of seeing my name in print, I saw monkeys in the toilet and flowers on the ceiling. That's when Gabe escalated his affair. Blind Lars had encouraged him to get away, to attend out-of-town teaching workshops because he was stressed with all his wife was going through and needed a break. When a friend called Lars to tell him how sick the drugs were making me, he insisted I had to trust him and Dr. Reed.

Surely he heard the tone of my silence, *You've got to be kidding.*

A week or so later I caught Gabe in a lie, and he admitted he was seeing someone.

Months later friends told me people had been whispering about his flirtations and infidelity for some time, possibly a few years. Meanwhile, his lies had been sucking me into the pit of darkness. If Gabe had been honest, would I have gone to the therapist in the first place? Probably not. The lies would have been out where I could see them, instead of inside, driving me crazy.

As he drove around the bend and out of sight on Easter, I didn't know I'd finally given him the excuse he needed to save face with his family and friends. I didn't know few blamed a man for leaving a crazy woman for a sane one, whether he knew he'd made her that way or not. I wish I had known. Outrage might have healed me on the spot.

Instead, that spring I sat on the deck and watched our fat domestic mallards chase the sleek wild birds away from their mates. The birds easily lifted off the creek and flew away. Nature wrapped me in her arms the way the Pacific used to rock me in its cradle when I was a girl. Drugs took my mornings from me, but God's mercy was without beginning or end. The eagle that flew above our land drew my eyes away from the pain and questions. Solitude became my friend.

By the time Gabriel took our kids on vacation to Washington and California the summer after he left us, I was ready to be alone with myself. Fear wasn't the threat it had been. When Calli called from the motel a few days later, laughter came easily. They'd gone to visit with Gabe's uncle that night. He didn't know we were separated, and asked where I was. Gabe didn't answer. Consequently, a lone rocker was vacant the whole evening. Now and then someone would look at it as if I was going to knock at the door any moment and join them.

Like smoldering coals in the ashes of my life, my passion for writing promised a revival. *Daughter of Fire*, God called me. *Will you follow me through the alleys of the dark side where daylight is never seen, follow me to the grave, and trust me just the same?* Daughter of Fire sounded like the name of a warrior. One smoldering coal told me not to give up.

I was ready for my mother-in-law when she called to gloat. The inferno was sweeping Yellowstone Park on my television screen when the phone rang. "I hear Gabe's met someone new," Mom Gaynor said excitedly, carving her "I won" in my soul.

"Yes, he has." I knew what was coming. For the first time in over twenty years, I finally felt calm about her predictability.

"Well, what's she like?" the woman who called herself a Christian asked cheerfully.

"I hear she's young, blonde, has a hot red sports car and a husband." Had Gabe finally met up to his mother's expectations?

"Well!" she said, "there must have been problems in your marriage!"

"Yes," I said calmly, "there were."

She hung up without saying good-bye.

I was relieved. I had never wanted to fight with her over her son. I just wanted to be happy.

As broken as any of the lame and blind that Jesus told to get up and walk or open their eyes, I needed a miracle. Shrouded in shame, I needed to be forgiven. Feeling as dead as Lazarus, I needed to wake up. The fires of destruction had stripped my soul. Feeling barren and brittle as dry bones, sifting the ashes for hope, I needed to be loved.

Divorce dumped me on the doorstep of my identity in November of 1988. The day before I signed the papers, God spoke to my heart, *I will be found by you and bring you out of captivity. Identify with Me.* I didn't know what He was talking about, unless it was the language he'd painted on the walls of my mind to protect me from the prison of labels. With my pen, I painted those pictures on paper with words. Armed with metaphoric images of faith and love, a warrior can fight insanity, I found. Armed with hope and purpose, a broken woman can withstand the crippling effects of prescription drugs as well.

With faith and a little rhythm, dry bones make music. Working two jobs, I was proving to myself who I was. Within two weeks after Gabe left, I started substitute teaching in spite of the drugs that kept me in a fog until nearly noon each day. Working as a waitress in a family restaurant since June, I was able to afford a nice condo in Bozeman, across from the high school. Nevertheless, serving food for a living was a long way from having a glossy cover with my name on it featured in the local bookstore. Lars Mitchell said Xanax would calm my nerves, but my hands trembled constantly.

In the fall, I was hired as assistant librarian at the elementary school, which made me determined to write books instead of shelve them. Somehow I had passed the National Teachers Exam and would start night school at Montana State University, winter semester. I needed sixteen credits to teach in Montana.

Not until I walked out of the lawyer's office after signing the divorce documents did I realize how Gabe's name had changed me from the woman he'd married twenty years before. It wasn't because I couldn't have been free. I didn't know how to be. With the warm wind ruffling my hair, I felt safe, full of hope and purpose. Then I remembered what time of year it was. My favorite—Indian Summer. I couldn't wait to get home and take my shoes off. It wouldn't be easy, but I wanted to walk barefoot with God.

8

A Fire Burning

Unless you've been close enough to a locomotive to feel its heat through the wall, like I did that morning at Martin's Cafe, a photograph of an engine is just a ghost of the real thing. Knowing God is like that. You have to feel his steam burn your soul, or else he's just another photograph hanging on the wall of your mind. You can burn candles under it; kiss it morning, noon, and night; and frame it with any doctrine you choose. But if you don't feel the engine vibrate clear to your toes, feel the steam loosen your tired muscles and hard joints, feel the power of His presence until you cry with relief that love is real, He's just a ghost that needs a nail to hang on. On the other hand, if a ghost is all you have to talk to, it's better than nothing at all until the real thing comes along.

Lou, the coordinator of Project Opportunity, was late that wintry morning in 1991, but God never is. I must remember that.

Like a gentle giant who had listened to a little girl cry long enough, it seemed as if He finally put His foot down the summer of 1990, because that's when the earth shook for me. Sunshine's child had grown into a brokenhearted woman, and it seemed as if that summer God said, *Enough*.

A lion with a golden mane, the sun owned that mid-June morning.

Sitting in my wicker chair on the patio of the condo, journal open on my lap, my Bible open on top of it, I hoped I smelled as good to God as the lilacs I had picked off of my neighbor's hedge earlier smelled to me. A couple of weeks before, I had quit my job as a waitress. My job at the library didn't start again until fall. Even with my brother's loan, I'd taken a risk to sit there on the patio with the sun smiling down on me.

I liked the way I smelled now that I wasn't wearing the food I'd served customers for the past two years. Resting my head against the back of my chair, I could feel beads of sweat drip between my unbound breasts beneath my cotton T-shirt. With my mind quiet, I listened to my own thoughts. It felt good to be able to recognize them among all of those that had been stuffed in my head by others. It felt good to enjoy being myself and to know who I wasn't. The woman in the mirror smiled back at me this morning. *You've come a long way, Lady,* I heard her say.

It sounded like something Curt would tell me. No sooner did I enroll in night classes at the university last year than God told me he had good things ahead for me. Never did I think He'd bring a man like Curt Brandon into my life, not until I had been healed a long time and was emotionally strong enough to love again.

From the time friends introduced us at McDonald's, where we met for coffee after church, I liked him. The men visited at one table, the women at another, postponing introductions until we all stood up to leave. I glanced Curt's way a few times and felt his eyes on me when I wasn't looking at him. Dwarfing the little table and chairs at the fast food restaurant, he had a presence that naturally drew attention. Like an ageless oak, he stood apart. The scars around his left eye fit a man who had weathered the severe storms my friend Kathy had described. Curt hadn't been divorced two months before he nearly died in a motorcycle accident, June 1984. At least six-foot-three when he stood and faced me, the smile in his sea-green eyes put me at ease. If he found anything about me that had disappointed him, he didn't show it.

Several months later, when summer days were long, the sun setting about bedtime, we were taking a walk together, just the two of us. We had just eaten dinner with our kids. Curt was thinking the same thing I was: together his and mine seemed like *ours*. Ryan and Calli joked with Curt's son, Chad, and youngest daughter, Gina, as if they'd grown up under the same roof. If Bree, his oldest, had been able to come to Bozeman for the weekend, our pretend-family would have been complete. With his hands in his pockets and a relaxed look on his face, Curt spoke first, "I said I'd never marry again, DeeAnn, but even with your wounds, you're better than any woman I've ever known. We both need to heal, but I can see us getting married in a couple of years."

Under my breath, I said, *Two years!* Yet I knew I needed time to become the woman I wanted to be, not for Curt and not for my kids, but for me.

Sitting in the morning sun, feeling clean as cotton ready for harvest, I noticed that my hands weren't shaking at all. I closed my eyes. Light penetrated the thin veil of skin that covered them. A ball of fire, so far away, yet hot. Somewhere within, there was a fire, and it was healing me.

Lies that made me sick were dead wood to truth's blaze. Thoughts were either friends or enemies and had the power to heal or destroy. Mornings were merciful as long as I turned to the empty page with my pen in hand, my heart open to the Holy Spirit's voice. A novel lay on the shelf in my room, the rewrite marinating in my mind. My files were thick with hope. Short stories were in the mail to potential publishers. My articles looked like the diary of a war correspondent stationed on the front lines.

Knowing that I couldn't count on my memory to get me through college after Gabe left, I used my writing skills to earn straight A's the winter and spring of 1989. My teaching credential was probably in the mail when my mind turned on me last summer. I'd never forget the summer of '89. The closet closed in; I went crazy and ended up in the hospital.

Looking back, it was still hard to understand what happened that weekend I became the nightmare I'd done everything I could to wake up from. Nevertheless, terrifying feelings and cloudy memories would erupt from within sometimes and I'd lose track of reality. After two-and-a-half years, the psychotherapist Lars Mitchell still didn't know what was wrong with me or how to help me. He called my flashbacks all kinds of things: hallucinations, dependence, anxiety attacks, an immediate need for gratification, inappropriate behavior. Lars tried to teach me to identify with Jesus—his Jesus, a candle with a short wick.

No sooner had Gabe married his lover last summer than Lars advised Calli to leave home. Crippled with feelings of abandonment that I couldn't explain, I was alone when darkness engulfed me. My kids were out of town for the weekend. Curt invited me to go to the lake outside Helena boating with him and his kids. The day before we were supposed to leave, he changed his mind. Over the phone, he said he needed time to think. I heard, "It's over." Another lesson in trusting a man. Slipping into a black hole, into another time and place, consumed with pain beyond reason, I took Xanax to get rid it. Lots of Xanax.

I ended up in the emergency room where nurses said I was on a chemical high, but not in danger. They told Carol and Diane, concerned friends who'd come with me, not to leave me alone for the next twenty-four hours. However, the next morning both friends left me alone after I assured them I was okay. Feeling detached from my body and fragmented into unrecognizable pieces, I went on a bike ride, did a little shopping, kept my appointment with the psychotherapist that was on call, and then returned home. Not one conversation I had with anyone stuck in my diluted mind. If the brain works like a computer, the blue screen of death was warning me something was wrong. It was a bad time for Curt to stop by to reassure me that everything was good between us. He didn't know I was drugged.

Sitting across from me in the living room, he sounded far away, like the boats that used to honk as they moved through the fog in Newport Harbor. He asked the same questions over and over. He answered mine again and again. "What?" I said, becoming more and more desperate as my mind gave me blanks when I needed bullets of truth and understanding. "Throw me a rope or something," I wanted to say, as I sank deeper into the dark waters of my soul. It was the same behavior I'd had when on Halcion, the sleeping drug. After two hours of confusion, the man who made me want to dream again drove away.

Swallowed in my black hole, I knew he was gone for good. Someone was gone for good anyway, maybe Dad, maybe Gabe, men who had used the last word to cripple me. Medicating the pain, I took my potent antidepressant. Lots of it.

The next morning, I lay in the hospital bed trying to recognize who I'd become. I thanked God Calli and Ryan were out of town. Nurses, doctors, the on-call therapist, and several friends waited to see whether my kidneys had collapsed. Lying there, I didn't feel like a warrior who had won her battles, but a crazy woman who'd lived up to all the sick labels. Over the phone, Lars threatened to commit me to the mental institution in Galen, where sick, poor people go.

"I'm a responsible adult," I told him, wondering whom I was talking about as a doctor and nurse listened in.

The hospital doors flew open when I left, I was so angry with myself. I'd been on the near fatal cure long enough. The grave had swallowed me and spit me out.

There was a fire burning within that could not be put out. That fire was my spirit, I realized, and it was stronger than my sick soul and body. I could heal myself.

Dr. Reed, the psychiatrist, said I'd plunged to the depths of hell because I was healing. The more healed I was, the harder I'd fall.

What if I fell harder the next time? I'd be dead.

Over the phone, I confided in Mom. She had told me before that drugs had changed me, and urged me to get a second professional opinion. My pharmacist, who had known me as a neighbor and friend since I moved to Bozeman, often asked me how long the doctors planned to keep me on medication. Friends, who knew I wouldn't take aspirin unless I was very sick, questioned the cure I was on.

Fearing for my life, I told Lars I was going off medication. For the first time, he said Xanax was addictive and to go off cold turkey would be extremely dangerous. He said something vague about flashbacks and rape but didn't discuss either further. When I read him an article I'd written, he encouraged me to keep writing. I still wonder if there was a short in our healing connection or if I was finally learning not to put "man" on a pedestal. The healing pools of Bethesda seemed to swirl in his blue eyes. The way friends who were also his patients talked about him, he could have been the angel that helped the crippled swim in miracle waters. Lars left Bozeman at the end of summer '89. He set me up with one of his associates, Gene Dover.

Gene moved into Lars' office after he was gone. It was as plain as one of those cubicles at H & R Block at tax time. At our first appointment, a fall breeze blew through the second-story window, cooling the uncluttered room. Gene looked at me with respect I didn't expect after what I'd done earlier in the summer. He said, "You need to trust yourself. You need to have confidence in your own thinking."

His response wasn't much different than Curt's had been when we talked after I got out of the hospital: "You fell down and got dirty, but look how far you've come. Let's move on."

Since then I'd seen less of the therapist and more of Curt and my typewriter, but not because anxiety didn't cripple me at times. Within me a fire was burning, a fire with a mane and a roar.

Sitting on the patio now, with the sun yawning above me, the past didn't seem to matter. Maybe endorphins were making me feel courageous. I imagined I was a warrior, and the lion my shield of armor. The day before the divorce, God promised to bring me out of captivity if I'd identify with Him. Surely he was speaking to me through the sun this morning.

Identity was a confusing word to me. How could Daughter of Fire identify with people like those who'd lived behind chain link fences at Patton when I was a girl? Patton was the mental institution in California Dad used to drive by on the way to the mountains. A friend once told me her mother was committed there. Doctors laid her on a bed, hooked her up to electric wires, and made her twitch like a rat in a research lab. She got better, then worse and worse. She was addicted to prescription drugs, my friend said, but no human should be stripped of dignity like that. Remembering myself in the hospital last summer, I shuddered.

The experts would probably say I was in denial if I told them none of my heroes thought truth came from a bottle of pills. Maybe they would be right. But I didn't care about being right; I cared about getting well. So I looked to the world around me for heroes, just like I looked to the sun this morning, hoping its fire would feed my own.

In response to President Reagan's challenge, Mikhail Gorbachev began to tear down the Berlin Wall last winter. Blow by crushing blow, the wall that had separated good and evil, bondage and free-dom, almost my entire life was being demolished, and I felt walls falling down in me. Somewhere in Russia there had to be a woman who'd been keeping a journal, waiting for the day she could write "Free at last" across the page. Her time had come. Surely mine was in sight.

This spring the aging Nelson Mandela walked out of the prison he'd entered as a young man. The fire in his eyes denied he'd been caged. A year before, China's military used tanks and machine guns to mow down thousands of Chinese students in Tiananmen Square when they made their stand for freedom. Their crime was thinking for themselves.

Feeling lion-strong this morning, I wondered if thinking for myself had been my crime at some critical point on the path of life.

The wicker chair squeaked as I studied my still hands. In the year since I overdosed, I'd gradually withdrawn from Xanax. Dr. Reed asked me to continue with my small dosage of antidepressant, but it would be next to go.

"I'm not shaking," I wrote, then lifted my pen to appreciate how straight and tall my letters were. Straight and tall for me, anyway.

I want to bless you with this job, the Spirit said, His steam hot inside me.

What job? I felt my pulse beat in my temples. *I don't have a job. Oh, God, don't do this to me.* A real job would either be there or it wouldn't.

I lay my journal on the wrought-iron table next to my wicker chair before I joined my kids in the kitchen. Looking like the sun had given her birth, Calli, almost nineteen, was standing at the kitchen counter in her shorts and T-shirt. I called her my Sunlet; she had her own light inside. Ryan was a senior. His smile would melt honey, and his hugs were warmer than the fertile earth that nourished the first planting of wheat.

I would never forget the look on those two beautiful faces when the kids surprised me for my birthday this spring with a party at Pizza Hut. They started the morning by having a bouquet of roses sent to me at school. Arriving on the heels of the delivery truck, their smiles would have made my day complete without the rest. The color of those roses were not of this earth. Salmon ice, I called it.

Dinner was just going to be the three of us, they said, when they drove me to the restaurant. No sooner had we walked through the door than a huge table of friends, including Curt and his son Chad, sang "Happy Birthday." Nothing had seemed impossible since.

Calli tossed Ry his toast. He caught it with one hand and then made a big deal of wiping jelly off his fingers and smearing it on her arm. Just looking at them straightened my back.

"Here, Mom." She tossed me a piece.

Licking butter off my palm, I thought how good it felt to laugh with my kids. They were always telling me what a good job I was doing now. I could still hear what they had said as we watched their dad drive away the year before, Easter 1988. With the clouds dark as doom, the wind blowing rain against the dormer window, and all three of us watching until he was out of sight, Ryan whispered, "We can make it, Mom." Calli said, "Just the three of us." I didn't know whether it was a prayer or a promise at the time. Now I knew it was both.

"Ry, Cal." I extended my hands out in front of me where they could see them.

"What, Mom?"

"Look. They're still."

They both hugged me hard. Still hands are better than promises. We were a family, the three of us. And within walking distance lived the man I loved.

Two hours later the phone rang. It was my good friend Carol. "Would you be interested in working as a literacy teacher for Project Opportunity, DeeAnn?" She described the perfect three-quarter-time job to me, including benefits, independence, and dignity.

9

The Job

Sitting on the other side of the desk from me in Bozeman's Project Opportunity office was the man who could change my life. As the director of a statewide program, Ron Sturgis was younger than I had expected and crisp with confidence that comes from success rather than undeserved blessings like mine.

"You'll be working with a lot of men who are facing their worst fear of not having a reason to get up in the morning," he said, "the fear of not being able to provide for their family."

I didn't expect him to ask me the same question that had been on the application, but he did. "What would you say to a man who had just been laid off from the job he'd already given over half of his adult years to?"

"Money is not what makes a man important to his family," I said. "Love and commitment are, but self-respect is the key to confidence. I would find out what kind of work the person loves and train him to be good at it."

I didn't tell him that I used to be good at almost everything that mattered to me. *Let me prove that I still can be.*

Ron said he'd call in a few weeks to let me know if I'd been hired.

In the meantime, I battled my worst fear: What if I hadn't heard God's voice, but made it up, like crazy people do. I doubted anything I couldn't touch, hear, or smell. Living her own life now that Dad had married—yet again—Mom came to visit at the right time. She reassured me I'd healed since Gabe left, and that I could make a career of writing some day.

No sooner had she left for California than a Realtor showed up at my door, looking like he'd beamed in from another planet. Absorbed in the list he held in his hand, he asked if I'd gotten the notice he slipped in the door a week or two before. I locked my fingers together to keep my hands from shaking. "No, I didn't get your notice. What did it say?"

"The owners of the condo are selling. You have to be out in two weeks."

I asked him to come in so I could sit down.

He said he'd try to buy me some time. People were jammed into communal housing waiting for rentals to become available. The worst news was yet to come.

It had been a month since my interview with Ron when he called to tell me he'd hired a high school math teacher for the job that was supposed to be mine. It didn't matter how sorry he sounded. The job I was promised by the One-Who-Had-Never-Lied-To-Me, was taken.

As soon as I hung up the phone, I rode my bicycle to Curt's condo to tell him the bad news. It was early August. In less than a month, I had to go back to my job as assistant librarian at the elementary school—shelving books instead of writing them. The only man I'd ever known who believed in my dreams more than I did told me to hold on to God's promise. About midnight, I listened to Curt Brandon breathe as I lay in his arms. He was asleep, but I was anxious and afraid. *Oh, God, please speak to me.*

As soon as the sun came up, I rode my bike home, ran to my bedroom to get my Bible, and turned to one of the Scriptures the Spirit spoke to me in the night. Sitting on the edge of my bed—as if it was the rim of the world I could fall from any minute—I read, "You know that his Spirit teaches you about all things, always telling you the truth and never telling you a lie."

Like the bugle before battle, the words sounded in my heart, and I cried with relief that I wasn't crazy. Someplace, sometime, God would bless me with a specific job. The one I wanted was already taken.

School would start Monday. The Thursday before, I was standing on a ladder putting up a bulletin board when the librarian told me I had a phone call. It was Ron, the director of Project Opportunity. "You want a job?" he asked, sounding happy, as if I was his first choice. Ignoring my stuttering, he said, "The high school teacher quit. He got another offer in Washington where he's wanted to move for a long time. You are the new literacy teacher for Project Opportunity if you want to be, DeeAnn."

"I do. I can, I mean."

"How long before you can start?"

"I'll ask my principal and call you right back." My principal was a gem of a man and a good friend.

I started the following Monday. Before work I stopped at the flower shop to buy myself a rose. It would be a weekly routine to remind myself that I wasn't dreaming.

A young businessman who was waiting for his order in the flower shop said, "You're buying yourself a rose?"

"Yes." I laughed. "It's come to that."

He wrote something on a card before the clerk brought his roses—a bouquet and one rose, individually wrapped. Smiling, he handed me the single red rose with a card attached to the wrapping. I was still stammering as the door closed behind him.

The envelope read, "To a beautiful lady." On the card, he'd written, "You shouldn't have to buy your own rose!"

I read the card over and over as I walked the block to my office. I felt as if I could do anything, be exactly who I wanted to be. Algebra? Accounting? They weren't obstacles, but rather opportunities.

A heavy-set young woman met me at the open door of the small basement office I shared with the coordinator. "I need to talk with you."

Her bright eyes had a spark of defiance.

"I'm smart, but I get mental blocks when I take tests."

"I used to get mental blocks," I said.

She smiled and motioned me to lead the way into the room that resembled a large walk-in closet. My office.

By the time she left an hour later, we were becoming friends. I leaned over the red rose on my desk and inhaled the smell of God.

10

Bit to the Bone

Like a bitter woman, winter bites to the bone in Montana. I've been bit by both enough times to use caution when exposed, but the winter of 1991 caught me unguarded. Maybe the dark feeling that came over me when I drove by the horse ranch where we bought Calli's thoroughbred the spring before she turned sixteen was a premonition, but I missed its meaning if it was. Normally I would have taken the freeway home from Livingston because it was faster, but that day, after I spoke with Terence, I took the frontage road instead. After reminiscing earlier at Martin's, I was thankful to be alive. Slowing the car to a crawl, I enjoyed the soft lines of gray hills that rolled into deep purple masses.

If the mountains, valleys, rivers, and big sky of Montana hadn't sung to me in that silent language they have when I lost the heart to sing my own songs, I wouldn't be celebrating new beginnings. Nature was the mirror of sanity in an insane world, the voice of wisdom that linked me to infinite hope. Winter was a presence that had its own music, as did spring, summer, and fall. Taking walks was better for listening to ice crack on the rivers and snow fall on snow, tiny paws on cotton. I would have fit in with the Indians and settlers who traveled by foot, horses, and wagons over a hundred years before, but today the car windows were rolled up tight as two lips with a secret, and "country" was on the radio.

January was its usual freezing self around noon, so at a crawl, I was careful of black ice as I approached the horse ranch where we bought Swamp Fox, a three-year-old thoroughbred, five years before.

Right away, I could see that it didn't look like the same place in winter. Concealing trunks I knew to be dense and gnarled, branches were piled high and wide, reaching out like arms of skeletons in a mass grave. If the day had been any grayer, the clouds any lower, I would have thought I was driving through sacred burial grounds where victims cried out, "Don't forget what happened here!" That's how haunting the landscape was. Like figments of my imagination, the ranch house, barns, outbuildings, and fences were there, but they weren't. Like etched fragments and shadowed forms, they hovered.

I shivered to think that it was the same place Calli had fallen in love with Swamp Fox on sight. The day we came here to take him home, Gabe, Calli, Ryan, and I drove down the gravel driveway under a web of sprawling branches. Thick tree trunks promised quick access to limbs big as God's arms, the kind a kid could sit on and daydream. They reminded me of the apricot trees we had in our backyard when I was a little girl, the ones that used to keep me content and sticky sweet for hours. White fences and weathered wagon wheels separated the ranch from the rest of the world as if it was a piece of heaven devoted to making the dreams of young girls and boys come true. Grazing on gold-frosted pastures, where Chinook winds had melted crusty snow overnight, was the chestnut beauty Calli wanted for her own. We had come early to get ahead of the storm that had been forecast to blow in around dinnertime, when we planned to be safe and warm at home.

The ranch's owner walked out of the house and motioned us to park the horse trailer in the unlit barn that was the size of a small indoor arena. His cap shadowed his eyes so I couldn't see them, but his ruddy face was as worn as any piece of leather I'd ever seen hanging, tough with history, at the old saddle shop in Bozeman.

Calli jumped out of the truck, the halter in her hand, and headed to the field to get her horse. A gust of cold wind nipped my bare skin before she closed the door, and I suddenly wished we were on our way back home. By the time Gabe opened the doors to the stall of the trailer, Calli had returned on Swamp Fox, riding him with just the halter. Not long off the racetrack, he quivered when he walked, but that didn't bother his rider. She was in love.

She threw the lead rope over Fox's back, the signal to enter. Instead, he shifted nervously from hoof to hoof and backed away from the trailer. A few more tries and the owner took charge, mumbling that Fox may have had a traumatic experience with horse trailers when he was younger. The wind picked up, sounding like it was going to tear the tin roof off the barn, one brutal yank at a time. It reminded me of the way I'd seen sharks rip sea lions apart while they were still alive. Penetrating my jacket and Levi's, it felt mean enough to tear me apart limb by limb, too.

Normally I loved how wild storms claimed the earth, man, and beast long enough to purge us of pride, but that day it seemed the furies of hell rode the gales. For a terrifying hour, the gentle, trusting animal we'd bought the week before fought to stay out of the trailer stall, as if his life depended on it. While the rancher whipped, yanked, and cussed, Swamp Fox twisted, bolted, dropped to his knees on the dirt, cut his back leg on the lower edge of the trailer, banged his head on the upper edge, and foamed at the mouth before he found himself locked behind steel doors. Our family's pleas to wait so we could bring Calli's trainer and a bigger trailer were ignored.

Heading home, I weighed the damage. Exhausted, Calli had tears running down her flushed cheeks. Ryan's huge eyes misted until white and brown ran together. Gabe clenched his teeth to control his anger. My heart was still beating so hard I couldn't take a deep breath. Finally Ryan looked at his sister. "We can heal him, Cal. We healed Newt from being afraid of the bridle. Remember?"

It was true. The two of them had gentled a huge quarter horse we'd boarded. Newt wouldn't let them get near his right ear with the bridle. Ryan rode him the most, so for a couple of months, he talked to him, brushed and combed him, and got him used to having his ears touched. Sometimes Calli helped. Then one day Newt let them slip the bridle on without jerking away first. The two of them had helped him heal of flashbacks without knowing what had caused them. "Fox will be all right," I said. "At least, he won't ever have to see that rancher again."

Today, driving alone, the haunting landscape reminded me of the rancher's mean edge. I had seen it before in my own dad. Brittle branches, withered by wind chill into scrawny lifeless fingers, reminded me of him. His temper was as unpredictable as the gale that had ripped the barn. Being his favorite hadn't spared me from feeling the bite of his leather belt on my bare legs and bottom, but it was a look in his eye that dared my heart to beat when he was mad. I never understood how he could call me his Annie, his Pumpkin, and then let that belt loose like a pack of dogs after a baby rabbit. My older brother, Rod, got it worse than I did. Baby Beth had Mom to protect her, I thought at the time. When I was old enough to ask why, Mom blamed Dad's childhood with an alcoholic father for his vengeance. For her, that seemed to be reason enough.

Through clear patches in the mist, thick trunks—gray as concrete tombs—almost begged spring to release them from death's grip. They begged to feel sap pulse to the surface and bring them to life again. I didn't know if the rancher still owned that place, but his spirit was there, and it felt like it would be there after the earth disappeared from the universe, just in case anyone doubted who was in charge. For all I knew, the guy could have been crippled and confined to a wheelchair inside his home, but if he was like Dad, who'd survived a couple of heart attacks and open heart surgery, he used illness to sharpen his con. Dad could draw tears from stone. He drew them from my heart when I thought I couldn't feel anymore, didn't want to feel anymore. But to forgive him was to offer yourself as a sacrifice to his dark side, no matter how he'd tried to conceal it over the past few years with his ritual of repentance and dry tears. Forgiveness was raw meat to Dad. The rawer, the stronger the scent, the quicker he'd show up licking his lips.

Last fall he showed up in Bozeman with his new wife—who was about my age—and her kids. He invited me to come see them at the campground west of town where they parked their trailer. After filling me in on all the things he was buying and doing for them, Dad offered me fifty dollars, which I rejected, the way I'd rejected anything that would give him power over me long before I was ready to be weaned from a father's love. Apparently he got the message. Just before Christmas, he signed his card to the kids and me, "From Bill Jones and his new family." At first I thought he'd struck me off his list of life, but then I realized he'd severed our tie long ago and was just doing what came naturally to a man who was the center of his own world. If Dad had ever been able to afford to buy the ranch he dreamed of owning when he moved us from Colorado to California in 1950, I imagined that today it would have looked like this one, a mass grave of skeletons crying out for justice. Mine wouldn't have been among them. I'd given up on justice. All I wanted was peace of mind.

"I forgive him," I whispered to God for the millionth time—a sacrifice of love between me and Him. I thought how easy Dad would have been to hate if he hadn't had another side too. When I was a girl, I kept my tender feelings to myself. Mom would never have guessed how much I wanted to be her beloved first child or her favorite last rather than the provoking middle child that I was. Instead, Dad favored me with special hugs and touches that made her jealous and made me feel ashamed for needing attention so badly. Mom took my anger and defiance to mean I needed the switch or the palm of her hand when all I wanted was to spend time with her, even if it meant drying the dishes while she taught me to sing "On the Good Ship Lollipop" and sweet songs in French, like she had before I learned to talk back.

Dad knew me better than Mom did, I thought back then. He'd study me from his easy chair, his eyes gathering raw diamonds from an abandoned mine. "You okay, Annie?" he'd ask, making me feel like I was sitting in his lap when I wasn't. I used to think he could read my mind and between the lines. A fiddler of emotions, he played my heart to the tune called "Daddy" until sometimes I thought God was probably like him, instead of the other way around. I'm ashamed to admit it now with those scrawny wooden fingers reaching out for me from the clouded grave.

Now that I was healing, it didn't matter. Dad had taught me a lot, more than I wanted to know, in fact. As much as I wanted to feel safe in a world where God promises jobs that don't seem to exist, I'd probably always have times when I'd look behind my back and around the dark corners of my mind for an enemy I could feel but couldn't see. But that didn't scare me now that I knew those times would be less and less. My fight with the dark side had been a proving ground, and I was due for a promotion. Maybe I'd done all the right things for all the wrong people. I risked losing my heart before I knew I could lose my soul.

Scarred with lessons they learned from man, the purple mountains proved that, at a distance, pain fades into magnificence. I wanted to believe that my pain had given me depth.

Glancing over my shoulder to take one last look at the eerie ranch scene, I decided to get on the freeway as soon as I found an on-ramp. I didn't have to wait long. Snaking ahead of me on the tracks that paralleled the highway, a train headed toward Bozeman Pass. Miles away, a dark tunnel opened its mouth wide, a toothless black hole waiting to swallow the train one car at a time.

11

The Good Times

Maneuvering through the slick Bozeman Pass toward Bozeman, I brace myself for heartache. Around the bend, in the meadow below a mountain, is the last real home I had with a husband, kids, dogs, cats, kittens, horses, ducks—the illusion of security.

I embrace that illusion with all my heart, wanting to believe there was love between us—Gabe and me. I want to believe love held us together, just as betrayal tore us apart.

Memories of the good times come back to me. What I thought was the worst storm in Bozeman's history hit the weekend we moved in. It was Thanksgiving weekend 1985. Trim for the doors and windows was stacked high on the deck, but we had water and lights.

The whole family was worn-out from working nights, then driving back to the place we rented in town to sleep. We'd broken ground in late spring, thinking we could finish it by fall. Gabe had wanted his dad and mom to come help us. I guess that says it all about who was in charge. After four long months, they were so frustrated and disappointed in their son and his wife that they packed their bags and left for California. About the same day, winter blasted in early, leaving us with enough work to keep a construction crew busy. If my mom and dad hadn't come to help for a couple of weeks and friends hadn't shown up with hammers and heart, we might have gone bankrupt—paying a contractor, plumber, and electrician—before we ever moved in.

Nestled at the back of the meadow at the base of our mountain—thirty-seven acres total—was the home that still looked like it would heal the heart from whatever broke it. The day that Gabe and I drove down the driveway in his pickup with our last load of the move, cats and dogs braved the storm to meet us while we looked for Calli and Ryan among the welcoming committee.

Why don't the kids have the lights on? I wondered, shivering from the cold as I opened the back door. "Calli? Ryan?" I called loudly enough for them to hear me from their upstairs bedrooms. My only answer was the wood fire that crackled, spit, and roared in the Blaze King stove that separated living room from dining room.

I called again. No answer. When I entered the living room, a huge Christmas tree glowed from all the lights that twinkled off shiny balls that seemed to float rather than hang from branches. There was an ornament for each memory of all the years we'd spent together, loving, sharing, forgiving, and building a family bond that flowed deeper than flesh and blood.

With pure glee and team spirit, our two kids answered my stunned, "How, when, who?"

"We did it!" They were ecstatic.

"We took an ax and walked a long way up the mountain." Ryan performed the drama.

"And then Ryan climbed this tall tree I wanted." Calli could hardly get the words out, she was laughing so hard.

"Yeah, she told me to go up." Ryan pretended to be offended. "And then I chopped below the place where I hung onto the trunk. Pine needles were poking me everywhere." He burst out laughing.

Calli was holding her sides when she said, "And the part of the tree he was holding onto fell with him all the way to the ground."

Electrified, they rolled on the couch together.

"You've got to be kidding." I couldn't keep my eyes from the festival of lights they had planned, delivered, and presented in a matter of a few hours. How they found the decorations in all our stuff, I couldn't imagine.

"The rest of the tree's outside," Ryan said.

"You mean this tree was bigger?"

"Yes." They cheered. "We rode it down the mountain!"

As I drive by the scene of memories, the ache in my chest tells me that our family's love was real.

Regrets creep in when I crank my neck to take a long look at the changes the new owners have made. If I'd been the Mom I should have been, I would have kept it after Gabe left us. By opening a bed and breakfast, I could have paid off debts.

The new owners had built a new barn. A two-story addition to the house extended from the kitchen to the mountainside, as if they planned to live and die there.

Has anything ever felt that permanent to me in my whole life? Sometimes I feel like one of those crabs I used to pick up as they moved from shell to shell in the tide pools at Laguna Beach and Corona Del Mar, California. This shell holds memories for me though, and I swallow hard. Horses graze in the snow-covered pastures where Calli pulled Ryan on his sled behind Shawn O'Lark, the quarter horse that taught her to ride. Shawn's hoof had finally gone bad when he was eighteen years old, but his mind was still sharper than most people's when our veterinarian took him to babysit his two-year-old son.

We all hoped Swamp Fox, the young thoroughbred, would grow up to be like Shawn, and we weren't disappointed. After he settled into the routines, Calli began to work on loading him in the trailer. Tammy, her trainer, suggested parking it in the pasture and propping the stall door open so he could go in and eat his portion of hay every day. Fox missed breakfast and dinner a few times because he wouldn't go into the trailer to eat, but no one hit or yelled at him. Finally he made the big step up into the stall on his own and enjoyed eating oats out of the bucket before he started on fresh hay.

His big test came that fall. Calli entered the cross-country event at North Hills, and we had to trailer Swamp Fox there. When the day of the event arrived, we started loading him early. Actually, Calli and her trainer loaded Fox. But Gabe, Ryan, and I felt like we were the ones on trial as we willed, prayed, and calmly praised him for every step he took toward the stall. Until Calli finally stopped in the middle of everything and looked at us like we were overdoing it, we thought we were indispensable. Fox walked in on the second try. The autumn breeze was a good sign, I thought. Indian Summer had come early.

We arrived at the grounds in plenty of time for Calli to ride her trainer's two-year-old Warmblood in the event before she rode Fox in his first cross-country race ever. I figured that if she got that huge black beauty over all the high fences, the rock walls, creeks, and hay bales, she could do anything she wanted to with Fox. Many people who came to the event had already heard about the young rider and her new thoroughbred. They seemed to be just as aware of

Fox's youth and inexperience as they were aware that Calli had fear of neither one. The large crowd that gathered to watch the race was tense and unusually quiet.

The announcer raised his hand in the air to get the crowd's attention. He paused, then dropped it as he yelled, "Go!" I held my breath as if I was under water. At first Calli rode with an ease that evoked cheers from the crowd. Fox broke into a reckless pace, but the teenager kept her poise, triggering gasps and applause from the spectators and other contestants. She urged him higher than he'd ever been before, hardly missing a stride.

We followed their every move. When Fox stumbled, it seemed the crowd's gasp kept him from falling, they were so in tune to the pair. Nearing the end of the course, he broke into a dead run, bolted to the left, and Cal rode him at an angle until it seemed she brought the wind itself under control. At that point I didn't care if she placed or won, I just wanted her to stay on. They took the last fence with no problem.

When all the races had been run, the judges gathered on the porch of the rustic cabin to announce the winners and hand out ribbons. Breathless, her eyes sparkling, sweat beading her tan forehead, and sun shimmering on her hair, Cal rode up to accept her ribbon for second place. After she said thank you, I could hear the soft giggle that broke into a belly laugh as she rode away.

I wiped my tears that day, and I wipe them now as I drive toward home on the freeway, but for different reasons. "I'll make it up to you, Calli and Ryan. I'll make it up to both of you."

They've been forced to grow up too fast, and it worries me. Nineteen years old now, Cal works three jobs and goes to the university in Bozeman. From her description, she must have made quite a picture in her pottery class, walking barefoot in wet clay while her wide-eyed professor watched. He was probably held captive by the gold highlights that sometimes spark off her long thick hair.

Ryan's always on the go. He never forgets to give me a hug and say good-bye before he goes out the door, not even this morning when he was in a hurry to get up to the ski hill. The Bridger Mountains have been his second home since he took his first lesson when he was about five years old. His olive complexion is broken by white circles around his eyes, where his goggles have protected them from the sun. My son's face used to be lit up by the smile I always look for but seldom see anymore.

Extreme skiing seems so dangerous, but to him, jumping off cliffs is the rush that makes him feel alive. He told me the other day that he wants to die doing what he loves, not lying in a hospital bed, paralyzed by drugs with a machine breathing for him. Ryan wants to live for Calli and himself.

For the first time in the twenty-three years I'd known Gabe, I didn't feel guilty for being angry with him. Nevertheless, I had too much to make up for, too much to live for to be unforgiving. I had a job, two kids, and a man who wanted me to marry him.

The way Curt calls me "woman" makes me feel like I'm the only one he's ever known.

12

We Had Love

Spring calves had brands and tags the last time I drove to Livingston in 1991. Winter bit down hard and left its teeth marks on my heart. Grams died in January, and I missed her. Dad died in March, which was a relief that I didn't bother to explain to anyone because I didn't understand it myself. Curt didn't seem to need an explanation. My brother felt the same way I did. That was enough comfort for me. Then Calli, my Sunlet, died. And I died with her, only to find what it means to live. Nothing's been the same since.

In pastures nearby, calves romped over patches of snow. A relentless winter and stubborn spring mirrored the way I was feeling. Not even the seasons were celebrating. It was a time to mourn. The words seemed to come on their own, "This isn't how it was supposed to be. This isn't how it was supposed to be."

If I thought about the pain, I wouldn't be able to drive, so I thought about Hank, Stuart, Terence, and some of my other clients who still needed support from Project Opportunity. They wouldn't have anywhere else to go now that the Bozeman office was given notice: Insufficient funds. Mid-June was the closing date. With the end of May approaching, I was finishing paperwork and missing my clients already. In March, Hank crawled under his truck to work on it while it was running. He died of asphyxiation. Anyway, that was the story Ron Sturgis told me.

After Stuart found out his lifeline wasn't going to have anyone on the other end, he dove into a swimming pool and didn't come up for air. Terence was making progress, and I could have helped him reach his goals if I had more time. Vince seldom missed our classes together the way he had when we started. I was glad to show Ron the final tests of over thirty clients when we talked at our last meeting in Helena, the state headquarters for Project Opportunity. Their scores had soared. Others would succeed where they'd failed before, if we had more time.

According to Ron, a coordinator from one of the other cities might come to Bozeman once a week, but he wasn't sure yet. We couldn't count on Lou anymore. A few weeks before, our coordinator didn't come into work one day. The secretary called from headquarters to tell me Lou was suffering from flashbacks of Vietnam and wouldn't be able to function under any kind of stress for a long time. I still hadn't talked with him, but hoped he'd call to say good-bye.

Good men had died of despair, yet God continued to bless me with this job even as it was coming to an end. Ron recently offered me a teaching position that was opening up north, but I couldn't leave Bozeman with a son here and a new husband who had three kids of his own. While we looked for a house to buy or rent, Curt's son Chad was living with us in his dad's condo. His sisters lived in Helena with their mom.

After I told Ron I couldn't move away from Bozeman, he asked what he could do to help me find another job. I wanted to write full-time. Consequently, he and the director of another employment program were in the process of getting funds for me to have my dream. I knew who was behind it all. God promised to bless me with this job when it was taken. I guess He wasn't going to stop now that it was almost gone.

Hank was dead. Yet Calli had proven that this life is the cocoon stage for all God's butterflies. I was somewhere between heaven and hell, where survival seems possible and impossible at the same time.

The ranch where we bought Swamp Fox didn't look like a graveyard today, with the sun sparkling off roofs, branches, and white patches of snow. Thank goodness. I couldn't take a graveyard today.

This wasn't the way it was supposed to turn out when Curt knelt in front of me and asked me to marry him on Easter Day, 31 March 1991. We were in Helena celebrating his friend Rick's birthday when Curt shocked everyone, including me. Ever since his ex-wife Vera divorced him, Curt told good friends he'd never marry again, so they made him ask me twice. He didn't hesitate to kneel again, and I didn't hesitate to answer.

On the way home, we planned our future together: the house

with five bedrooms, one for each of our kids, an office for him and one for me. We'd need a big garage for bikes, cars, water skis, and kneeboards, we agreed, wanting to believe that our lives were on the mend. Sounded like heaven on earth, for sure, this time.

Looking back, I can still remember the landscape as the sun went down. I told myself I'd never forget it. The highway took us through barren hills and frosted fields. No one could survive there without food and shelter. Or manna from heaven. That's the absolute power nature was manifesting as sunlight trimmed the horizon. This was not a place that man had made. If the lone skeleton of a tree on the windswept mound would have exploded into fire, I would have asked Curt to stop the car and listened for God to call our names. The silence felt that loud to me.

I didn't notice Curt turn off the stereo, but when I looked at him, I knew he was listening to the silence too.

He took my hand in his big warm grasp and pulled it to his chest.

I take this woman, I heard in my heart.

Do you take this man?

Under my breath, I said, "I do."

The sun dropped out of sight, leaving the white bones of the tree to the cold moon and the starless night. Paradise had a stark, severe side, but it was as sacred as the Resurrection we'd celebrated that day.

Calli wasn't supposed to get sick three weeks later.

It was a week before my birthday and two weeks before the wedding we planned to have at our friends' house in the country. This spring was supposed to be a celebration that would dwarf all the hard times and give them meaning. She wasn't supposed to get a disease that defied test tubes and the best medicine to identify it for nearly two weeks. For almost three days she was in Bozeman Deaconess's intensive care unit while a team of Bozeman doctors tried uselessly to diagnose her disease. Gabe, Curt, and I agreed Calli should go to Billings where pulmonary specialists could diagnose and treat her. Gabe rode with his daughter in the helicopter that flew her to the Billings Deaconess where she lay, medicated and paralyzed by machines so she wouldn't have to breathe, for almost ten days. That fatal disease ravaged Calli's lungs while we stood helplessly at her side.

She'd been in Billings a couple of days when her boyfriend Mike brought his guitar and sound equipment to her hospital room. I thought the nurses would shake their heads and say "Absolutely not." Instead, they paused outside her room or came in to listen while he strummed his and Calli's favorite songs. He played along with the tape a professional singer had made just for her when she got sick.

I never gave up believing she'd live. Believing was all I could do with those machines and the disease in control of her body. I thought God would work a miracle—the one he'd been strengthening my faith for all these years—and that's what I told all her friends when they called the hospital. Calli wasn't in the hospital but a few days when Gabe and I, together, lay hands on our daughter's body and prayed for her healing. I looked at his bowed head as I had so many times over the years when we'd prayed for our children or each other. With all my heart, I wanted Calli's body to be our altar of reconciliation. I prayed that the power of love and forgiveness would heal her. When both the hospital chaplain and priest asked permission to anoint her with oil, we thankfully agreed. My hopes were high when the doctor took Calli off the ventilator so she could breathe on her own, but coughing tore holes in her lungs in two more places. Partially conscious for the first time since she'd come to Billings, tears ran from her fluttering lids as she tried to open them. The doctor immediately anesthetized her again.

Early the last morning, the hospital staff mopped around me—getting ready for the next patient already, I thought painfully—as I sat in a chair by my daughter's side. Surrender was the only answer. "She's yours, Father. She always has been."

Family and a few friends gathered around while others who'd spent the night in the hospital filled the huge waiting rooms. The first time Ryan saw his sister in the Billings hospital a few days before, he went into shock. His body was paralyzed and he couldn't breathe. I feared for his life until the nurses helped him function again. Now he sat near his sister, ready to go the distance as long as she needed him. Her boyfriend Mike was playing a song about a golden sleep on the guitar as best he could, until tears made singing impossible. Calli's breathing stopped before her heart did, and I waited for God to breathe His life into her and give her back to me. I guess He did, just not the way I hoped for.

Today, as I drive toward Livingston, there's a stark side to heaven that I don't like to think about. Nothing's turned out the way Curt and I planned it on Easter. Our pastor, Reverend Blackmore, married us while Gabe rode with Calli in the helicopter to Billings. Ryan says he's moving in with his dad and stepmother for a while right after he graduates in a week or so. His dad promised him a new truck for graduation, and a stepbrother will be born in July. I've moved in with Curt. Chad's with us, but his little sister is afraid her mother will commit suicide if she moves to Bozeman.

Soft as my daughter's breath when she sleeps, a fragrance wafts by me. It's so sweet my head's spinning, yet the windows are up and I don't have perfume on. There aren't any plants, candy, or roses in here. It's so strong, I may have to stop just to inhale for a while. *Calli? Calli, is that you? Sweetheart, I love you.*

She's here, just like the morning after I left her in the hospital for the last time, the image of her heavy on my heart. She was stretched out under the sheet, the smell of her skin still on mine. My empty arms ached to hold her and never let her go, especially not into that black hole where I couldn't see her, couldn't see if she was safe, if she was eating all right, getting enough sleep, needing to talk, needing me to leave her alone. From the time I left her at the hospital until I went to bed that night, heaven seemed like a myth, a cloud of mist that had evaporated when I needed it the most.

Dawn light woke me the next morning, but loneliness reminded me of what day it was, the first of forever without Cal. I looked at her high school graduation picture where I'd taped it on the cover of my journal and stood it by our bed the night before. I made heaven out of the things that were available—a chair, a journal, and a wallet-sized picture.

Oh, God. I cried silently.

Listening for His voice, I heard her voice instead.

Mom, she said. *Mom.*

Grief is making me crazy, I thought, but it wasn't just her voice I recognized. I could feel her spirit, her familiar presence.

Cal?

She laughed. *Yes, Mom, it's me.*

Heaven was on earth where I always prayed it would be, and I was ready to accept I couldn't hold her. She was here. That's what mattered.

Honey, I didn't get to tell you I'm sorry or say any of the things I wanted to say.

No, you were being strong for me and everyone else, and you didn't want to let me go until you knew it was what God wanted.

Cal, I have so many regrets. I let you and Ryan down in so many ways.

Don't feel guilty, Mom, she said. *I have a peace you don't understand. And joy. You thought I'd always be there. I did too, but this is better. There's no room for regrets. You have too much to give others. You'll understand some day. And Mom . . .*

What, darling?

Thank you. Thank you for loving me. We always knew that we had love.

Calli, my memory is gone, except I remember I wasn't there when you needed me.

I have a lifetime of memories, Mom, not just one day. We'll look at them together soon. Then she was quiet, but she wasn't gone. She was spirit now.

Curt stirred next to me. "You okay?" he asked.

"Yes, yes, I am," I said. "Curt, she talked to me this morning."

"Who?"

"Calli."

"I told you she wasn't gone."

A half-dozen hot pink roses in a vase on the kitchen counter caught my eye the minute I walked into my friend Kathy's kitchen the next evening. She had invited Curt and me over for dinner earlier that day. "Where did you get those beautiful pink roses?" I assumed her husband or son bought them for Mother's Day, which was that Sunday.

"DeeAnn, I have something to tell you." Her voice trembled. She took a deep breath. Through the years, we'd found our sense of humor in the midst of life's crises, including each of our divorces, but the death of a child is unnatural, like striking the key of a piano and not hearing a sound.

Letting her breath out in a rush of words, my friend said, "You know how I have to see things for myself to believe them. Today Eternity was spliced into earth time all day. I could hear angel wings. Angels have talked to me today."

She paused, as if waiting for me to nod or fall over or break into pieces. I listened. "They told me to set a place for Ryan and his friend Jesse for dinner. I couldn't get hold of Ryan, but I know he's coming. Then, there are the roses. I went to Safeway after I left you at your place this afternoon. When I walked through the door I heard Calli say, 'Get Mom some roses.' I walked over to the flower department and started to pick up a bouquet of white ones, but she said, 'No, get the hot pink.' 'Do you want me to get her a card?' I asked. 'No, just tell her that I love her.' "

"Hot pink was her favorite color." I was crying now. "It was the color of the cummerbund she wore with her tux to the Senior Prom last year." Her friends always said Calli had her own style. She could have worn the black evening gown she tried on at the mall. When had she grown into a beautiful woman?

Ryan and Jesse showed up just before we were about to sit down at the table for dinner. Kathy looked at me as if to say, "See what I mean?"

By the time we got to dessert, Ry started talking about his adventurous childhood as Calli's younger brother. She tried to teach him to ride horses the way her first trainer, a cowboy at the college, had taught her, by holding on with her legs and letting go of the reins, her arms outstretched wings at her sides. Like a bird on a horse, she flew in circles forever, it seemed.

I knew what he was talking about; I'd watched her for hours. But Ryan's legs were shorter than hers, and his horse was almost as wide as he was tall. All of us laughed until our sides hurt as he told story after story. Then I remembered what Calli told me that morning, *I have a lifetime of memories, Mom. We'll look at them soon.*

I felt so close to her in the days that followed, as if our thoughts were one. She knew what she wanted at her memorial: The Young Life leader who went with her and a group of her friends to a youth camp in Malibu, Canada, had a story to tell that would help all those who came to her memorial understand that she was happy and safe. The summer before her senior year—a couple of months after Gabe left—she was excited to go someplace she'd never been and make new friends. As the leader told the story to the crowd that filled church pews and aisles near the walls, his eyes were seeing it all as if for the first time:

"As the boat entered the harbor of the remote camp in what seemed like Paradise, we could see teenagers from all over the nation waiting on the dock to greet us. A guy yelled to Calli, 'What's your name?' "

" 'Calli,' she yelled back."

" 'What?' he said, and a few other guys joined in the game."

" 'Calli,' she shouted."

"And then they began to sing her name, spelling it out, a letter at a time, 'C-A-L-L-I! C-A-L-L-I!' until the boat docked."

My daughter got a welcome she never forgot. *This is what heaven is like*, Calli was telling us. *I'm someplace I've never been before and have new friends. I love you all.*

In front of the crowd, Ryan promised his sister, "I'll never forget you, Cal. We'll never forget you."

We never will. The parking lot at Martin's Cafe is full, but I squeeze my compact car into a slot. With her fragrance strong around me, I don't want to get out of the car, but I've promised a young client who's hired on as a cook here that I'd stop by to drop off the books he needs to study for the GED. *I don't want to leave you, Cal.*

Reluctantly I get out of the car. *Surely this isn't how it was supposed to be.* A man holds the door for me as I walk into the old train depot café.

13

Gathering the Children

Walking on the icy sidewalk toward the Western Cafe, I think time's nothing more than the glue that connects the slippery path of a child's prayer. Looking down the street at the familiar neighborhood of old houses, I see a few with gnarled tree trunks standing in the front yards like ancient sculptures that have lost arms, heads, and legs. The city park has become a field of snow, and I see hockey players practicing on the ice rink. The safe scene doesn't look like it's in a valley where mothers are asking why so many teenagers have died in the past decade.

Too many teenagers have passed away in this valley for me not to wonder why. The first one that I remember was a graduating senior boy who committed suicide two years before Calli died. There have been several suicides and fatal vehicle accidents, a skiing accident, a drowning, and another fatal disease besides Calli's. These are just a few that I know of. And while we mourn those lost to the epidemic of shootings around the nation, including the one not too far away in Butte, Montana, bomb threats have left the corridors and classrooms of our own high school vacant from time to time.

How does a mother keep her children safe from harm?

When a child dies, there must be an explanation and a solution, especially when that child is your own. After she died, I relived phone calls I made to her doctor the week before she became too sick to save. Her fever went down toward the end of the week, but it still hurt her chest to breathe deeply, so I called him. If her fever's down, she's improving, he insisted.

A mother should have known—if she was any kind of mom at all—was what I told myself then, and still do sometimes. After she died, the lung specialist in Billings said it wouldn't have made any difference. The germ they hadn't been able to identify had probably been fatal from the moment Calli breathed it. I hung up without telling him I'd seen God work miracles; He could do anything if He wanted to.

Sometimes I feel as if I'm standing off at a distance, watching my life happen. Others wrestle with the question of why so many tragedies could happen to someone who tries as hard as I do to get life right. Is getting it right as important as I've always thought it is? Other parents who loved Calli have gone through torment as they've walked the bases, trying to make sure they've covered them all so their children won't end up like mine. Some think it was her dad's fault for breaking her heart. Maybe others think it's my fault. How terrifying it is to think my God could be so small. Why believe at all? It's heartbreaking to think a loving Father would take out a parent's sins on a child. Why am I alive then? Whose child is safe from His wrath? I have to ask myself.

Death makes pilgrims of us all. In the wilderness of grief, we each find our own way to safety.

Anger was not what I heard in God's voice as I walked across the street from Curt and my motel to see Calli in the intensive care unit a few days after we arrived in Billings. I was thanking God that the doctors and nurses were so hopeful for her complete recovery when He said, *This will be hard on you, Annie, but there is no other way.*

Like a gust of wind blowing through my mind, I heard, *There will be sorrow for the night, but joy comes in the morning.*

I couldn't bear the burden of a love that would let a child suffer in the first place, let alone a love that would let mine die. It seemed like the week before she'd gone to the swim center to practice doing flips in a kayak. Her friends had invited her to take on the Gallatin River during spring runoff. She'd just started riding thoroughbreds again. She'd just started; she'd just begun. I've had thousands of nights and mornings since.

Today snow's falling on the ugly limbs and branches that form a web above me, reminding me of the aspen that grows outside my office window. Curt pruned it last summer, the same day he sprayed weed-killer on all the young shoots that were growing too close to the foundation of our house. He was nearly finished when I heard him sawing away as if he were doing me a favor. My husband chopped off smaller limbs with his hatchet while I sobbed in my office, feeling as if he'd cut off my own arms and legs. It was too late to tell him I would rather hang ornaments from those roots if they shot through the walls than let him destroy the illusion the hedge of trees gave me when I looked out my office window. Even before they leafed out every spring, the web of limbs and branches made it easy to convince myself I had the best of both worlds, the best of both heaven and earth. I lived in town, but it felt like country, not a neighbor for miles around. I barely stopped him in time before he lopped off all that was left of the tree just outside my window where I loved to watch birds flock to my feeder all year long.

It's not just the ugly branches I miss, though. I didn't give my love the right to strip my illusions down to the neighbor's chalky white wall. Until Calli died, I hoped someday I'd be able to give her heaven on earth. She gave it to me instead. I've held the real world in my arms.

Truth cuts to the core of a woman's existence with the sharp edge of tempered steel. The promise of freedom, it carries a burden of responsibility no human should have to bear without God. A love that blooms in darkness, it is enduring. Reason becomes dead weight on wings of faith. These truths are written on the chalk wall of my heart now that the illusions are gone.

Or are they gone? Perhaps the hope that I'll see Paradise on earth is an illusion, but a child's prayer denies it. There is a story about roses that grow in the Balkans and supply the world with their attar or perfume. Workers gather the roses in the darkest hours between one and two o'clock in the morning when the perfume is the strongest. In the light of day, the petals lose forty percent of their scent. Perhaps God gathers his children when the power of their fragrance reveals it is time. One of Calli's friends told me my daughter knew all there was to know about love and was ready to move on.

When God said, *This will be hard on you, Annie, but there's no other way*, no one had called me Annie for a long time. I'd almost forgotten it was my name. I couldn't believe she'd die. The truth was more than I could bear. It still is sometimes, so I gather her fragrance in the darkest hours to get me through until morning comes.

14

The Valley of the Flowers

A patch of ice on the sidewalk sends me flying, but I catch myself before I fall. The sound of tires on snow and the smell of bacon and Bea's cinnamon rolls makes me realize I'm already there, just across the street from the white stucco café with the brown awning over the small entryway. The Western looks just like it did yesterday and the day before. It's sure not anything special to look at, yet I come here daily—and have for years—as if it's the hub of paradise.

I've walked a mile of my life this morning. In Bozeman I've known more heartache than some have in their whle lives, and less than others have in hours. Yet I woke up this morning thinking maybe this is the day. This is the big day I'm going to see something in a new way, a new light, and Paradise is going to reach out and hug me around the neck like an old friend who's been lost. Where have you been, girl? he'll say.

I'm not the only one who thinks this valley is special. There's a Native American legend that shows how extraordinary it is. I have some Indian in me, Mom says. Dad said it too, but he swore his great-uncle was a half-breed thief. I never heard the details.

As I wait for the flow of cars to either stop or pass so I can walk across the street to the café, I think about the legend of "Valley of the Flowers." In it, a child—a woman-child in spirit—puts an end to war in this valley and changes it forever. I think of Calli.

War is not new to this part of the country according to the story John Richau, a half-breed, told pioneers. The day once-hostile tribes saw its heavenly side, this valley became neutral ground. The Blackfoot, Bannack, Crow, Flathead, Nez Percé, Shoshoni, Sioux, and Snake camped side-by-side from then on.

The way I understand it, when deadly enemies, the Nez Percé and the Sioux, met at the mouth of Bridger Canyon one morning, only a miracle could have stopped the bloodshed. For two days they fought, and blood soaked the earth like rain never had. The sun was radiant when it rose on the third day, as if marking the hour of deliverance, but the tribes saw only death as they closed in for the kill.

Moved by laws beyond nature, darkness moved over the sun. Stars shone brightly against the night sky. Stunned and terrified, the warriors listened as a pure feminine voice moved toward them from heaven. Singing out of a white flame, a spirit appeared on the mountain, later called Mount Bridger. Not a warrior looked away as the flame moved toward the blood-soaked field. Growing larger and larger, it finally fixed itself at the top of the pass. As if nothing more than a velvet blanket in God's hands, darkness disappeared.

Aglow in flames was the stone maiden, so the story goes. The Crow legend calls her Evening Star, the spirit of a child bride who lost her sweetheart to war.

She said, "Warriors, children of the Great Spirit, sheath the hatchet and unstring the beautiful bow. Shed not the blood of your brothers here, lest it mingle with yonder foaming water and defile the 'Valley of the Flowers' below. There must be no war . . . . All must be peace, rest, and love." [2]

According to the legend, Evening Star never stops watching over the valley. Legends are true, aren't they? This one has to be.

In a large photograph on the wall of the Pioneer Museum, the original jailhouse, a Crow maiden stands in front of a humble log dwelling. The open range spread like a carpet of freedom at her feet. Made of mud and God's spit like the rest of us, she reminds me that in spirit we're all flames with a voice, if we choose to be. Is this what I'm here in the Valley of the Flowers to learn?

Looking toward the Bridger Mountains, it's easy to remember all the nights I've seen them outlined by a star-studded sky. There's usually one star above them that's brighter than the rest. Some days heaven's easier to see than others.

If you've ever seen the Bridger Mountains painted pink by a twilight sky in winter, you know what I mean. If it's cold enough, a

---

[2] Annabelle Collier Phillips "Valley of the Flowers," as ". . . recorded for posterity by Mrs. E. Lina Houston in her book, *Early History of Gallatin County, Montana.*" Except for the quote, I've told the legend in my words.

thick fog rises from the foothills and it looks like the whole range is floating above the earth. At those times, it's not hard to imagine this valley mirrors its eternal twin. It's not hard to remember why it seemed like the Promised Land where my children would be safe compared to living in what I saw as Charles Manson's diabolical California twenty-six years ago. There are still nights when that one star is so bright I wouldn't be surprised if it's the white flame, the spirit that's been watching over the valley since the beginning of time.

Is she speaking to me today?

Having seen the power of a child's prayer this morning, my mind wanders up Bridger Canyon, Kelly Canyon, Moffit Gulch, and the other trails that run like loose threads from a ball of yarn all over the valley. Brooding over the land the way God did over genesis waters, husbands, wives, and children paid the price dreams are made of to settle this land. They raised cattle, sheep, and families and logged, mined, and farmed in temperatures too cold, conditions too rugged to do anything but harden the metal of their souls. If you've ever seen a photograph of an old mail truck stuck in gumbo, you know the settlers weren't alone in the crucible.

I don't think anyone could identify the seed this dream grew from or where it's going from here. No one but the Creator, anyway. He knows why I'm here.

Cars going both east and west have stopped. How long have they been waiting for me to cross the street?

When I was a child, I imagined God's Kingdom on earth to be one big happy family and I wanted to be a part of it. When I was in college, a friend showed me a book called The Family of Man. Page after page, photographs of men, women, and children from all over the world looked like a family album, one I could imagine my own picture in. Cheerfully, I thought love makes relatives of strangers, friends out of enemies, children out of grandparents. The clock of creation ticks backward.

Now that I'm old enough to have grandchildren, I still dream of seeing Paradise on earth. Yet if I had a book called The Family of Man in my library, I'd add a caption on the cover: "Jesus entrusted himself to no man because he knew what was in a man." It's another lesson I learned in Bozeman, Montana—one I didn't want to learn anywhere. But as I walk into the café, I'm feeling the family of man in a special light, where our weaknesses are noble.

Looking around for Curt, I see the Strobel family having breakfast at the long table in the back room as they have for years. I see old friends who have taken a break from ranching or daily chores and jobs. We haven't known each other for our whole adult lives like some of them have, but when I'm around these people, I feel like I can stick out the worst winter blizzard of my life, if it's still up ahead.

At another table I see Bud V., who's seventy-three years old. From what he's told me, Bud knows about thirst, both man's and the land's. He was a little boy when the dust storms nearly choked the life out of his dad. With topsoil layered in mounds against the house and property fences, his father had to work for a neighbor to keep his family from starving. To this day, Bud openly thanks God for every drop of rain, every blade of grass, his health, the food on his table, everything. It's all a gift, as far as he's concerned. With his generous wife by his side, it probably is.

Sitting next to Bud is Joe K. His iron will makes him look like he's taller than the others, even when his little wife isn't standing next to him. The grasshopper plague followed the dust storms, and when Joe was thirteen years old, living in eastern Montana, the grasshoppers ate his shirt off the fence. Being the oldest, he left home so his dad would have one less mouth to feed, one less to worry about starving to death.

Art Morrow walks by and squeezes Curt's shoulder as a greeting. I picture Art as a little boy, pulling his wagon from the other end of town all the way to the junkyard that used to be on this end, over half a century ago. After the Story Mansion was torn down to make room for a new school, he gathered copper roofing and sold it at the junkyard for a nickel.

John Ham is here now. We sit down at Curt's table at the same time. John's usually late because he feeds livestock first. Standing to leave, Burl Hamilton offers his chair. He's the one who keeps me on schedule by asking if the book's done yet. There's no point in explaining that this one's different from the others. There's an auction today, a big first-of-the-year sale where ranchers sell last year's calves while the prices are high. Some of the men will see each other there later. It's been years since I went with my ex-husband Gabe and the kids to see what a good horse was going for. Canning prices were high, so it was not a time I like to remember. Good horses were sold for dog food, or maybe their meat was sent to Europe. I don't know. But the auctioneer's call was music to my ears. I'd like to go back for the music.

The conversation relaxes now, like a slow dance between fast ones. "Dad used to have rodeos at our place when I was a kid," John says to Curt. Like me, my husband loves to hear about the old days when bad times were a good reason to get together with friends.

Les Walton's joined us now, and soon his wife Audrey will come. Les had a ranch up the road from John's for years. He smiles in a way that looks like the sun rises from his heart. "We'd drive the whole family in wagons through a blizzard on weekends to go to each other's homes for potluck and pinochle." You can tell friendship means a lot to Les. Both of his parents were dead by the time he turned twelve. He's another one who packed all he owned in his sleeping roll and went to work as a hired hand. Like the others, he never complains how he had to fit school between jobs as a kid, enlisted when he was old enough to do his duty, and then worked hard to make a living for his family every day of his life.

"There were a lot of kids like me," he says.

None of these friends pity themselves, and it helps me remember that I didn't pity myself when I was growing up either. Even if my brain and body hadn't shut down when the pain got so bad, from what I've remembered, Annie's been the best part of me all along.

These are the knights and ladies of my round table. I know I'm a romantic, an idealist, and a little loony, but when a woman finds out that almost everyone she ever trusted in her life betrayed her, she creates a world she can live in out of what and who she has around her. It could be Paradise. Only God knows for sure. God and His daughters, Calli and Evening Star.

15

The Colonel

Intense as starlight, there's a knowing that's in me today. Like a secret begging to be told, it's here, and I look around to see if anyone else notices how bright it is in the Western Cafe. There's music in the conversations you can listen to for hours and not get bored. Maybe it's a Song of Roots that pulls me deep into my soul until I come to Annie, open as a four year old who loved to chase baby lambs in the corral.

Is this you, Cal, shining on my heart? Are you and Annie in cahoots, using a child's prayer to open my eyes? Nothing's been the same since you died—or broke free is what I want to say.

Josh Ham leans across the table after I sit down. "Tell me about the husky again." The familiar smell of the earth is on the five-year-old's clothes. It's a kid smell, Calli's and Ryan's smell when we lived in what I thought would become Paradise, outside of town.

I know what Josh wants to hear. This is a game we play. It is a game, but it's memories too, remembering how a child's eyes open wide like the trust that's in his heart. Talking about the good times is healing for me still.

"My son Ryan got Syke when he was just a fluffy puppy," I tell Josh.

He puts his elbows on the table and moves closer so he can hear every word, his blue eyes springs of curiosity. His sweet mom invited us to his birthday party a couple of weeks ago, and his eyes have the same sparkle now as they did when he tore open his presents.

I think about my son's fifth birthday and want to kick myself for getting caught in Reverend Harmon's web of laws, then adding a few of my own to make his god proud. I invited Ryan's small kindergarten class to Village Inn for pizza, but told the teacher no one was to bring gifts. Birthdays were about friends and love, not things money could buy. My son's family would buy him a few presents, but the kids just needed to come to the party. Ryan was happy, or acted happy, as if he'd been given every wish on his list, but I wasn't happy as I asked myself, What's happened to me? What's happened to Annie? I don't want to think about it now. Maybe on the walk home.

"Syke was smart." Josh begins, anxious to hear the whole story.

"And his eyes were ice blue just like his daddy's."

"Tell me about the chickens," Josh says.

"You mean the neighbor's prize Banty roosters, don't you?"

His blue eyes get bigger, waiting for me to tell him the whole story of how Syke grew until he became the scandal of Bear Canyon Estates by following the instincts he was born with. "Hens, roosters, sheep, and deer had been safe on the mountain until he got big enough to take them down."

"My dog helps Dad and Grandpa round up the cows."

When my brother was Josh's age, Dad used him to herd sheep the way the Hams use their dogs.

"Your dog was born with instincts to herd cattle, Josh, and she's obedient too, isn't she?"

He nods but doesn't budge when Lana, our waitress, sets his big breakfast in front of him. Knowing how the regulars like coffee, Patty and Stacy arrive with full steaming pots at the same time.

"Eat your French toast and bacon before it gets cold, Josh," his grandpa says, then goes back to trading stories about the good years on the Ham Ranch.

That's it! The light I've been waiting for. It's the stories Mom used to tell that sheltered me in the storms of childhood. Through her eyes, I saw my father as the young man who lost his job at the grocery store rather than lie. He was an inventor and a hunting guide. I saw him as the boy she fell in love with in high school bookkeeping and married a few years later, against her mother's will. On Mom's tongue, every story had a happy ending. It must have nearly killed her to call me, the summer of 1993, when she knew I'd almost finished my story of healing, which included memories of the rapes. I'd been waiting. I told God that I wouldn't expose the truth about the rapes unless I knew Mom would be okay. Until the day she called, she'd denied everything. "How could you forget how special you were to your dad?" she often said, making me feel like I'd raped him, instead of the other way around.

I had only a few chapters left to write when Mom called with a purpose, "Have you finished the book, DeeAnn?"

I'm close, Mom."

"Finish it, then, and publish it. I've remembered enough to know it's true."

"Like what?"

"Your dad said I didn't really know him."

"Did he ever call you a leech?" In my memories, Dad had called Mom, Rod, and Connie Beth leeches and threatened to kill them if I didn't do what he wanted.

"DeeAnn, I loved your dad, but he was the easy way out when I married him. I'm so sorry. I'll tell your brother and sister the truth too." Rod and Connie were fighting as hard as I was to heal. They were survivors long before "survivor" became a household word in America.

I waited for Mom to tell me what she remembered.

"Your dad said he had friends and a life that I didn't know anything about."

Well, I knew them. Today they could be sentenced to life in prison in some states for what they did to me."

For the first time, I felt like Mom stood up to Dad for me, even though he was dead.

Until today, I hadn't thought about the stories Mom told me—and tells me still—as my shelter in the night.

Like a sapling under a sprawling oak, "The Colonel" sheltered me. I'd never seen him, not even in photographs, but he was as real as the heat off the land that kept me warm, the rugged Rocky Mountains that kept guard, the song of the meadowlark in the morning. Mom made sure I knew him. Colonel Albert Pfeiffer was a legend in Colorado, and he was my great-great-grandfather. He made me special no matter how many times I wet my pants when Mom said I was old enough to know better. One of the bravest men in the West, "The Colonel" made me feel brave every time I heard how he fought for white men and Indians alike and made treaties he tried to keep. Letters from his friend and commanding officer Kit Carson were treated as sacred as the Holy Bible at our house.

The Colonel adopted Indian orphans and raised them as his own. Noble as I thought he was, it seemed natural he would marry a princess. She was a Spanish princess, Mom said. And her wedding dress was made for royalty. I don't know how many years the storybook couple was married before a tragedy changed the Colonel's life forever. They were soaking in healing waters near the fort, probably to treat a bad skin condition he had, when an Apache war party attacked them. Like savages, they cut the fetus out of her womb. My great-great-grandfather ran naked for miles with an arrow stuck in his back, a wound that finally killed him later in life. It never entered my mind that he was a drunk when I found out he drowned his pain in alcohol and took his vengeance out on hostiles. He was "The Colonel," after all.

This was my inheritance. A land of womb songs, rugged wilderness, and heroes. This was one of the stories I heard and asked to hear again as I was growing up.

Maybe the Colonel was Annie's Jacob. He fought man and God for his identity as a soldier in the volunteer army. I must have assumed the genes made me a soldier, too.

If the Colonel's image wasn't enough to cover family flaws, Mom made sure I knew who his daughter-in-law was. The last few years that I lived in the valley of the Rockies, I stood on the sidewalk next to Rod every summer, where I shifted anxiously from one foot to the other, peeking around Levi's pant legs and print skirts to see down the street.

When is the parade going to start, Mommy?" I'd ask. Then the band would strike up, and my chest would fill with vibrations from the drum. Unable to stand still, I marched in place between my parents.

"Where's Grandma?" I asked every year that I can remember.

"She's coming, Sweetie. See the stagecoach? She's in there." We waited for the Colonel's daughter-in-law to come by.

Dad swung me up in his arms to see better. "How's this, Annie? Better?"

"Yes." Better. Much better, I thought, as I watched the parade and felt the warmth of those strong arms around me. Softly, I touched Dad's tan felt hat and quietly inhale the smell of his sweet pipe tobacco and aftershave.

Straining to see inside the coach's window, I found her, the little wrinkled lady with the wonderful toothless smile, waving gloved hands, first one and then the other. I'd held those small hands. They told me about love, about hard work, about age. Strong hands and happy eyes are how I remember Great-grandmother Pfeiffer.

There wasn't a trace of sadness in those eyes. No one would have known that her mother's wealthy family had abused the daughter of the French fur trapper, Francis Chamberlain. Colorado cattle barons, they used her as a servant after her mother died.

I visited Great-grandma at Aunt Lena's house, a place I'll never forget: two-story red brick with stone walkways and dirt paths, a little creek with bridges wide enough I wouldn't slip off of them. Leafy trees smelled friendly, like my aunt's house. When we went to visit, the solid oak table was filled with fried chicken, potatoes, and gravy. There was an upstairs bedroom where I took naps and watched cracks travel across the ceiling. Old, forever strong, and safe. My inheritance.

Heroes are important to a little girl, and Mom gave them to me. Although there was one I chose for myself.

I can do that! I thought. All the kids sat around the sweet-smelling Sunday school teacher while she explained the game.

"Every time you remember a verse, I'll put a star by your name," she said. "The first verse is John 3:16, 'For God so loved the world that He gave His only begotten Son . . . .' "

Those wonderful stars. The teacher was still quoting the verse but all I could see was stars. *One by my name . . . Rod will help me.* My brother was three years older than me and in first grade. His love made me taller when Mom and Dad's world got too big for me.

Rod was the one I ran to whenever Mom's eyes spoke trouble or Dad's laugh stopped before it hit his belly. He was the one who walked me to the outhouse in the dark at night. Patiently, he waited outside the door while I talked to him, kicking my feet and looking up at the cold moon through the cracks of the wooden box. Rod was always the big brother and made sure I didn't get too close to the canal when we drove Bessie home to be milked. When we took walks, he dug a hole for me to squat over so I wouldn't get in trouble for wetting my pants.

Rod wasn't the Colonel. He was there when I needed him.

Josh hasn't moved since his grandpa started telling stories. He's wearing the cowboy hat that's too big for him today, but he won't let Cliff pad the lining. Josh's ears keep it from falling over his eyes. He has other western hats that fit him perfectly, but I suspect he's feeling grown up today. He's going with his dad to the feed store and probably to check on the mechanic who's working on the baler. Josh will grow into that hat long before his mom and dad and the rest of us are ready to see it fit him. His roots will have to sustain him until he's old enough to understand the truth he can always count on is within him.

I wouldn't be alive if I didn't know that.

On the other hand, regardless of the stories Mom told to protect my identity, I grew up in a country that lost faith when I was depending on it the most. Until spring 1998, at the library book sale, I didn't know I'd been fighting a battle that has escalated into an apocalyptic war on man's soul in my lifetime. I didn't know one seed of thought had exploded in the modern mind like dandelions in springtime. The thought: Truth is a figment of the imagination.

Pushing my chair away from the table, I tell everyone good-bye and let Curt know that I'm walking home. I don't tell him I'll probably walk by the library because I'm following a child's prayer today.

16

The Modern Mind

The elderly volunteer who is working as cashier at the library book sale is so crippled she leans on the table for support as she takes my dollar bill. Smiling, the little woman with curly, short, silver hair counts change into my open palm. "This is a good one." She nods reassuringly as she hands me my book about Dietrich Bonhoeffer, the theologian who was executed by the Nazis for plotting with others to assassinate Hitler. He said something that makes me wish I could talk to him in person: Christians may have to find a new language if their faith is going to survive. The volunteer's eyes look into mine. She deeply inhales the secret she thinks we share.

At home in my office, I pick up my bulky treasure and begin to turn glossy pages, beige with age, when a portion of a magazine falls on the floor. Bright as a flashing traffic signal, *The Modern Mind* claims the top half of the page, which is a faded eggshell color and torn at the binding.

"It's very old," I say out loud and look for a date in the opening paragraph of the editors' joint introduction.

> The mind is its own place, and in itself
> Can make a heaven of hell, a hell of heaven.

These words, written by the poet John Milton in 1667, ring startlingly true in the year 1958.

"1958!" I can hardly believe my eyes. This magazine, written forty years ago, says thoughts can give life or destroy it.

I've opened a window in time and am thirteen years old again: There it is, that blast of light, bottled somewhere in Riverside, California. Funneled through an invisible pipe that reaches from earth to eternity, it moves above me in a circle. Etching a path in the night sky, it travels for hours like a needle on an old 78 record. Losing myself in the parade of stars, I imagine they are forming a band, playing trombones, clarinets, trumpets, and drums that keep beat as the parade marches out of sight. I don't have to wait long until the blast of light has gone full circle, announcing to the whole world something we ought to know about is going on in town.

As excited as if we were following a rainbow to a pot of gold, I loved it when Dad drove the whole family through town until we reached the giant spotlight where it was moving round and round, face open to God, like a reflection of his own. At last I would look out the car window, follow the milling crowd, only to find we'd come to another "GRAND OPENING" of a furniture store, a car dealership, restaurant, or some other business that I didn't need, didn't care about. I felt like I'd been tricked again. Nevertheless, the next time and the next, I'd see that blast of light and feel that shiver of excitement, think I was going to explode with curiosity unless I got to see the occasion for all the commotion. I begged my brother or my folks to get in the car and drive until we could find out what the spotlight was doing in town, as if whatever I'd been waiting for in my short life might actually happen when I wasn't around. When I was old enough, I drove myself.

Forty years later, here I am again, my eyes wide open and my heart beating with anticipation, as if I have never followed that spotlight to location after location, expecting to see the heavens open up and rain goodness on the earth, only to find I've been lured by another business promotion.

This time is special. I can already feel the electricity in the air the way I do before a thunderstorm that shakes my faith in nature to the ground, soaks it hard, and leaves me feeling clean, as if I'd been baptized again. Could truth be the blast of light I've been racing to find my whole life? With such a long list of spotlight specials, I ought to know when I've found the real thing by now. *The Modern Mind* has waited a long time for me to find it.

Set apart in a box by itself is a startling announcement: "Never before in history have men and women been so conscious of the power and the problems generated by their own minds . . . . The basic problem is anxiety—anxiety about what we believe; about the way we live—or fail to live; about the new world of outer space . . . . Millions of Americans are trying to escape this anxiety by silencing its insistent gnawing with tranquilizers or alcohol . . . ."

This sounds like a Bill Moyer's PBS special on addictions. I imagine today's headlines: "Prozac, Top-Selling Drug in the Nation."

Shivering in the cold light of truth, I read on, feeling as if I've done the impossible: Standing in Bozeman, Montana, on this side of the millennium, I'm watching the spotlight circle the sky in 1958. It's warning the whole country that something's going on we should know about. Maybe heaven opened forty years ago after all, and I've waited this long to be in the right place to see it.

"Taking a pill . . . may dispel anxiety temporarily, but it does nothing to combat the basic problem that lies at the root of anxiety," the article says. Like watchmen guarding the gates of man's soul, America's leaders and experts—"clergymen, reformers, politicians, intellectuals," surgeons, psychotherapists, theologians—warn us we won the world war for freedom in 1945 but are confused and helplessly out of control in the battle for our souls. "Americans have lost faith!"

Bottled lightning released at last. Have I discovered the boot camp I spent my childhood in? When I was thirteen, I felt a darkness gathering in my soul. I didn't know that a dark cloud was also building in my country's soul. A bird with a broken wing can survive among predators if she has to. So can an eagle, it seems, but the symptoms of its injury reveal themselves, crimson tracks on snow. Predators know the scent.

On another page is a black-and-white photograph of Dr. Paul Tillich, a Harvard theologian, who says, "Everyone must have some kind of faith in order to live . . . . When a person loses faith, he loses the center of his being . . . . He may develop deep feelings of anxiety." Psychoanalyst Dr. Eric Fromm says, "Without faith man becomes sterile, hopeless, and afraid to the very core of his being."

The light is not so distant from me as it was when I was a girl. The stars aren't marching anywhere, either. They never were. Just billions of suns burning themselves out, truths on fire for everyone to see. According to the magazine, Americans became part of a herd instead of individuals when they moved away from the land, family farms, and ranches to suburbs where they worked for corporations.

As if under a spell, masses succumbed to the science of "adjustment" offered by popular psychology. "Parents are told how to adjust to their children, husbands to wives . . . . If everyone on the block gardens, you, too . . . must sprout a green thumb."

Getting along had its costs in 1958. It sounds like the American language was changing. Was America's soul shooting away from itself, a comet on a crash course to a hell of its own making?

Dr. Fromm said, "There are certain ideas that can severely damage a person's ability to possess faith. By far the most dangerous of these . . . is the disheartening conviction that all values are relative and that 'truth' is a figment of the imagination"—

Not at my house it wasn't. At my house, truth was that slippery pearl at the core of endless arguments.

When I was ten years old, Mom finally got the bigger house she'd been wanting since we moved to California five years before. The roomy white house with green trim on storybook windows was two doors down from the field where a new junior high would soon be built. In the daytime, I felt safe walking to the elementary school that was several blocks away. A few two-story ranch houses stood like remnants of the good life among rows of modern homes that filled blocks and formed suburbs on lots that used to be fields and pastures. A retired doctor and his wife lived next door to us, and behind our street another sprawling development was under way. Close as we were to our neighbors, the only hollering I ever heard was at our house, so I thought only my family fought over money. I thought it was just my brother, sister, and me that drove their mom to make threats about what would happen when Dad got home if we didn't stop fighting.

My neighborhood smelled good. A billion blossoms in the spring, eucalyptus year round, and rain that called honey from the earth made me happy when nothing else could. Smog hadn't settled in yet like it did before I left California. No sooner did I turn thirteen than a sadness gripped my heart, and no matter how hard I tried to think about things that made me happy, it wouldn't go away.

Until I read *The Modern Mind*, I didn't know that the nation's heart was as heavy as mine.

17

If the Foundations Are Destroyed

Walking home past the library, then two blocks back to Main Street, I think about how *The Modern Mind* dropped into my hands at just the right time. It gave me the bigger picture, a cosmic painting that my story of healing fit into. Emerging from layers of contrasting hues was a psalm: "If the foundations are destroyed, what can the righteous do?" They will see God's face, it says.

Were America's foundations destroyed? Did the language change? What shape was the cloud that moved over God's face?

The soldiers who fought in World War II had suffered unbearable hardships and endured. The article says they faced their fears and anxiety with courage, "courage of a higher order." I didn't know anything about *The Modern Mind* when I was thirteen years old, and what I knew about soldiers I'd seen in movies. All I really understood was how to hit the tetherball until it nearly broke from its rope and that God knew where to find me when I needed him.

Most of my friends thought you found God at church. I knew he hung around the eucalyptus trees. According to the article, in 1958 most Americans believed in God, and the majority went to church. Yet surgeons, politicians, theologians—a whole lot of experts—said Americans had lost faith. What do the statistics mean? In the year 2000 if a person wants credibility with professionals and the public, he or she quotes statistics and polls like the religious quote prophets. Surveys may only question 50,000 Americans—a fraction of the population—but their findings have the power of a map that locates buried treasures. What does it mean that most Americans still believe in God today, that over three-quarters of the population "identify" themselves as Christians and less than half go to church? Or that witchcraft is growing right along with those who "identify" themselves as non-believers?

I've read amazing stories in the Bible where waters parted, stone walls tumbled, armies fled, and prison gates opened because one person prayed or a few believers obeyed God. So if only a handful of us pray in faith, the possibilities for healing and transformation of us as individuals and a nation are staggering. What do the polls mean when compared to faith?

Maybe statistics are like digging for fossils: one bone can lead to the whole skeleton. So who, or what, did a startling number of Americans, especially Christians, really identify with in 1958? What caused us to lose faith thirteen years after fathers, sons, mothers, and daughters paid the price for freedom with their lives?

Will we ever know? *The Modern Mind* offered scattered bones of truth in hopes of revealing the bigger picture. When I was still waiting for breasts to bloom on my chest, a lot of Americans' identities depended on wealth, status, and having a marriage like those they saw in the movies. I know the movie part is true because my girlish dream was to be as beautiful as the actress Ann Blythe and have a husband as handsome as the actor who sang to her in the movie *Indian Love Call*. It's also probably true that wealth and status were as important in church as they were in jobs and neighborhoods, if the schools I went to were any example. I envied the popular girls who could afford to wear new store-bought dresses and matching skirts and sweaters instead of clothes their grandmother made them, like I did.

If Mom had gone to every church in town, she probably wouldn't have ever felt like she had the right thing to wear. I told her it didn't matter, but what did I know? Apparently reality was what you could see, touch, and spend back then.

Maybe it still is. Today reality is also the prescription drug or over-the-counter remedy you swallow with food or milk that makes life tolerable.

The new church Mom took us to was closer to our new home near the junior high. Even I could see that people looked at your face there before they looked down to see what you had on. The rotund pastor wore round-rimmed glasses and smiled whether he knew your name or not. He didn't perch above the congregation in a nest like the pastor at the cathedral with the stained-glass windows had, but stood at a podium instead. Since I'd gone to special classes he taught when I turned twelve, I was a member and could take Communion. Regardless, darkness had formed a deep hole in my heart, and it hurt.

Now I realize that I probably wasn't the only one who was hurting. The article says whether people were sitting in pews every Sunday or not, during the week many were nervous, anxious, driven. Dad's hands trembled constantly, and I felt sorry for him, thinking he worked too hard. I wished he'd go to church more often, but back then I didn't know pastors were taking tranquilizers and having breakdowns like the men and women in their congregations.

The editors of *The Modern Mind* refer to a segment of the magazine that wasn't in the clippings I found. It was on self-destruction. Whatever it said was probably written on my soul because I felt its heaviness every time Dad drove us by the stark stucco village on the way to the mountains. Mental illness wasn't a term people said out loud when I was thirteen. Prozac and Xanax hadn't been concocted yet. Antidepressants weren't as common as household cleaners, either.

"Crazy" was a word my brother, sister, and I whispered in the backseat when we drove by Patton, the mental institution on the way to Big Bear Mountains. The name Patton sounded like a harsh threat to me. Maybe my spirit knew things I didn't. Locking people up who are already locked up inside seemed insane. The first time I saw the neglected landscape, it was enclosed with chain-link fences made of strong wire and steel, the kind that would keep a vicious dog from attacking little girls. I asked Mom who lived behind them. "People who are very sick," she said. I didn't know what she meant until the year I saw previews of the movie *Snake Pit* on television. The dark village would have ruined my trip to the mountains for years to come if I hadn't made myself notice the trees that were growing tall along walkways and near the buildings and the flowers that bloomed in cultured patches on the lawn. Straining to see how the people who lived there looked, I found one or two men and women who didn't appear to be any different from my parents and teachers.

What caused a person to lose control of his or her mind? I wondered. Was a girl born with the seed of madness in her soul? Surely no one would choose to be insane.

Since then, I've seen sane people make choices that a sick person would know were wrong. Voices like the French philosopher who was popular after the war reveal a side of truth, too. It's a side I've felt in my dark moments just as I felt it when Dad drove by Patton on the way to the mountains. Jean-Paul Sartre said, "God is dead, and man is alone, abandoned on earth in the midst of his infinite responsibilities."

Milton's phrase seems to penetrate the walls of time: "The mind is its own place." God is dead to some people, maybe to most people at some time, but does that mean He doesn't exist at all?

How many of those buildings at Patton housed men and women who had dreamed of finding heaven on earth, only to find out that the earth was hell? What if they were the ones who knew the truth and didn't know how to live in a society that was being destroyed by lies?

I imagine a special ward, a timeless warehouse of patriots, survivors of Vietnam, World Wars, Wounded Knee, Jim Crow's South, the Civil War, and the American Revolution. Here, guards keep watch lest the truth gets out to the sleeping masses. A cry rings down the corridors of time, "Give me liberty or give me death!" The cry of a madman, or is it?

"I have a dream," Martin Luther King Jr. proclaims. And someone, maybe at the FBI, shudders as if he's heard a ghost.

In 1958, heaven and earth, fantasy and fact, truth and lie all shared the same screen on television. For the first time in history, Americans didn't have to leave their living rooms to be on the front lines of war one minute and rocketing into outer space with Sputnik the next. A white girl would think she couldn't stand to see one more helpless Negro jailed or murdered for doing things she took for granted. There was enough bad news on television and the movies to prove the Kingdom hadn't come to earth, enough information to harden a grown man's conscience. Yet a little white girl thought she could change it all if she could get God on her side.

At least with television, you could flip the channel to *I Love Lucy*, *Range Rider*, *Space Patrol*, *This is Your Life*, and the real world would be transformed into a fantasy you could live with. I didn't watch much television, but watched for the spotlights that circled the sky instead.

Meanwhile, advertising continued to become an art of deception on television, billboards, and in magazines, but I was too young to realize that the drug, alcohol, and cigarette companies had found paradise in America's misery.

When I was thirteen, there was a reason freedom didn't have the same ring to it as when I was younger. Putting my hand over my heart, I said the Pledge of Allegiance every morning at school, thinking it was just me who felt trapped. There were days I said the Pledge like it was the only prayer I had left to pray. My prayer for heaven on earth was buried with my tears where it would be safe. Right after the teacher took roll, I said some parts louder than others to show God that I meant them with all my heart: "I pledge allegiance to the flag of the United States of America . . . one nation under God . . . with liberty and justice for all." With our hands still over our hearts, the whole class would sing "America the Beautiful." I felt like everything that was wrong in my home and the whole world was going to be all right. Then we'd have an air raid drill. The startling, shrill repetitive squawk would start up out of nowhere. I crouched under my desk, held my hands over my ears to shut out the noise. It was hard not to imagine they were the real thing. Many nights I lay awake and worried about the cold war. Every time a jet flew over, I wondered if it was from March Air Force Base or Russia.

I told myself I was just growing up. I wasn't a little girl anymore. I hadn't felt innocent since I turned ten and learned Dad was having an affair with his secretary. I was twelve, had just started seventh grade, when Mom packed what she could in suitcases and took Rod, Connie, and me with her on the bus to Bend, Oregon. Dad had gone ahead of us to look for a job, he said, but Mom didn't believe him, and she was right. We got off the bus the day before his lover was supposed to arrive.

In our new town, the smell of cedar permeated the air. I liked the small junior high better than the crowded one I'd attended in California. I liked hunting for agates with friends of the family and the look on Mom's face when she felt her marriage was safe. Dad still yelled at Rod too much. He chased him outside, his fists shooting like balls of fire in the air. My brother was smart, athletic, and handsome. That's about all that was wrong with him.

About the time the ice on the banks of the Deschutes River began to thaw, we moved back to our old neighborhood in California, where Mom wore a smile on her face and kept a book on her bedstand that I'd see her reading during the day sometimes. Before spring blossoms bloomed, Mom's smile was gone. And so was mine. Being thirteen didn't feel very good.

Santa Ana winds threatened to tear up palm trees when Mom picked me up from school one afternoon. "Why don't you laugh anymore?" she asked. "Why are you so down on yourself? You have so much to be proud of; you're a beautiful girl."

I couldn't talk, and couldn't cry either. She'd seen how Dad's hands moved over my body like I didn't have any clothes on, tickled too close to my small breasts and crotch like he had the right. She knew I fought with him constantly. Mom had seen him lay his head in my lap, heard me insult him and push him away. When he cried and told me that he was only pretending to love Mom, I told her. She got mad at me instead of him. My brother defended me, but she wouldn't listen. I'd beat my tetherball until my fists bled. She'd watch from the kitchen window.

That day in the car she asked me why I wouldn't talk to her. Mom didn't want to hear what I had to tell her. I wasn't sure I liked the book she read all the time, *The Prayers of Peter Marshall*. It didn't give her the courage to take a stand with Dad. Maybe she thought she was standing when she forgave him again and again and asked us kids to do the same. It seemed that to Mom, faith was what helped you endure things you shouldn't have to.

If the foundations are destroyed, what can a girl do?

The day was warm and sunny when I was walking under the eucalyptus trees. Thinking no one knew how lonely I felt or that I wanted to make friends at school, I heard a loving Voice speak to my thoughts, *Show an interest in the other boys and girls, DeeAnn. Ask them questions about themselves. Use your own experiences to help you understand others. You'll have lots of friends.*

I didn't question who was talking to me. I knew.

That year my English teacher made me an example to the whole class. "You can tell that DeeAnn feels good about herself because she's happy, outgoing, has lots of friends, and gets good grades."

The innocent will see God, the Bible says. I didn't feel innocent. I felt angry.

18

Mr. Lee

Mr. Lee was seven feet tall. Until the day I walked down the hall at Ramona High School and saw the twelfth grade English teacher who taught my brother that he was smart enough to do anything he wanted to, I'd thought any man who was bald had to be old. Walking down the hall past the handsome giant with the deep voice, I knew I had to work hard the next two years if I wanted to be in his English class. It was geared toward smart kids. Mr. Lee only taught kids who had shown they had the potential to do something important with their lives. In order to be in his class, you had to be invited. My brother had been invited. Because I was his sister, I never thought I wouldn't be on the master teacher's list.

But when Mr. Lee posted his list on the wall outside his office just before school was out the end of my junior year, my name wasn't on it. I thought he'd made a mistake and made an appointment to talk with him personally.

Even as he sat at his desk the day I went to his office, he stood out in his small room like Gulliver stood out among the little people in *Gulliver's Travels*. I introduced myself and shook his hand. He asked me to sit down.

"Mr. Lee, I want to be in your English class next year. I'm not on your list."

He looked surprised and a little amused. "Oh, you do?" His voice vibrated off the walls. "Well, Miss Jones, apparently your English grades didn't reach the required mark this past year."

"My brother Rod was in your class three years ago." I hoped that genes would make up for the grades I hadn't made.

Closing the distance between us, he leaned over his desk and looked me in the eyes. "Being your brother's sister is not

enough. We cull the students who come to my class carefully."
His voice was so low, it rumbled in his belly.

"But I can do it." Wasn't culling something Dad had done with
potatoes on the farm? I wasn't sure I wanted to be culled like a potato. I wanted to be special, and I thought whatever Mr. Lee could
teach me about the English language would help.

But, Miss Jones, you're not on the list," he said in plain English.

"Could I come to your class for a semester, Mr. Lee? If I don't
meet up to your standards, you can kick me out."

"You'll have to work hard, Miss Jones." He raised his voice
enough to make me shiver. "Harder than you realize right now."

"I can do it." Can't I? Why was I was trying to make my life
more difficult than it already would be with a fourth year of Spanish
and a first year of French, both with the same grumpy teacher who
had nearly flunked me first semester? Mr. Piper was almost as old as
my parents, and he'd been a bachelor too long. Anyway, that's what
his students had decided. The only reason I enrolled in his class
again was that I wanted to go to college. I'd also heard he was getting married to a Mexican woman from Mexico City next summer,
and I'd noticed lately that he smiled at me even when I gave him
the wrong answer. He must have loved this woman a lot.

"So you think you can?" Mr. Lee said. "Then you may come."
He conceded, bowing his head like a prince to a peasant. He wrote
my name on the list where it belonged.

I was Rod's sister, after all. My brother had joined the Army.
But he'd been fighting on the front lines at home for most of his life,
so fighting the cold war abroad probably didn't scare him at all. Dad
had threatened to shoot Mom when they argued one night. Rod
had been going to Riverside Junior College, but not long after the
threat, he signed up for the military. I thought he wanted to fight in
a war he could win, for a change.

Dad threatened Mom again. Hoping I wouldn't lose my brother
forever, that he'd come home once in a while, I told Dad our family
was falling apart and asked him to do something to fix it.

"I will, Annie." He promised, then moved out of the house and
into an apartment where he would call Mom late at night and ask
her to come quickly. She'd drop everything and squeal out of the
driveway, leaving Connie and me alone. My sister knew where Mom

had gone. She was the one Mom had taken along to find out what Dad was up to when he didn't come home at night.

I thought our family was the only one in the middle-class neighborhood that was crumbling to pieces, but I never asked my friends if their families had problems. The middle class didn't talk about their problems to other people.

Regardless, I knew Mom's life as Dad's wife was not normal. She had substance, the inner strength to manage Dad's home office full-time, run his errands, keep creditors at bay, keep the house spotless, do the yard work, run kids to appointments—all while her heart was breaking. She took tranquilizers sometimes and read *The Prayers of Peter Marshall*. Meanwhile, Dad kept us all guessing what he'd do next as he soared to extremes of devotion and dove to the depths of betrayal. He cried and said he was sorry. But he didn't change. No wonder no one discussed private matters in public, I thought.

Angrier than my cocker spaniel that spent her days in torment while the mockingbirds dove at her, cackled at her, and almost laughed when she ran in circles, my way out of despair was to set goals like learning to write in Dr. Lee's class and making plans for college.

Feeling guilty for my sharp tongue and quick temper, I hoped the Holy Spirit would help me be more like Jesus if I attended weekly meetings of a Christian organization for teenagers. The star basketball player talked about how Jesus changed his life, but most everyone seemed to know that as soon as his term as president of the club was up, he'd be back to drinking, partying, and switching girlfriends like they were new shirts he was trying on. Life was a struggle while I waited for God to answer a child's prayer.

My first kiss had been a flop, so romance seemed like a mystery I'd never get to experience. Throughout high school, I wrapped my heart in dreams, my mind in goals, and my body in standards that were so high no boy could measure up, not even the senior baseball star, "Pinch." The team counted on Nick Rossini's home runs and pitching arm whenever the score tipped for the opposing team. Nick called me "his girl" before we ever met. After cheerleading tryouts, I heard from friends what he'd said about liking me. He never knew "his girl" threw up before their innocent dates until I finally told him I didn't want to get serious with anyone, didn't want to date just one person, even if he was the sweetest guy I'd ever met. The first real kiss—the only one that lasted longer than a sneeze—that I thought I'd waited for all my life was the last real kiss until I met Gabe at Denny's restaurant two or three months before I graduated from high school.

So when I took my seat in Mr. Lee's class, my senior year, I thought God wanted me to know he was listening to my prayers. I thought our family would move to a ranch before Mom and Dad did something we'd all be sorry for and kill each other. I hoped we'd moved to a ranch the way we should have when we first came to California.

Meanwhile, I drove the car Rod left me when he joined the Army. Even before I had my driver's license, he taught me as much as he could about driving when he came home on leave. The rest I learned at school. My brother didn't get angry when I ran his car over our hedge trying to learn how to use the clutch and brake at the same time. When Dad walked out on the front porch bare-chested, I knew we were in trouble. He'd been taking a nap. "What are you damn kids doing?" he shouted. Sitting in the car behind the wheel, I bowed my head to hide my laughter while my brother tried to explain from where he was standing next to the car. "I'm calling the cops," Dad barked as he went back into the house. My brother turned to look at me and shook his head when he saw I was holding my hand over my mouth. He didn't blink months later when I told him I passed my driving test by only two points above failing.

But I was in Mr. Lee's class now, and it was as hard as he promised it would be. Stubbornly, I stayed home on weekends and read every book he assigned until I learned from authors like Willa Cather and Thomas Hardy that I wasn't the only girl who had to deal with family problems. Some people who had done the right thing their whole lives still struggled to survive with the people they loved and the families they were born into. Doing the right thing had to be enough in itself. It was what growing up was all about.

I got A's on vocabulary tests, but Mr. Lee loved his red pen more than life itself, and it ran like blood all over my writing assignments. He didn't grade on a curve because he was God and he didn't have to. On a good day, I'd see B-blood everywhere. As a ritual, Mr. Lee would call out our names, then hand each of us our papers as we came to get them in front of the rest of the class. "Miss Jones," he'd say, sliding his deep voice down to the netherworld. I got up from my seat, approached him one step at a time, and reached for my assignment. He looked at me from over the top of his dark-rimmed glasses for a few seconds, then released my paper. That look made me feel good. At least he knew my name. He knew I was doing what I said I could. The day came when he pinned me to the floor with that look for a while, then he smiled until his face was all teeth and made me glad I was stubborn.

19

Santa Ana

Year after year, California's Santa Ana winds tore Christmas decorations down, but there was nothing anyone could do to change their course of destruction. From the time I was old enough to prefer being by myself, I stood in their path and reveled in their stinging force.

With my eyes closed, I imagined nature's howling giant had exhaled. Separating my short hair to the scalp with the force of his breath, he dared me to ignore his power to both build and destroy. Electrified, I'd smile at Santa Ana and face him down, knowing I could never blow hard enough to break his composure. It didn't matter; confronting him was enough to give me the confidence I needed to seek him out when he returned, whether it was the next day or the next year before workmen took Christmas decorations down.

Old Santa Ana wasn't alone in his awesome role on earth, and I knew his twin well. The waves of the Pacific unleashed their muscle on me, and I loved, respected, and learned from them as if I'd been born to. The wind and the waves can be forces of destruction, yet they've carved my identity on the face of heaven and earth. Without them, I wouldn't be me.

The term paper that my world literature professor at Riverside Junior College assigned, the spring of 1964, wasn't an accident, but I didn't know it then. I needed to write that paper not only for what I'd learn as an eighteen year old, but for when I went back to it almost thirty years later as the bird with a broken wing God said I was. I needed to write that paper so that when I was in my prime and Santa Ana came back for one more try, I'd be able to stand in his path, face him down, and remember how confidence in my own thinking felt.

———————

The Santa Anas were tearing orange groves up by their roots, the fall of 1963, a prelude to their New Year's performance. My own roots were feeling heaving tugs and had been since I'd graduated from high school, though I didn't like thinking about emotional upheavals in my life. In my small world, God's existence was tossed around like a beach ball or anything that could easily be replaced at the five-and-dime store. None of my friends seemed worried about the truth of His existence. They had dads they could depend on.

When my brother's friend Stein stopped by for a visit, the summer of 1963, before I started college, his news seemed harmless—another yank to ignore—but years later, I realized it wasn't. Talking with Stein one summer night probably made writing that term paper on freedom's tie to faith inevitable.

Stein stopped by to visit the family and see how my brother was doing in the Army. The boy had grown into his muscles and was a young man now. He'd be going back to the University of Santa Barbara where he majored in biology. Feeling like two gypsies traveling the frontiers of the mind, we stayed up way past my bedtime while he taught me about, what I thought, was new theory of man's biological origins. Stein told the story as he understood it from Charles Darwin's work, *The Origin of the Species*.

Wide-eyed and full of questions, I felt the way I had when I was swimming in the Pacific, like I was in over my head. My worried mother would call from shore, "You're too far out, DeeAnn!" I pretended not to hear her, turned toward the horizon and swam for the next swell.

Seduced not so much by Darwin's imagination as the German hunk who was sitting next to me on the living room sofa, I listened intently. Close enough to make me notice things about his lips I'd ignored when I was younger, he described how a tiny cell was the beginning of bigger things to come. The language of science rolled off Stein's tongue. Words were poetry on his smooth lips, and I liked the way his blue eyes danced when he spoke them: ontogeny and phylogeny, entropy and atrophy. Words marched in Stein's phrases: natural selection and survival of the fittest. The theory of evolution: how life on this earth began and progressed.

Stein was making music with words when my mother rushed out the door. Tires skidded on pavement as she hurried to the apartment Dad shared with his mistress. When Mom didn't come back by the time Stein left, I went to find her. To my amazement, Dad puffed up like the hen-house rooster while two women fought for his love. Mom acted like she was saving him because he couldn't save himself. His mistress was wearing the big diamond wedding ring he'd said was going to be my mother's.

I thought of my earlier conversation with Stein. He said man evolved from an ape. I'd never heard of a monkey that lied to get its way. Stein could afford to indulge in new theories, but I couldn't. I needed something real to believe in, like the voice that talked to me when I was walking under the eucalyptus trees.

Nevertheless, gypsies of the mind that we were, I welcomed Stein with a big smile when he showed up at my door the next week with his entire collection of English literature and bluegrass record albums I couldn't afford to buy myself. There was so much to learn, and I couldn't wait to get started.

A tug here, a tug there.

Sweat beaded on my skin as I walked home after swim class at Riverside Junior College one especially hot afternoon in the fall of 1963. My brother was on the other side of the world in the Army. Mom had moved us into a cozy home in the old part of Riverside I'd always loved. Dad had moved home again. She wanted to keep him there, regardless of the trouble he caused.

We were all standing in the dining room when Connie reminded him that he said she could borrow the car. Dad changed his mind, probably to make her beg. He might say yes, or he might say no. He was in control. I hated his games. Mom looked at me to keep quiet. She knew I'd tell him what I thought of him for playing with my sister's trust, and then there would be a fight. I told him anyway. He came at me with his fists flying. Those cannons didn't land on my back and chest until I was in my bedroom on my bed as close to the wall as I could get without falling through it. Dad stopped hitting me when I wouldn't cry. Tears would have been an invitation for more pain. Crying would have meant he had control over me.

When I went into Connie's bedroom, she was stretched out on her bed, white as a corpse and numb to the touch. She couldn't move any part of her body, yet tears were running from the corners of her eyes. He hadn't touched her, but what he did to me must have triggered something in my sister. I went to call the doctor, but Mom said to put the phone down. Defending him, she said Connie Beth would be fine. Dad hadn't meant to hurt any of us. Because I was afraid another fight could damage my sister permanently, I complied.

Connie didn't die from emotional pain, but she was never the same after that. Vulnerable is the only word I can think of to describe her. Vulnerable as a bird with a broken wing.

Maybe Dad belonged in a cage, after all.

More determined than ever to get an education so that I could make a safe home for Connie, I went back to school the next day, then went to work at the village café. Next summer my friend Deb and I were going to take the bus to New York where we planned to get jobs at the World Fair. Dreaming was as close to heaven as I could get, it seemed.

———

I needed to write the term paper on faith for my world literature class, the spring of 1964, although research stirred more questions than I ever got answers for.

Sitting on my bed, my back against the wall, my legs stretched out in front of me, I had a book in my lap and others lying open around me. Some I'd checked out at the library; others I borrowed from my professor's personal collection. Feeling as if I was moving through the corridors of time and space, I researched the impact of faith on my country and me. Surely this was how Alice felt when she walked through the looking glass to the strange world on the other side. I didn't know the authors as major characters on the world's stage the way my professor probably did. I knew them only by the way their presence sucked me into the light and shadows of the soul. Understanding was the fish on the hook that flipped and squirmed until it got away. At least I could say that I knew how it felt to catch it for a little while.

It's funny how you conjure the faces of authors and characters you've never seen. I imagined the Dutch theologian of the sixteenth century looked much like Friar Tuck in the legend of Robin Hood. As I read and reread passages of Soren Kierkegaard's works, my image changed. A jolly, round Hollywood type became a cynical wise man. He tried to tell his colleagues that something was drastically wrong in Christendom, but they called him a heretic for being honest. Undaunted, he said that Christendom was the cobweb that clung to the fruit of the Spirit, instead of the sweet juice from within it.

The web felt lifeless, sticky, easy to get caught in, and nearly impossible to get free of as I read on.

Suspended in the shadowed corridor of time and space with Fyodor Dostoyevsky, I imagined him scrawling his manuscripts in candlelight. Intense, obsessed, and tortured, he searched for eternal answers to human questions, just as I was. I read and reread one particular chapter in his novel *The Brother's Karamozov* called "The Grand Inquisitor." (Not even for a grade could I venture into *Crime and Punishment* again, although I knew it had an important message for me. Like a monster from the deep, the corridor swallowed and digested me until I felt the bile in its stomach when I tried to get through that novel the first time. But it had been assigned.)

Dostoyevsky didn't have a face. A figure of light and shadows, he had one foot in heaven and the other in hell, and he painted the images of both too well. Shriveled and deformed as an abandoned cobweb, his voice as sharp as the guillotine and scorching as the fire that raged around its victims who hung where they were bound on the stake, the Inquisitor told Jesus, his prisoner, he must burn for what he'd done. The Son of God gave humans the burden of freedom when all they wanted was the security of having someone else tell them what to do. Man wanted bread to eat, not choices, the Inquisitor said.

On the dark stone walls of the timeless corridor, words appeared as connected sparks of life: Freedom, faith, God, a horrible burden? Feeling as if I'd walked in on an execution and seen God die, I was afraid that a part of me could die, too, if I didn't take care of it.

The important chapter had meanings I was missing, a message that I needed to heed, but I had so many books to read, so many thoughts to consider, so many notes to take. I'd procrastinated too long already. My subject was deeper than the ocean I loved to swim in. Though it was drowning me, I couldn't get enough of it.

By the time I read Friedrich Nietzsche, the imaginary stone walls closed in completely. I think it was in a play he wrote that I read "God is dead . . . and we have killed him." I had to know why.

Feeling as if the burden of freedom was on my soul, I waded into the works of contemporary theologians. Reinhold Niebuhr, Martin Buber, Karl Barth, and Paul Tillich were among the authors my professor recommended I read. The subject I'd chosen for my term paper was relevant to my life and times, a requirement of the paper, the professor had said.

Dr. Tillich's book *The Courage To Be* lit up like talking fire in my hands. It lit up the way I'd wanted the Bible to, but it never had, except for the paintings. His message still warms my heart: True faith is the courage to stand when the Inquisitor says, "Tomorrow you burn."

Through the ageless corridors, all the great voices seemed to speak as one: "A young woman should know who she is and why she exists."

The night before the paper was due, my mind blocked completely. A force stronger than the Santa Anas made me believe I could be who I wanted to be, not in spite of Dad and the heartache in our home, but because of it. I'd hoped that writing the paper would help me decide who that was. Understanding freedom wasn't as easy as I thought it would be. With the clock ticking away precious hours, I called the professor to ask if I could have another day. When he didn't hesitate to grant my request, I wondered if he knew I'd swum out too far this time. One of my best friends came over that night and typed while I wrote. We finished just before dawn. She went home, and I waited for morning to come so I could deliver my burden.

Feeling as if I'd mined my soul for gold and missed the main vein, I walked up to the professor's door and rang the bell. Muted tones flowed like ribbons of velvet through the smooth stones his old house was built from. I was studying them when he opened the door. He smiled and took my paper. I said thank you and walked away. A few days later, he returned it with B- scribbled at the top and "redundant" written under the grade in red ink, as if I didn't know it already.

———

The morning's half gone and the sun is melting snow on the sidewalk as I walk slowly up Willson Avenue toward home. In just over two hours since I left the house this morning, I've followed a child's prayer through a wilderness of memories, a wilderness it seems I've wandered in most of my life, even all the times that I thought I found the Promised Land, heaven on earth.

Is reality as complicated as I've made it to be all these years? Probably not. In a world where a woman is identified by the number on her credit card and checking account, reality is taking a deep breath of fresh air.

20

Ever a Seeker

The fall of 1964 Dad and Mom moved us to a ranch, the closest that we ever came to my dad's dream. The whole family was glad to leave behind memories of last year's nightmares with Dad's mistress and the fight that left my sister temporarily paralyzed. We had a lot of practice leaving heartache behind.

Sitting alone on acres of tumbleweeds was the stucco house, which looked like a quaint adobe ranchette to me. The first time I saw the swimming pool in the backyard before we moved in, it was half-filled with dirty water and leaves that had probably blown off the two trees in the yard. It was a fixer-upper. Mom said I could choose the color to paint my bedroom and pick out curtains to match. Dad came home from work almost every night we lived there, acting like he'd been doing it for the past eight years instead of making life hell. He read the paper while Mom fixed dinner. He asked me what I was learning in school and called me Annie, like I was his hero. I took it as an answer to a child's prayer, although it seemed like I'd never been a child, at least not one I could remember.

Shaking her head, Mom would smile when she called me a dreamer. I wondered if she was remembering another young woman who had dreamed of being an actress. Mom had a beautiful voice. I loved to hear her sing when she put me to bed as a child. She also played the piano, but we didn't have the money to buy her one. When Mom made excuses for Dad's meanness, I pictured her lost in her music on stage at Carnegie Hall or playing a role and getting paid for it instead of giving center stage to Dad, while she did all the work for nothing. It wasn't about the money, but the respect she deserved and didn't get. Somewhere inside, Mom had a song she'd forgotten. It was important for me to know that a person could abandon herself, even a woman with all of Mom's talents.

1964–65 was supposed to be my last year in Riverside, and I wanted to feel the heat of God's hands on my wounded heart. A piece of clay that had been stomped by life's heavy boots, I was soft and ready to mold with a light touch. It was a gentle Southern woman who showed me that songbirds sing not because life's perfect, but because they have a song. Thirty-five years has not erased her from my memory any more than it's erased the salty, damp smell of the ocean from my senses, the spicy smell of eucalyptus trees, the song of the meadowlark, the living prayer my mother taught me. Dr. Stallings fits among them in my heart.

My professor had given up a career in international law to teach kids like me. Working part-time as her secretary, I learned she didn't do anything without having a good reason. No one would have known how sick she was unless they'd seen her like I had one Friday in her office. She rested her head on her desk. Too sick to pick up the phone and call her husband, who was the superintendent of schools in a town thirty minutes away, she said, "This happens sometimes," and asked me to make the call. I waited with her until he came to take her home.

Monday morning she walked into the children's literature class she taught, looking sharp, snapping quips, and asking questions, making me think I had awakened from a bad dream. I never saw her sick again, but when Dr. Stallings told me one day that she wanted to prepare her three children to be on their own by the time they were each fourteen years old, I wondered if she knew she was going to die young.

I knew what she meant by preparing her children, because she treated us the same way. Sitting at one of the student desks with a stack of books in front of her, she'd wait until she could see our souls through our eyes, then recite works from memory. They became my favorites. Caldecott and Newbery Award winners, classics, Madeleine L'Engle, John Ciardi, Lewis Carroll—who and whatever she thought would ignite sparks in our imaginations. Quoting Ralph Waldo Emerson and Walt Whitman, my professor linked God to his creation in a way no minister ever had for me, as truth breathed through her lips.

Alert as if she were presenting a *prima facie* case to the Supreme Court instead of stirring her students' curiosity in children's literature—so the catalog called it, but this was a course in life and thinking for yourself—she opened each class with a passage or poem. The room was as quiet as the night waiting for the stars to come out. When Carl Sandburg's words emerged from her soul, I knew that I was "Ever a Seeker," too.

> There was a time there was no America. . . .
> Then came a later America, seeker
>   and finder, yet ever more seeker
>   than finder, ever seeking its way
>   amid storm and dream.

Holding Thoreau's *Walden* in her hand, she'd look at us in a way that made me feel she could see my heart. Then she spoke, soft as a train whistle in the distance coming my way: "If a man does not keep pace with his companions, perhaps it is because he hears a different drummer." She paused. "Let him step to the music which he hears, however measured or far away."

Noble thoughts knew no age limits, according to my favorite professor. Neither did the responsibility to have them. She was trying to expose us to her favorite thinkers so that no matter who our mothers and fathers were, or who shot our president or what the human cost would be for Vietnam and justice delayed in the rights of Blacks, Chicanos, Indians, we'd know that we had choices: I could choose who I wanted to identify with and who I wanted to become.

Reverence for Life was the name of the large book Dr. Stallings held up for us to see. She explained that it was about Dr. Albert Schweitzer, the man she hoped would win the Nobel Peace Prize that year. Later I borrowed the book so that I could study the photographs of African children, their parents, and lepers who had no family at all except for their friends in Lambarene, the village Dr. Schweitzer built deep in the jungle. Those faces weren't twisted with pain and anger, and they weren't haunted with death or agony, not like the faces of some of the black people I'd watched being hosed and beaten on television news. From the pictures in

that book, I could tell Dr. Schweitzer was as concerned with healing the soul as he was with healing the body.

Medicine was the last job on my list of potential occupations.
Teaching was probably only one step above it until Dr. Stallings
worked on my heart. By the time she finished with me in her argu-
mentation and debate class the next semester, no one but my brother
would stick around to have a discussion—my thinking was so sharp,
the shyness and mental blocks gone. I decided to become a teacher,
the kind that heals hurting children and teaches them to believe
in themselves.

When night falls, morning always comes. As a college girl, I
looked forward to the hard times to see the good that was going to
come out of them. My friends said I had a lot of faith. Mom said
there was a name for people like me: I was an idealist. Dad said I
lived in a bubble that was going to pop someday.

It didn't matter. The Word came to me through a Southern
woman's lips and moved over the waters of my soul. I thought I'd
follow its current and see where it would lead. It's flowing still.

21

Songbirds and Cowbirds

Not far from home, I turn the corner where one of my favorite houses stands. In the backyard, the owner has bird feeders everywhere. She's hung them in the trees, planted them on long poles in the ground, and tucked a few in places I wouldn't have thought of. As I walk by, I see a fat squirrel eating out of the feeder that's nailed to the tall old pine tree closest to me. A flock of chickadees hop from branch to branch around the blue bottles that decorate naked limbs. Fondly, I think about Dr. Stallings. Whenever I've been in danger of losing touch with what's important, I've turned not only to her example of courage but also the thoughts of the writers, poets, and great thinkers she introduced me to.

The words of Dr. Albert Schweitzer have since helped me understand that I wasn't the only woman who had to struggle with lies. He was awarded the Nobel Peace Prize the same year he died, 1965. The doctor saw the darkest threat to mankind back in the thirties. Prophetically, he warned man to beware of the "spirit of the age" that robs people of confidence in their own Thinking. He capitalized the word Thinking, like God had breathed on it.

The dark spirit doesn't work through brainwashing in obvious ways but through the social, religious, and political institutions of society, he said. While men and women are wearing themselves out trying to pay the bills, it wears, tears, and erodes their eternal ties until they're not sure about God and Truth or who they are anymore.

My favorite quote was the message the doctor gave to the children: "Tell them that the truths they feel deep down in their hearts are the real truths. God's love speaks to us in our hearts and tries to work through us in the world. We must listen to that voice; we must listen to it as a pure and distant melody that comes to us across the noise of the world's doings."

A couple of years ago I saw a documentary about the plight of songbirds that made me think about the doctor's warnings. Today, as I anticipate their return in the spring, the link between man, nature, and the bird with a broken wing seems stronger than ever.

Twig by twig, hair by hair, root by root, the birds will form the deep cups that hold their eggs until they hatch, wombs in the treetops. We'll look forward to a new batch of songsters, and some of us will fill our feeders faithfully, hoping a few will choose to stop by to eat and sing a tune. But I won't be surprised if they don't show up this year, because in some states songbirds are dying in their nests while the cowbirds multiply every year. It's one of those twisted things nature does when man forgets who is God.

Apparently the crisis has been caused by the human population expansion in rural areas. The documentary showed naturalists doing research in wooded areas that used to thrive at a safe distance from the population. Today the forests border fields and pastures that farmers and ranchers have been forced to cultivate as Americans migrate from cities and suburbs back to the country they abandoned during the dust bowl era and after the war.

Naturalists, while careful not to disturb the birds, identified songbird mates as they built their nests deep in the woods of Indiana. I felt as if I personally knew each bird by name. When they returned to the nests to count the eggs the birds had laid, it was as exciting as having an Easter egg hunt in the backyard when I was young. You could feel trouble brewing when the cameras switched to the cows that grazed in the pasture that bordered the woods. Big old cowbirds seemed expendable, as they did nothing more than flock around plump heifers and dozing bulls. I took an immediate dislike to them.

By the time I watched those cheating, loafing, parasitic beggars plant egg after egg in the songbirds' nests, I was raving at the television. I didn't care if God created the cowbirds. They were trespassing and stealing. They were like people without conscience who turn paradise into hell. When the songsters eggs started cracking and splitting open to reveal tiny fragile birds next to huge, honking, gulping cowbird chicks, I wanted to call somebody, even the president, and ask him to send in the reserves.

The scene that broke my heart was when the mother songbirds, who were unaware of intruders, dropped their babies' food down the throats of the greedy chicks. Feeding after feeding, day after day, week after week, they fed those fat deceivers until their whole gifted nursery had starved to death. Meanwhile, the cowbird chicks grew fatter and noisier as they took practice flights in the safety of the woods until they were mature enough to leave the nests. Next year they'd be back, and as welcome as car trouble in a rainstorm.

I took the documentary as a warning: Look out for the cowbirds or they'll take over your nest when you're not looking; although, I'm still not sure who the cowbirds are.

Because I've felt particularly tender toward meadowlarks since childhood, I can't imagine my world without them. The fields and pastures, the foothills and meadows where they've built nests for years, places that I've purposely taken drives or walks so I can hear them sing, are now blacktop parking lots, malls, business parks, and busy streets—housing tracts and landscaped developments. Yet I'm not sure property development is the worst threat to the young songsters or the children who are as open and vulnerable as Annie was. The population explosion was not the worst threat to a girl who was determined to dream, to fly—with her wings hanging limp at her side.

Maybe the worst threat to my mind wasn't visible to the naked eye. Perhaps a dark spirit, the "spirit of the age" is a predator that starves the soul of truth while it feeds the imagination lies. Man gives it power by choice—unless Dr. D was right when he said an addiction to the dark side can be put on a person from the outside.

Through my adult years, I found myself asking one question often: What is truth? Since the Voice of Truth saved my life, I hear other adults asking the same question regardless of how many years they've sat in pews on Sunday mornings. It's a good question. I'd like to think that if mankind knew the answer, the earth would be heaven and children would be safe.

22

Beyond the Naked Eye

The bite of February's cold winds doesn't keep me from the nature trail. The path that used to be a track for the Gallagator—the train old timers rode when they didn't want to ride their horses or pack wagons—has become the trail of a child's prayer to me.

My glasses are fogging up, so I stop and pull a Kleenex out of my purse. An image pops into my mind of the first time I saw myself in glasses. I was fourteen when the doctor said I needed them to see the blackboard at school. It was hard to get used to seeing my eyes framed in dark blue. I had to adjust to seeing clearly what had been blurred before. One day I took my glasses off in class and realized how long I'd tried to read fuzzy words and numbers without prescription lenses. There are things in life I don't see clearly still, like What makes smart people do radical and irrational things to change their world? What makes the difference between a visionary and lunatic? Were the zealots who died at Masada heroes or depraved individuals?

Perhaps the emotional atmosphere around the presidential campaign of 2000 is making me wonder. The contest is triggering extreme reactions from friends who aren't normally outspoken. There isn't a cloud in the bright blue sky today, but a storm angrier than I've seen since the fifties and sixties, when revolutionaries and activists were rioting and leaders assassinated, is brewing in the world around me. The presidential campaign isn't through primaries and the media's already predicting—or stirring up—a cock fight. Few would deny words have the power to create and destroy when elections come around every two and four years. Mention one name at the Western and a smile turns to a frown; mention another and someone who's normally quiet starts tapping his spoon on the table. Mention World War II or Vietnam and you can feel the bond that I like to think makes us Americans. What would it take for one of the Western's patrons to stand up and passionately shake his or her fist in the air and shout, "No one's going to take one more freedom away from me!" Would everyone in the café cheer, or just me?

Maybe I never grew out of my need to confront the opposition. I was an argumentative girl. By the time I entered college, Mom used to warn me not to discuss religion and politics with anyone but my brother. She didn't have to worry about me bringing up science because I didn't think it was a controversial subject. But now I think the topics are all mixed together; like the wind, they all fan the fire inside me. From what I've observed, coals of passion smolder within my silent friends as well. Are they too tired, or perhaps too wise, to be zealots for freedom?

Do I listen more than I used to because I've grown up a little? I hope so. I still don't know for sure what made smart people, including me, follow the pastor who said all the right words well over twenty years ago. I desperately wanted to believe in man's nobility and God's unconditional love back then. I was beginning to hear His voice in ways I hadn't since He spoke to me under the eucalyptus tree when I was thirteen. When I read in the Bible that Jesus gave his life out of love for mankind, I was ready to die for Jesus if He asked me to.

From Scripture, I got the impression that a real Christian gives up family, money, and good sense to follow Jesus. Did Pastor Stone Harmon see what a fool I wanted to be for God when he led me down the crowded path to find the Kingdom of God on earth? Or was he as afraid of the Church's disapproval as much as I was?

What made me different from the dreamers that historian Adam Zamoyski writes about in his book *Holy Madness: Romantics, Patriots and Revolutionaries, 1776–1871*?

The dates tell me that my great-great-grandfathers could have been among the passionate visionaries who turned European nations into "cults." But Albert Pfeiffer and Francis Chamberlain sailed for America instead. Why didn't the Colonel stay in Holland where democracy and social reform were thriving in the first half of the 1800s? Why didn't the French fur trapper stay in France during the same period Zamoyski says Europe, America, and countries in South America saw Paradise on the horizon? The vision of a New Jerusalem, heaven on earth, was so bright in France it seemed angels mingled with man to achieve the impossible. Like water on dry ground, social, political, and economic reforms soaked through society's cracks, and freedom was the harvest.

I follow tracks in the snow made by others who walked the trail before I did this morning. With my head down, eyes on their tracks, I put one foot in front of the other.

I wish my great-grandmother Pfeiffer was alive. I have questions no one seems to be able to answer. Was her father-in-law, the Colonel, a Freemason, like Mom says? Dad taught me all I knew about Freemasonry when I was a little girl. He was proud to be a member of a society that has secrets. I thought Masons were good men who didn't like Irish Catholics, black people, or wealthy Democrats the way Dad ranted whenever Adlai Stevenson, Hubert Humphrey, or President John Kennedy spoke on television. According to Dad, President Eisenhower and Richard Nixon were honest Americans, so I figured they must be Masons, like he was.

When President Nixon and his advisors were exposed in the Watergate cover-up in the seventies, I felt sorry for all the people who'd trusted them. By then I knew Dad could con a leopard out of his spots, but for a president to lie to "the people" made me think I'd better look to the Church for guidance. The nation was not going to lead me to heaven on earth.

In the late 1800s, it was probably the other way around for some of those who longed to create paradise on earth. Spiritually dead in its laws and doctrines, it seems the church lost its hold on both heaven and earth for a while. National leaders took their followers to the brink of paradise, but social and economic reforms weren't enough for all citizens. Whether it was in the 1700s, like Zamoyski suggests, or long before, all kinds of gods filled the spiritual void. The Illuminati—the name that raised the hair on my arms in the seventies—was a pagan cult, an offshoot of the Freemasons. Feared by governments for its aim to abolish political states and create one government, it allegedly survived for fifteen years, then vanished.

But the Freemasons thrived. Freedom wasn't all that grew in the mystical cracks of rejuvenated democracies. Freemasonry flourished in Europe. And some of our founding fathers brought it to America. Until I recently found a tome of Masonic moral dogma and rituals, which is over a hundred years old, I thought Dad had taught me all I needed to know about the group that gave him pride. On the first page is a photograph of a sage who looks older than God. He says he wrote the book and included the teachings of just about anyone he thought sounded interesting. I could see what he meant as I followed threads of thought leading to Zoraster, the Greek Mysteries, Druids, God, truth, moral virtue, brotherly love, and liberty and justice for all. The ancient wizard must have loved Egyptian symbols—pyramids and triangles are among the ancient drawings. It seemed he'd spent his whole life thinking and wanted to write his conclusions down.

I wonder if the Colonel carried a tome like this one along with his Bible? Or was he disillusioned with both and looking for something real, like a God who would talk to him when his wife was murdered by the Apaches? Or a Redeemer who would wash the blood off his own hands and give him a conscience he could live with?

With his wife dead, and political radicals screaming for extermination of the Indians, would Albert Pfeiffer have sympathized with the French poet Ferdinand Freiligrath, who in 1848 wrote, "We stood on the threshold of paradise—but the gates were slammed in our faces."[3]

As the Colonel drank one glass of liquor after another, would he have sympathized with Dostoevsky's dreamer who was about to commit suicide when he found the "other earth?" The citizens of Paradise didn't' need scientific theories or military force, but thrived on love and truth—until an outsider taught them to lie.

Zamoyski suggests Charles Darwin's scientific discoveries about life's origins gave philosophers and reformers ideas in 1848. They envisioned nations where the strongest ruled the weak. Man was god by natural selection. Decades later, Stalin didn't need the Church to justify the Gulag, or the prison state within the state. And to a madman like Hitler, creation was finally as God had intended; through genocide, he culled the inferior Jewish race from the "pure strain," which was whatever he said it was.

---

[3] James Eastwood and Paul Tabori, *'48: The Year of Revolutions* (1948): 56, quoted in Adam Zamoyski, *Holy Madness: Romantics, Patriots, and Revolutionaries, 1776–1871*, (New York: Viking, 2000), 358.

I suspect philosophers and reformers never anticipated the slaughter to come when they dreamed of organizing the humble masses, the rights of the strong determining the rights of the weak. It wasn't such a new language they spoke, using scientific principles. Man had been using the name of God, or gods, as credentials for slaughtering the innocent since before Christ was born. But why would anyone follow sadistic criminals like Stalin and Hitler?

Thinking of my own country's history: Why would anyone follow a leader who hung Negroes from branches and burned their bodies to ashes, or slaughtered Indians for their land? In the year 2000, the Aryan nation promises the Holocaust of World War II will be nothing compared for what they have in store for the Jews. There aren't enough laws to control the evil man is capable of.

If mankind doesn't live by the laws of the heart, how will the Kingdom will ever come to earth? Love God with all your heart, and your neighbor as yourself. Is it possible? I used to think it was.

The tracks in the snow lead to the bridge. The river is bubbling, cutting shapes in the ice that's frozen up to the banks. The tracks stop at the rail. Did he or she jump over it into the freezing water. Should I? Of course not. But the Reverend had credentials, and he said he could help me find the Kingdom of God on earth if I would die to myself.

How can a man or woman who isn't free lead others to freedom, whether he or she is a parent, pastor, president, or psychologist? Since I nearly drowned in Pastor Harmon's church, I study the tracks of those who have walked the trail of dreams before me more closely now.

I wonder if ideas are like these old trees I see on the nature trail. You can chop them down, but unless you pull the roots out, they'll grow back again, somehow. I still hear and see reports of a secret society that's trying to take over the world.

"Passing on the left." I step aside and wait for the jogger to pass. This trail seems remote, but yards away it's bordered by older homes, apartment buildings, and condos. Like a new wave of growth, the hill in the distance is covered with expensive houses. What forces are molding my country and determining its course for decades to come? Is there anything modern about the modern mind of the years 1776 or 1848 or 1958 or 2000? Most of us are wondering why marriages don't last, why children have to suffer for the shattered family core.

I'm wearing a new pair of glasses, but they don't help me understand the times I'm living in. Looking beyond the naked eye, I imagine a scene: While mankind makes history and writes fat books about it, there's a Voice that doesn't make headlines. In Truth, love speaks to the heart of children, like it spoke to Annie's. Whether they're abused, sick, homeless, or taking trips to resorts with wealthy parents, children hear Truth speak to their hearts. History happens as they find they're way back to it as adults, one way or another.

I'm following a new set of tracks on the trail now. They seem to go clear to the end of the path. I stop at the pruned rose bushes the way other mothers who've lost their children visit their graves. This is one of the roses that "won the West," the owner of this house told me once. Father Hugo's Rose, the fragrant yellow variety, was one of the only two roses hardy enough to survive in Montana's climate. I suppose Calli knew that when she told me there was something "really yellow" ahead that summer day.

A woman has to look beyond surface appearances for the truth about anything. Heaven comes with a price. One withered bare rose bush reminds me that love lays down its life—only to flourish in Paradise.

But I was the adult. Calli, the child. Sometimes I don't hear answers to my questions. The Spirit is quiet.

23

The Razor's Edge

The Western is nearly empty when I get there after my walk. The wall furnace is blasting hot air at me, thawing my frozen cheeks. Our rancher friends are moving a little slower as they come in for breakfast or a quick cup of coffee, but their greetings come with a smile. This season is another that can make or shatter lifetime dreams in Montana. After calving season, planting begins, but so may drought and forest fires begin if forecasters' predictions are accurate. These ranchers and farmers are used to living on the razor's edge of paradise. I hear no complaints, even though they've been up all night, or most of it, checking cranky cows, pulling calves, using winches if they have to, hoping with all their hearts that the new bull or heifer is healthy. Calves are being born dead fifty miles from here. One rancher said no one's sure why, not even the veterinarians.

John Ham sits down next to Curt, across from me. He's probably already fed the cattle, checked his herd at the edge of town, and been to the garage that's getting a part he didn't have in his shop. His and his son Cliff's herd doesn't calve until closer to March, which is still early enough that branding's done in time to seed.

"How's it going?" Curt asks John.

"Someone left the gate open on the south field. The fence is torn down. Same place the ground was torn up when they tried to put a road in last year." He shakes his head.

We all know what that means. "Someone" didn't get permission, doesn't have the right, but thinks he's God and can do anything he wants to.

"There was a time when neighbors looked out for each other." John's voice is as soft and low as the rumble of a locomotive moving toward you from a distance.

In my head, I add, *Now they tear down your fences and rustle your cattle.*

"I think I know who's responsible." He gives us a look.

Is he talking about the man who's trying to force the Hams out of the canyon or a forest service worker the same guy has probably paid off to harass them. When the slick manipulator moved here from back East, he didn't know which end of the horse to feed. John helped him learn.

"Does one man ever know another?" John says.

Something from *The Modern Mind* comes back to me, "Without others to tell him what to do, he is lost." There's a new breed of rancher now. No sooner do some city folks buy property than the camouflage appears, shinier than polished chrome: the Levi's, boots, cowboy hat, and Carhart pants and jacket, a brand-new rig with a fancy long horse trailer in tow. The Hams enjoy friendships with a few of them, but others aren't here long before the soft metal and empty core exposes itself, usually with a haughty attitude toward those who work with their hands for a living. But when the first hard snow hits, weights tip the scale. The transplant from blacktop and high rises needs his driveway plowed and calls his neighbors for help. Some regret they didn't show more respect to their link with civilization when their fields were green and the roads easy to drive on.

While John and Curt talk about finding parts for their old trucks, I continue to file and fit life together. Sometimes I feel as if I'm sitting in a classroom when I'm at the Western, learning lessons about humanity, which usually teach me about myself. Nature gives lessons too. She's no respecter of class or stock portfolios. Cast in the image of her maker, her cauldron renders pure metal only. Come feast or famine, the wisdom of the earth cultivates faith, truth, and loyalty in those who serve her. There's no arguing with her justice.

I'd love to be able to say that I'm pure metal and have never dressed in camouflage or known the consequences of taking my values from those around me. How I'd like to be able to say that once God spoke to me I didn't have to worry about my eternal identity and crumbling foundation, but I can't. And I can't blame my weakness on the city, because that's where He spoke to me when I was a girl, and often later. Can I say that I've never been deceived, never been duped before by anyone as phony as some of our politicians?

No, I can't say that either. I've even fought for the enemy, or liars, when I thought I was fighting for truth. Wealth doesn't identify the soldiers who know which side they're fighting for, whether it's good or evil, but neither does religion. Faith wears no costume. It strips down naked in front of the whole angry world.

This is definitely a day to think and look beyond surface appearances. It's a day to look for the bigger picture because the smaller one challenges a woman's courage. The dark side has had eons to perfect its con. It could win the election in November regardless of who becomes president, like Zamoyski suggests it won in France and the rest of Europe in the 1800s—subtly, through a campaign on the mind, a thought at a time. Whether a woman believes in God, Mohammed, or just the person she sees in the mirror first thing every morning, she's not immune to the dark side.

"No one's taking my guns away!" Booming like a cannon at dawn, a man takes a stand a few tables away, and I look to see if he's standing on the table, shaking his fist in the air. Anger has its place. This election may save my country from its worst enemy, complacency. We're so divided as the campaigns build steam, it's impossible to tell whether our next president will be a conservative or a liberal. I don't know where tension's strung the tightest or what the core of the conflict is. Issues are as blatant as signposts, but there's something deeper going on. I'd be the last to try and identify the songbirds and cowbirds, elitists and republicans, patriots and traitors. My own emotions color the way I see others. Passions inflame every issue.

It's not hard to understand how America fractured into civil war over a hundred years ago. Taxes, campaign reform, military reform, racism, education, health care, and protecting the environment are the explosive subjects covered by journalists and news networks. With every shooting, gun control is on the line, along with the Second Amendment, the right to bear arms. I don't see Montanans giving up their right to hunt and protect themselves. With the endless scandal over campaign contributions, there's more fear than ever that President Clinton has sold us out to China, or to about any country that makes him an offer that he can't refuse. Who's going to care about our national identity if the president doesn't?

Fear, distrust, and rage run like electric wires through society, and every time someone blows a fuse, we're all jolted. The massacre at Columbine High School in Littleton, Colorado, haunts us all. How could two students plot and execute fourteen classmates and a teacher without anyone—not even their parents—knowing in time to stop them? How could the warnings have been missed by officials? Because I was born in Colorado, have history and family there, I've wondered many times what my life would have been like if I'd grown up on the farm instead of in California. The horror of Columbine has triggered questions I don't have answers for, especially since my own daughter died in the state that I thought was as close as I could get to "home" when we moved here in 1974.

The way city dwellers migrate to the Northwest en masse, especially to Montana, makes me wonder if they're suffering a kind of post–traumatic stress disorder from the violent war on their souls. Most of them probably don't weigh the costs of living in the century of wars—World Wars I and II, Korea, Vietnam, Desert Storm, and military interventions in Somalia, peacekeeping efforts in Bosnia. Not even two decades can pass without heavy losses to the family core. Wounds need time and space to mend. Yet frayed nerves and life-shocks become more routine than a good night's sleep. Who has time to grieve and heal?

If you ask Curt, he'll tell you that herds of flatlanders move to Montana every year to have the best of both worlds. Like me, they want city and country, but no one with a pulse would deny that many are looking for something more, perhaps within themselves. Whether they want to buy a few acres or a whole mountain range, a river must run through their property, their thirst is so strong.

Some say that Robert Redford's responsible. His movie *A River Runs Through It* triggered a human tidal wave. *The Horse Whisperer* was another lure that tantalized the imagination. I'll never forget the three hot dry days I spent on location in Big Timber as an extra in some scenes that never made it to the big screen. With the land that God created, the help of a few props, and the skill of artistic masters, cameras told the story that I was glad I hadn't lived. But as I watched the movie on the big screen over a year later, nature's voice was the most powerful of all. It was the star of the show. It's no wonder that ever since those two movies came out, people have crossed oceans and driven U-Hauls clear from the east and west coasts to buy their share of the one place on this earth where they think time stopped before man fell on his face in the Garden.

Cameramen used artistic illusions to reveal truth about the land, and I applauded them. They saw through those lenses what I see all the time, regardless of the season. An artistic illusion can convey truth. It's the sham that I hate. The intent to deceive. It's the spin doctors that make me cringe. It's the half-truths that trigger my outrage. Imagination is another word for heaven, if it's focused on truth. Deep in our hearts we know the difference, but sometimes we have to dig through layers of debris to find the nugget that changes everything.

I guess I'm looking for a nugget like that now. I don't care if I have the best of both worlds as long as the one I have is real. I wonder if deep in their hearts, the Americans who migrate to Montana aren't looking for the real world. Quite a few stop at the Western Cafe when they arrive in town, and some come back after they've settled in. No one wants to believe there isn't a place left on this earth where children are safe from harm. They want to plant their roots in the earth while they still can. I don't blame them. Maybe *The Modern Mind* of forty years ago is also the mind of 2000 that hasn't found what it's looking for. People are searching for something more, like an identity that can thrive in a hostile world. Like the songbirds, we build our nests deeper and deeper in the woods, or at least farther and farther away from violence and high crime rates in big cities, hoping our children will be safe. But the cowbirds come anyway—whoever, or whatever, they are. The war on man's soul never ends.

In an interview, Albert Schweitzer was asked to advise the children. "Tell them that the truths they feel deep down in their hearts are the real truths. God's love speaks to us in our hearts . . . ."

If God's love speaks to me in my heart, is He angry too?

With my mind so full of questions, I don't stay at the Western long. Yearning for a child's faith, I follow where Annie leads. As I walk home through old neighborhoods where the past is transformed with fresh paint and new windows, she takes me into the imaginary classroom of a boy named Adam.

24

Adam

It's possible that one of man's secret scientific experiments for creating paradise on earth is going to elementary school in Bozeman right now. His first day of school last fall may have gone something like this:

The teacher is calling roll. "Adam T. Cooper?"

A little boy with shaggy white-blond hair waves his hand in the air.

The teacher smiles. "Just say 'here' Adam."

"Here." The six year old smiles back at his teacher.

Dressed in Levi's, a navy blue T-shirt, and tennis shoes—none of them new—Adam looks like he probably comes from a family where both parents work hard to keep food on the table.

The teacher passes out a large sheet of construction paper to each child and explains, "I'd like to get to know each one of you better. Would you draw me a picture of your family? Mom and Dad. Sisters and brothers, if you have any."

"Nana lives with us. Can I draw her too?" A stout girl with carrot–red hair wants to know.

"Yes, of course," the teacher says. She's not much taller than one of the easels in the back of the room. "Nana, too."

Adam stares at the blank sheet of construction paper, like he's waiting for his family to appear and tell him who they are. He wishes he could draw the soft flannel blanket he wraps up in at night while his mother's working the graveyard shift and his dad's asleep on the couch. He selects the black crayon and makes a big circle for his father's head. If he could spell, he'd write "Adam T. Cooper, Sr." under it. Holding the crayon snugly, he draws a small black circle next to the big one.

Adam's a clone, and he knows it.

He also knows he's special, because his father told him so. The other clones the doctor made died from terrible complications after they were born. Adam, the strongest, survived. He knows he's a secret, but he doesn't know why. When Adam was born, human cloning was against the law in the United States. And it still is. Yet some people believe that because of Adam, man has a chance to create the perfect world. Because of Adam, man has a second chance to create heaven on earth. Nothing will be left to chance. His dad said so. He also said that when the world finds out about Adam, their family will get rich off talk shows, tours, and scientific research—the doctor promised. Some day Adam may understand what his dad his talking about.

This morning he wants to find a crayon the color of his angel's wings. Her name is Trina. She's there when Adam goes to bed at night and when he wakes in the morning. Adam hasn't told his dad about his angel yet.

Will Dr. Schweitzer's advise to the children apply to clones like Adam? "God's love speaks to us in our hearts."

Man can't control all the variables. We don't even know what they are.

I stop in front of a charming old home that needs a fresh coat of paint. The ornate iron fence that encloses the big yard is leaning in several places. The striking contrasts between yesterday and today and unknown tomorrows weighs on me like time weighs on the iron fence. What if the day comes when haystacks are gone from the horizon and the kittens that used to hide in them are clones?

What good will it do to be angry about changes I don't want to happen? What do I have to be afraid? In my heart, there's a prayer and a promise leading me home.

I'm sounding more and more like a young woman I used to know.

25

Tinseltown

Tinseltown was the last place I expected to find the answer to a child's prayer. When I drove through Los Angeles on the freeway, early September 1965, the small community of Garvanza that had been the life pulse of the "Magic Region" at the turn of the century was gone. [4] Scattered among the nation's museums and libraries, like footprints of an eternal being who once visited earth, are letters, paintings, books, and photographs—documents of a vision Garvanzans shared. The Old World across the Atlantic had a decadent stain. America was their hope for a new spiritual civilization.

The dream of heaven on earth seems to ignite sparks that never to die out from century to century. The community of Garvanza gathered in eastern Los Angeles in the 1890s. Inspired by the purity of the Indian culture and the sacred bond Indians had with God and nature, the wealthy banked artists, naturalists, archeologists, and writers who traveled among the tribes in the Magic Region to document their way of life. It's possible that the founder Charles Lummis, the son of a minister and educated at Harvard, alerted his friends to the plight of the Indian race, which one of their leaders called "a bird with a broken wing." With truth their noble pursuit, the lie their common enemy, the idealists fought passionately to protect their dream. Ultimately, the relentless force of materialism diminished their work to a commodity. Nevertheless, from the California coast to the high deserts of Arizona and New Mexico, Garvanza's torch blazed for a little while.

Its fire still smolders among high rises, industrial fumes, sirens, and the philosophical descendants of strangers who moved to town,

---

[4] Helen Laird's, *Carl Oscar Borg and the Magic Region*, (Layton: Peregrine Smith, 1986), is descriptive of this era in America's history. One of Borg's paintings hangs on the wall of the public library in Anaconda, Montana.

moved in less than two decades after the Garvanzans did. Equipped with an arrogant attitude and enough money to build paradise without God if they wanted to—and they did—materialists put heaven on the market.

Feeling as if I'd taken a wrong turn off the freeway of dreams, when my parents dropped me off at my tiny apartment in Brentwood, I tried to get a whiff of the Pacific but choked on whatever was clogging my lungs instead. The Watt's Riots had reduced a community to ashes not far away from my stack of stucco, so I didn't know if I was inhaling smoke or smog. It wasn't what I'd had in mind, but without a job and a roommate, my acceptance at the campus that curled up like a seashell on the shore of Santa Barbara didn't matter. At the University of California at Los Angeles, I had both a job and a roommate.

Her name was Sable. A work of art herself, with a long thin frame, huge blue eyes looking out of an oval face, and thick wavy hair, dark and long, she tried to expose me to the soul of the City of Angels so I'd see beyond the shiny stuff and smoggy sky. Wrapping her hair in a sleek turban, she took me to the Museum of Modern Art, where pop art sculptures looked like artists had gathered rubble from Watts and molded it into shapes and figures that only the night would recognize. In awe, Sable murmured names I didn't want to remember, names of contemporary artists who were famous for their deranged, chaotic works. Insanity was in style. I turned away from sculptures made of cereal boxes and cans, string and wire, nuts and bolts. What were they supposed to be anyway?

Sable also liked Modigliani's rigid angles and lines. One of his paintings hung over her bed, a portrait of an austere woman that was staring right through me when I woke up each morning and when I shut out the light at night. Another painting stood next to Sable's bed. She covered it with a blanket she pulled off now and then. "It makes me sick!" she'd say. I preferred the painting of a mother breast-feeding her child to having to look at the frigid eyes of the woman I decided was a spinster.

My roommate's tastes were different than mine. Over my bed, I would have had a dramatic ocean scene, crashing waves and boiling skies, or splendor poured like silk on quiet waters at dawn and twilight. If I'd known about Carl Oscar Borg, the Swedish painter and a Garvanzan, I would have preferred his realistic paintings of hills rolling to the seashore and primitive staircase dwellings carved out of the side of the Rockies by American Indians, mansions in the sky. But the money I earned working three different jobs went to pay for food, rent, classes, and supplies. Born half a century too late to live where money wasn't god, I felt like a stranger in my own world sometimes.

The campus that sprawled like royal velvet over the hills and valleys looked like a haven. However, in an anxious society where truth was in question, it was the utopia of extremes. Activists staged protests over Vietnam while Christians sought a compromise with God on the Biblical story of creation. A week-long seminar I attended on campus put a face on the modern mind. The auditorium was packed with nuns, priests, clergy, and others who I thought were searching for truth like I was. Maybe we were all infected with the disease of doubt and needed to prove our faith. Nothing was real unless you could prove it, in the sixties. Anyway, that's how I felt. Everyone became silent when the lights were turned off. The presentation began. In graphic eloquence, businessmen presented *The Phenomenon of Man*, Teilhard de Chardin's effort to unite evolution and the resurrected Christ, in theory.

The Jesuit priest, who was also a paleontologist, relied on the laws of entropy and atrophy to carry mankind from the tiny seed of creation to its ultimate destiny, a blossom of perfect light suspended in the universe. If I'd never heard of the Inquisition or the Holocaust, never seen bloody Civil Rights marches or smelled Watt's revenge, if I'd never seen my mother cry in the dim light of her bedroom lamp at night, I still would have had my own heart to prove him wrong. Mankind was not moving toward perfection in this angry world.

At the university, truth was whatever you wanted it to be. Drop a little LSD or smoke a little pot and the search was on. John Wooden's championship basketball team dominated conversations; team spirit was better than no spirit at all. As I served hot dogs, cokes, and cookies at Pauley Pavilion's food stands, it was impossible for me not to feel the tension and excitement through the concrete walls. Swallowed in the estranged family of man, I'd never felt more alone, never felt more challenged, unless it was when I'd faced Santa Ana and the Pacific tides.

The environment of doubt and uncertainty about truth and God's existence increased my faith. He was more real to me than if he had been the topic of every class discussion, the reason for the banners, rolling drums, and pounding feet on the floor of the stadium. My hunger for things money can't buy was being satisfied in Tinseltown. The unrest and conflict around me kept a child's prayer alive. It wasn't the last time I thought I knew what I wanted and got what I needed instead.

Maybe that's how it's going to be when I find paradise on earth.

26

If I'd Looked Back

When I left California for Montana, in the summer of 1974, I didn't look back as my husband Gabriel, our two children Calli and Ryan, and I drove out of Montclair—a distant suburb of either Los Angeles or San Bernardino, depending on which direction you were coming from. Family, friends, and hot summers were as much a part of me as the ocean, but I wanted to move on. I had dreams to live, a family to protect.

We planned to leave town before the sun went down that warm night in late August, but the lights didn't work on the U–Haul we'd be pulling behind our Vista Cruiser station wagon. It was close to dawn by the time we drove away from our first house for the last time. A train of U-Hauls, we exchanged the lead with friends who were also moving all the way to Bozeman, Montana. Safe in our car was the family that made me who I wanted to be: a mother and a wife, a woman with a purpose. We were moving to a better world, a place we had seen the month before, when we visited friends in Montana. In Bozeman we'd be safe.

Looking out the window into the night made me shiver. Just before dawn was not the best time to be driving anywhere in Southern California. The culture of crime and drugs was expanding to her borders. Charles Manson's kind of killer defied the rational mind, and it terrified me. A block away, in our middle-class neighborhood, a woman had been raped in her own house. The rapist hadn't been found.

A year before a gang leader had threatened Gabe when he caught the gang stealing bikes from the junior high where he taught. "Watch your family, man," had haunted us at tennis courts, on our walks, on bike rides, when the kids played in the yard, and after dark when we were moving targets unless the drapes were closed.

These were not the only dark stains I couldn't rub out of my mind, but they were the most relentless threats right up until the dry warm night when we left California for good. My California was the shell of what it had once been, beautiful as it still appeared to be. I didn't want surface appearances of heaven on earth; I wanted the real thing.

If life worked out the way I hoped it would, we'd buy some land in Montana. In a few years, maybe my whole family—Mom, Dad, Rod, Connie, Grandma Jones, and Grams Morse—would be visiting. Maybe they'd move to the Promised Land. Everyone would heal. It was possible. Anything's possible in Paradise.

If I had looked back in the damp hours before dawn, I would have seen those precious sparks of love I had felt in California. They were real. One by one, I gathered memories. Like shoots off special trees and bushes, I'd plant them around my new home when we arrived in Montana.

I'd never forget how much Mom loved Christmas. I keep saying it was the prayer she taught me that kindled my own to have heaven on earth, but it was probably the way she gave us Christmas every year that made me a believer. When she wrapped gifts in boxes and tied them with bows, it didn't matter what was in them, they were so exciting to look at. Until I was nine years old and got mad at her for lying to me about Santa Claus, the Easter Bunny, and the Tooth Fairy, she'd made me think I could hear Santa's sleigh bells, hear him call to Prancer and Rudolf, and see them as they passed by the moon.

Whether we ate at Grandma Jones's house or ours, Mom made rolls from scratch. No one at the table would have denied that if we hadn't had another dish on the table, those rolls would have been Christmas dinner by themselves.

Mom knew what she'd have to go through in a couple of weeks when the bills came due. She knew all hell would break loose in the living room where her husband and kids had sat around the tree and opened pretty presents. We all knew there would be a fight after Christmas every year because Mom spent too much money on gifts, trying to give us heaven on earth the only way she seemed to know how. If you had seen Dad's face on Christmas morning, you would know that she made him believe in the miracles, if just for a little while. For a boy to grow up poor, knowing a new pair of shoes was the only miracle he desperately needed for Christmas, other than a dad who was sober, had to be hard. Mom's love made up for all that, I thought. Hers and ours. Love was real.

Memories came easily as we drove the packed station wagon down dark streets on the way out of town. I could see the whole family gathered at Mom's house this past Christmas. Rod, Connie, and I—all there with our spouses and kids—half of them coughing and sneezing with winter colds. I was spraying Lysol disinfectant like a woman with a cause. One more month of confinement with sick toddlers was not my idea of fun. Sitting on one end of the couch was Grams Morse, her long braid lying on the breast of her "chummy" sweater, her face hiding behind her big toothless smile. Next to her, Grandma Jones laughed every time one of her great-grandkids did something cute. "Lordy, ain't she sweet," she'd say, and slap her knee. Dad had moved out again, so sometime during the day, he came by. Mom always invited him, like she didn't want to miss the miracle that was about to happen any time. My anger was real that Christmas, but I didn't show it. Christmas was Mom's big day.

Gabe's family loved the holiday too. His dad fixed fabulous pancakes while his mom cooked bacon. Like a fabric tightly woven, the Gaynors' bond didn't seem to have any holes in it. Yet as I sat next to Gabe on the carpet in front of the Christmas tree at his folks' house, I'd think of the hours I'd spent shopping for gifts we couldn't afford. To tell them the truth would not have been acceptable, so Gabe and I would just have to pay off the debt one month at a time. It took hours for the family to open all the presents. I'd smile and say thank you for the gifts, but I'd be thinking we were like oil and water, Gabe's family and I. Were we materialists and an idealist, hanging on the same frayed rope of matrimony?

The years had put meat on the bare bones of those two words for me. To be a respected idealist in a materialistic world, like Ralph Waldo Emerson, Dr. Schweitzer, and Dr. Stallings, you had to prove yourself.

Dad didn't have pride in his voice when he'd tell me that I lived in a bubble that was going to pop some day. But he got a look on his face I never understood every time I took another step toward independence. I'd worn one pair of sandals all year long and walked to campus at UCLA rather than let him manipulate me with his money. His blasted money. His measure of self-worth. His measure of happiness. His excuse for failing as a dad and husband. Sometimes I wished we had never moved to California.

Swallowing tears, I wondered why things couldn't have been different. Why couldn't I have done something, prayed something? It wasn't too late. There was Montana.

As I sat next to Gabe in our new Vista Cruiser, I could see how tense he was. For two weeks we had been packing, cleaning, saying our good-byes.

In the dark, he looked at me and laid his hand on my thigh.

I can't say that I didn't know what I was doing when I married Gabe. His folks' eyes lit up when they found out that I was putting myself through college and could help their son get through graduate school. They liked my independence when it came to making money, but not when it meant they had to give up control of their son to please me. I'd seen the signs, but I was idealistic enough to think that slow kisses on sandy beaches, long hikes in the mountains, carefree drives to Mexico, and a guy who couldn't stay away too long meant we had a future together. We became friends, a sure thing for a lasting marriage, I thought, as I looked forward to the day I could trust him with my heart. He was a man who gave what he could, but always held something back: the truth, the whole truth.

He had been hurt before, I told myself, as we drove through the countryside beyond Montclair. We would grow together. I was an idealist to the core.

No one could have told me otherwise. Gabe was the man that I loved. Raised in the Baptist church, he would be everything to his kids that my dad had chosen not to be to me, because money was more important.

But Gabe's parents reminded me of Dad. Charles Manson's California and the gang that threatened our lives had terrified me, but the thought of spending my life like my in-laws did, shopping and buying and storing goods for eternity, strangled my imagination. The thought of living near a woman who mocked my dreams as childish and criticized me for things that didn't matter—from the length of my hair to putting the toilet paper on the holder backward—seemed like emotional suicide. Bozeman, Montana, was the Promised Land.

Only an ocean, a Red Sea, between it and Egypt—my California in the seventies—would have made it any more desirable.

I didn't see a star in the night sky, but smoldering inside me was a spark I didn't talk about to anyone, for fear it would go out. In California I'd learned that God is real.

Two years before we left the state, Gabe, Calli, our one-year-old daughter, and I spent the summer in our motor home on a mountainous peninsula in Northern California. We'd owned a couple of different cars since we sold the motor home, but the memories of that summer would be with me forever. I could still see myself sitting at the campfire one night. The owners of the campground, Beverly and Troy Crane, had stoked it to a roaring blaze.

The Cranes weren't an ordinary couple. Running the campground in the summers gave six or seven of their eleven children jobs, but it seemed like a lot of trouble for a family that had plenty of money and a nice home in Santa Barbara. Still a striking beauty at fifty years old, Beverly, the mother of the brood, didn't pretend to have an easy life. She said things would have been different if she had been not only a good Catholic, but also a real Christian while she was raising her oldest kids. I understood from her conversations that God was all she thought about now. God and writing. One day she had driven all the way home before realizing she had left her twin daughters at church.

Sitting in one of the lawn chairs that circled the crackling fire, I watched campers from several campgrounds slowly gather to sing. Beverly said I'd love the music if I'd come. She and her husband were already sitting next to each other in their lawn chairs. Gabe was working nights as a guard at the gate to the peninsula homes. Calli was sleeping, so I came. But I sat alone where I could leave without being noticed.

The guitar player began to strum. Roaring and spitting like a wild thing, the fire lit up the faces of strangers who sang as if they had known each other their whole lives. Caught up in the spirit of unity, I hardly noticed when the solo began. My new friend Rita, whose husband had recently died of cancer, leaving her with seven children, sang "Amazing Grace" like it was her reason for breathing. Grief made her voice sweeter, thick as honey from the hive she had shared with her husband and lover, the father of her kids. Rita sang God's amazing grace into me until I thought I'd die of peace. Right after the singing, I hurried home before the strangers saw how close to tears I was.

About ten o'clock that night I was sitting on the couch of the motor home, wondering if I had locked the door, when someone knocked.

Beverly stopped by. She brought me a jar of pickles and said something about a Sister, meaning a nun, giving them to her for me. Then out of the starry night, she seemed to grab hold of one bright light. Beverly spoke words that only God could have known would count. "My dad was an alcoholic, DeeAnn. He hurt me really bad," she said. I'd never told her about my father. I never talked about what happened at my house to anyone in my whole life. What Gabe knew, he'd seen for himself. Yet Beverly knew. She said, "God wants you to know that He is your Father. He loves you with all of His heart."

She left.

I sat down on the couch and cried my heart out, probably for the first time since I had learned that beating the tetherball until my fists bled felt better.

The next day Beverly talked to me about forgiveness, about how important it is to forgive those who have hurt you. My list was not long. As soon as I was alone I forgave Dad, Gabe, and his parents. At that moment I knew God would never leave me no matter what I did. But I needed more. I needed to know I belonged to Him.

By the time Gabe and I drove home to Southern California at the end of the summer, nothing less than feeling God's presence and hearing his voice was enough for me. I wanted to feel steel meet steel, feel steam bursting from my pipes to prove God was inside. It didn't matter to me that the Holy Ghost was stirring up the American Baptist Church we attended, with gifts of the spirit. Nor was there anything special about the freestyle gathering in the park, where people like me who wondered what the charismatic phenomenon was about joined hippies on the lawn and drank wine from the same chalice—wiping the edge off before sipping God-knew-what from the slippery stainless steel lip.

The summer in the mountains with Beverly and Rita had only been the sprinkle before the downpour.

Silence made memories seem loud as Gabe and I drove away from my California under the starless sky. Calli and Ryan were snuggled together in the backseat of the car. I thought about the night that forgiveness had poured through the cracks of my broken heart again. The bedroom was dark and quiet when I pleaded with God to help me pray. Wounds were too fresh and swollen to distinguish one from another, anger too hot to touch, self-condemnation all consuming.

Before Calli was born, Gabe told me he hated me for coming between him and his parents. Conflicts with them kept the wound open. Words were lost in a desperate need to change before pain destroyed my marriage, leaving my two little babies with a legacy of divorce and abandonment like mine.

Needs I couldn't express made it impossible to do anything but curl up in a knot of anguish. Gabe was asleep next to me when a new language poured from my heart. God and I weren't strangers; that was all that mattered. Emptied of pain and anger, love was big enough to take care of everything, it seemed.

But fear wouldn't let go of me. In the countdown to disaster or deliverance (I didn't know which), I'd felt an urgency to leave California. The gang leader's threat to Gabe, "Watch your family, man," haunted us, but there was more to my anxiety. Memories of my own childhood were scattered and stubborn as crabgrass, but I never forgot the sound of boots running across our lawn when Mom and Dad were out together one night. Looking pale as a corpse, my brother had sat in a chair with a loaded rifle where he could protect my sister and me if the boots came through the door. The fear that Dad might use the gun on Mom was one my kids would never experience, but in Southern California, there were other dads like mine.

If God had sent a chariot to get us out of there and take us to Montana, I wouldn't have been surprised. So when the principal of an elementary school in Bozeman called Gabe to offer him a teaching job, with the potential of moving into administration in a few years, I couldn't pack my bags fast enough.

Poppies grew wild in California. Fields so orange they looked like the sun had dropped to earth in chunks made a young woman feel like anything was possible, if she believed. But staying there wasn't safe.

Thinking I had found the real thing, I may have left it behind. I believed I had a real Father in heaven who cared enough to lead me to the Promised Land. I'd asked enough times.

We'd been driving less than an hour, but it seemed longer at night. Scattered porch lights made me feel warm inside. I rolled down the window far enough to smell orange groves that hadn't yet been torn out for housing tracks and shopping malls. Lights were on in dairy barns; cows mooed. In the pastures, horses whinnied to each other. Was the love that had brought me to the state of sunshine taking me away?

If I'd heard a train whistle, I might have asked Gabe to turn the car around. Feelings that go beyond reason still have power over me sometimes. Over the years, just hearing a train whistle has brought tears to my eyes. That weeping sound grips my stomach until I want to double over. The train brought Dad, Mom, Rod, Connie, and me to California when I was a child. At night I slept on Dad's lap while he sat up on the seat. He felt safe. The black porter was also safe. His voice was deep as the beat of a drum, and I wasn't sure it didn't make the train move when he said, "All aboard."

The sun was shining like a diamond in the cerulean sky the morning we arrived. Grandpa Jones picked us up at the depot. Grandma may have been there, but I like to remember her home fixing breakfast, stoking their small potbelly stove. All the way to their house, I sat in the backseat. Too little to look out the windows at buildings, I looked up at the palm trees that lined the streets. Ever since, the whistle of a train has been a part of me, like the call of a lonesome soul begging to come home. It's real.

27

Riding Shotgun

By early afternoon we were driving through the Gallatin Canyon toward Bozeman, Montana. I inhaled the clean scent of pine. Absorbed in the safe sounds of the Gallatin River, I didn't notice the dark clouds until they cracked with thunder and poured rain, a baptistry in the sky.

For almost an hour, the shower washed away dirt and grime that clung to the surface of the car. Without scratch or dent, it was in mint condition, typical of the way Gabe took care of all the cars he had since I'd known him. Looking at his face, I could see dark circles under his eyes.

After driving all night, he'd given me the wheel about dawn. Outside of Provo, Utah, the heavy trailer had started swinging the car from one side of the lane to the other. All I could say was, "Uh-oh. Oh, Gabe?" He woke up just as the car stopped at the edge of the highway. Calli and Ryan were looking out the window at the steep incline we teetered over when their dad got out of the car and moved into the driver's seat. "We're okay," he said, and pulled back on to the highway. "Where can we get some breakfast?"

As long as his car had a shine, he could keep conflicts and disturbing emotions under control, it seemed. In our life together, I'd seen him blow up a few times. Usually emotions churned under the surface. He'd go out to the garage, get a rag and some car wax, as if they'd solve whatever was bothering him.

Driving through the canyon, I felt close to Gabe. The boy I married was growing into a man I wanted to grow old with. Just two weeks before, he'd risked his parents' disapproval and made the decision to move to Montana. He looked like he had the weight of the world on his shoulders now. The rain was washing away the dirt and grime of the past, but there are some things that are a part of us. Childhood is one of them. Gabe's cars were another.

His metallic forest-green Ford, a classic model, had stood out like an emerald jewel in the high school parking lot. From a distance, I watched him smother both his car and his girlfriend with affection, telling myself I would never let a guy control me like that. Four years later, our wedding party waved as Gabe and I drove away in his brand-new electric-blue Corvette. Two classic 'vettes later, Calli dozed on the floor under the hatchback to the purr of the engine. The price we paid for a motor home stunned his parents, but we sold it before the gas crisis could bankrupt us in the seventies. We replaced it with a new Volkswagen bus that served us well. We had planned to buy it in Europe, where I hoped we'd find jobs and live a couple of years. Instead Gabe wanted us to go camping with his family in Utah for a couple of weeks, then travel south to see his mother's relatives in Texas, then loop around to Colorado to see mine. We planned to come to Montana at the end of the trip, but his mom's disapproval changed that. We spent the rest of our vacation with Gabe's folks.

Finally, I thought, as I rolled down the window to smell the rain, the wet earth, and the mountain pines. As we passed dusty farm trucks burdened with hay bales and at least one dog riding shotgun on the narrow canyon road, I felt ready for the transformation ahead and hoped my husband did as well.

At the mouth of the canyon, the big blue sky stretched like a gossamer canopy over unharvested fields that carpeted the valley. Meadowlarks sang from fence posts. I was home, at last.

A week later, a Realtor—who we didn't know at the time was called Fast Freddy—sold us a renovated farmhouse four miles from town. There isn't anything else available, he insisted again and again when we told him we'd rather rent for a while. With the help of Gabe's brother we made the down payment and moved in right away. Our U-Haul trailer was due at the store the next day. As loans go, it wasn't much, but Neil said the matter would remain a gentleman's agreement between brothers. In other words, the responsible son wouldn't tell his mother that the irresponsible son was borrowing money from him.

Fortified with fresh air and open spaces, I was ready to shake tambourines with friends and neighbors at the community church when they invited us to come. There was a spiritual revival going on all over the country by now, but this valley felt so clean that I thought the land could revive the weariest soul. Every Sunday, the kids on either side of us, I raised my hands in worship, and sometimes Gabe clasped one of mine in his. Nevertheless, for me church was the one night a week when friends would come to our house and gather around our old majestic wood stove. We sang our favorite hymns until the kids fell asleep, then talked about our good God and how he'd blessed us all. On weekends we got together for dinner at each others' homes and helped with projects and chores, the way family does when you're close. With friendly ranchers as neighbors, I couldn't have asked for more. Soon enough I felt the community bond I'd dreamed of.

Calli and Ryan felt it, too, when winter storms turned the dirt road in front of our renovated farmhouse to ice. Gabe's folks were visiting us when a Chevrolet Blazer took the curve too fast, plowing into the ditch where it got stuck. Within fifteen minutes, cars were stopped everywhere. Neighbors laughed and visited like they'd been invited to park in the middle of the road in front of our house. Sitting tall on his tractor, Mr. Kirk came to the rescue, but not before a lady's German shepherd locked her out of her car. She asked to use our phone. Watching from the window of the sliding-glass door, Calli's and Ryan's eyes were bigger than ever. When I came in, Mom Gaynor was laughing. She told me Calli said, "Isn't it nice how everybody helps each other here?"

The spirit of hope, imagination, and forgiveness had caught fire in me. I was a wife and mom who knew who she was and what she wanted. I thought that I was finally home where I belonged.

I hadn't lived in Bozeman long before a psychopath dragged a little girl out of her family's tent in the middle of the night when they were camping. He took her home with him, where he chopped up her body, then scattered the pieces on a plateau that overlooks the freeway, less than thirty minutes west of Bozeman. It was the dark side of paradise. Like a fatal germ, one breath is all it takes to be infected, impossible to cure. I tucked the image of that evil deed into the farthest corner of my mind, where it wouldn't defile my idea of the heaven I'd found.

Sitting at the table in my kitchen, our second spring in Bozeman,

I watched the birds flock to the old cottonwood that sprawled from one end of the house to the other. Reaching over the roof, it almost touched the hill on the other side. My heart was full with purpose. From my chair, I could hear Calli and Ryan laughing as they played with Muffin's puppies on the carpet. The sun beat down from the huge church-like window that took up the top third of the wall, near the ceiling. Morning after morning, I came to my chair at the kitchen table to meet with God and wait as long as it took to hear his voice.

One morning stands out in my mind. He said, *I love being your Father, DeeAnn*. His love for me was as natural as the aroma of home-made jam that leaked from the pot on the stove. Several mornings later, I came to my kitchen temple, offering a small vase of daffodils I'd picked from my yard. He said, *Bloom where you're planted*. I thought I would. I'd bloom in the light of his love.

Surely, God would ride shotgun in Paradise and protect us all.

28

Meet Jesus, Girl

Over time, even decades, noxious thoughts can settle like silt in the river of faith until a woman's spirit is buried completely. Like cheap art, Jesus is on sale today, but back in the seventies and early eighties you would have thought he was the product for every man. If you didn't think for yourself, you'd get the name Jesus without the substance, and then wonder why religion didn't work for you.

Beverly and Rita, the friends I made at the campground, had wanted me to see how much Jesus loved me, but there was another crowd that marketed him like car wax. He'd give you the best shine in town.

Without much warning, new waves of Christendom rolled over me in Bozeman. Through traveling ministers, tapes, books, and television, I learned Jesus was a materialist, an overachiever. If you claimed his promises, you could be rich, prosperous, and miraculously free of debt, forever insured by God himself.

Grams was on a pension, and she was vulnerable to television preachers who sold forgiveness and prayer like the grocery store sold toilet paper and those thick paper towels she used to wash when they were dirty, then hang to dry. Over the phone, long distance, she would tell me that Reverend So-and-So was praying for me, and I'd fume inside. She was already giving a chunk of her pension to live in one of the nicer retirement villages in Riverside, California. It was a Christian establishment where either the heater cooked her like a Thanksgiving turkey or the air conditioning froze her until she feared she would never thaw out. Who knew what the TV preacher bought for himself with money Grams could have used to get a pair of shoes that fit her gnarled, arthritic feet when she shuffled to the store blocks away?

Why did she fall for his con, "Send a check right away?"

Meet Jesus, girl.

To Grams, God was real. What had the little woman done that made her think she had to pay for his forgiveness? No sooner would I flip by one of those TV gods, hear him warbling about miracles he could perform for a price, then I'd start telling him what I thought of phonies.

For some people a phony's fine, better than a Santa Claus Jesus who gives sticks and stones for Christmas because you've been bad.

Meet Jesus, he's keeping track, girl.

No wonder I couldn't wait to sit at my kitchen table every morning to hear His voice. Blooming where I was planted was impossible without His help. Sometimes other voices were so loud I had a hard time hearing Him the way I needed to.

It had been only a couple of years since we had moved to my Promised Land when we were shaking tambourines over a hotbed of conflict. Some said that Satan was responsible. Wherever God was moving, the Devil attacked the hardest. We were Christ's body, God's Kingdom on earth. The Devil was after us. What he wanted with a bunch of people who were more worried about thawing frozen pipes under the house than giving him trouble, I didn't know.

It seemed that in the church, the only way to get to heaven was to go through hell.

Where women were concerned, the body was there to make sure that your own thinking didn't deceive you because at your carnal core you were a descendent of Jezebel. Feminists were a good example of what could happen if you weren't under a man's authority to keep you on track. Feminists owned the word "identity" in the seventies. I saw all I wanted of their identity at the bookstore where I'd thumbed through one of their books called *A Woman and Her Body*. A woman with any self-respect at all wouldn't join a movement that had her practically standing on her head to look at her private parts with a mirror. Feminists were whiners. I'd chosen to be a snake-finding, bread-baking, flower-picking wife and mother. To me, identity was a personal decision, not a group phenomenon.

The church had its own brand of feminists, however. I thought I wanted to be one until I realized they wanted to control God more than they wanted to know Him. They cast out demons in the name of Jesus, but let bitterness root deep within. Wounded and mistreated by too many men in their lives, they revolted against chauvinistic church leaders with prayer. Spiritual warfare, it was called. Prayer warriors used Scriptures as weapons to bind and hog tie other Christians. They called on legions of angels to bring them a minister who would recognize the spiritual gifts they had to share. Consequently, many pastors were afraid of any group of women who weren't under their authority.

Sometimes Jesus didn't make sense.

Desperate to see the real Jesus, I looked for him in books. Watchman Nee, Corrie Ten Boom, and Dietrich Bonhoeffer had suffered and bloomed in captivity. I learned as much as I could about Alexander Solzhenitsyn, whose novel *The Gulag Archipelago* had been smuggled out of Russia while atrocities committed by the prison-state-within-the-state were still hidden to the free world. Solzhenitsyn, while still a prisoner, warned us of what can happen if you don't guard your faith and the spiritual foundations of your country.

Meeting Jesus was complicated.

At home with my family, I rested from the Jesus crowd. Most nights Gabe read Bible stories or chapters from our favorite books to the kids while they leaned against me on the floor or the couch and listened. We were blooming where we were planted, I thought. With logs crackling in the wood stove, and the horses, dogs, and cats warm in their shelters, all seemed right in my world.

While the church leaders debated ethics and the Moral Majority became a political force in the nation, frightening reports spread to Bozeman of an elusive world power that some called the Illuminati, symbolized by the eye on the back of the dollar bill. I clung to our simple family routines and a love that was real.

Flashing like a neon light in the back of my mind was the story I had read years before in college. In the story, people said they loved God but were slaves to whoever would tell them what to do. They gave up the burden of freedom for miracles and authority. No one ever mentioned the author of that story at church, Fyodor Dostoyevsky. So many of the great men and women I had studied were considered secular figures in a pagan world, part of the past I was supposed to leave behind if I wanted to be Jesus' girl.

We sang "Amazing Grace." We prayed for South Africans and for the end of apartheid. We wept with the Cambodians as we read *Anointed for Burial* at the end of the Vietnam War. We sent couples and young single men and women to Youth with a Mission. We sang "They Will Know Us by Our Love," but the gavel of judgment fell hardest on brothers and sisters of the flock. Yet so did God's forgiveness.

The pastor's hand on his shoulder, one young man stood at the podium, his sins hanging on him like old clothes on a scarecrow until he dumped them on us, one lurid lust after another, pornography to masturbation. He begged us to forgive him, one sinner to another. Believing he was delivered of his demons at last, he sobbed on the pastor's shoulder in gratitude. His confession probably turned more of us away from sin than any sermon we ever heard. No one wanted to be in the spotlight. Jesus saw everything and exposed it to the crowd.

Maybe Santa Ana had trained me too well. I was not good at religion. I never had been. And moving to the Promised Land didn't change me no matter how hard I tried to go along with the crowd. Whoever was asking me to meet Jesus, one unwritten law was not to be broken: A Christian who left one church to go to another was called a rolling stone. It was like rolling right out of salvation into the enemy's camp. You were unfaithful, rebellious, and disobedient to God. To leave the church was like filing for divorce. Subtle as sugar working on teeth was the message that when it comes to behavior and appearance, true believers are the same. Even in the Holy Ghost church, Thinking for yourself didn't feel good.

Sometimes "Come meet Jesus" had a frightening sound.

Afraid that I had come all the way to Montana only to find the Kingdom at war and truth buried in the rubble of souls, I went to hear a woman who had been invited to speak at the home of a Lutheran couple. A nun who didn't wear the traditional habit, she made me think of Rita and Beverly. I hoped she had a message for me.

To her small audience she said, "Too many Christians don't listen to God's voice. He wants them to talk with Him as their Father, their Friend."

When I showed her my journal, she told me not to be afraid of what was going on around me but to keep listening to Him.

The real Jesus never let me down.

If I had taken the time to watch the eagle that I saw fly from the highest crag of the mountain near our house, I would have seen that he flew alone.

29

Two-Inch Heels

I'm medium height if I wear two-inch heels. God created an original, but she got lost in the crowd.

When I was a child and Grams came to visit, I used to sit on my bunk bed and watch her coil her long black hair, form it at the curve of her head, and pin it in place with a wide wire bobby pin. Digging into her makeup bag, she'd pull out a tube of fragrant lipstick and line her lips in ruby red. Turning away from the mirror to look at me, she asked me what I wanted to do today or how I liked my teacher this year, something to make me feel important. Exchanging her robe for a dress, she didn't mention how tangled my hair was from wrestling with Rod or riding my bike. Grams slipped on her comfy shoes. I followed her into the kitchen where she fixed me breakfast in the orange skillet she'd brought for special occasions. Over fried eggs, bacon, and toast, she told me about the love of her life, Mom's dad. He'd operated a sheep ranch with his father in South Fork, Colorado. His mom was a school teacher. They came from back east, and during the summer their friends stayed in cabins they'd built for a Christian retreat. Grams loved to tell stories about her husband's sense of humor. Everyone had loved him, she said.

I wondered how Mom's life would have been different if her Dad hadn't died in a typhoid epidemic when she was two years old. She was his world. But Grams was his lady, I suspected, when I watched her dress for church or dinner out. She made an art of putting on nylons and heels (this was years before her feet twisted into knots). Earrings and a necklace came next. Finally, she cocked her hat on her head, paused a second in front of the mirror, then pulled down the veil far enough to shadow her eyes. I don't know what kind of perfume the little woman wore, she smelled of Ponds cream and Listerine to me. At ten years old, I thought it would take forever to grow into a lady like Grams.

She called me Darling, Sweetheart, or Precious, and told me what a lovely little lady I was becoming, except when I wrestled with Rod. Then she called me Gorgeous George, after the famous celebrity wrestler. If Grams had worn rags, her love still would have made her who she was. We spoke the same language.

When her husband died, Grams sent Mom, her only child, off to a Catholic school instead of letting her grow up with her cousins. Mom remembers nice nuns, cold showers, cooked cereal, feeling lonely and abandoned. Letters Mom found from her mother's married lover may explain why my Grams didn't want her around. The adulteress woman still seems like someone else to me.

———

The day God spoke to me in my kitchen and said, *I love being your Father*, I still wasn't sure I'd become a lady like Grams, even though I'd worn nylons, heels, lipstick, and earrings since I'd turned fourteen. Outward appearances didn't matter to me nearly as much as who I was inside. To God, I was real.

While my children dressed the animals like people or acted out Bible stories they made up themselves, and the washing waited, He fed the flame of desire that burned at my kitchen table. For the first time in my life, I wanted to be a writer. Fresh as carrots from my garden, original as my kids' plays, a language was growing inside me. I thought I had something to say.

As a bridal shower gift, I read a poem I wrote for the bride-to-be. One woman challenged me. Her bushy eyebrows closed the gap over her nose when she asked me in front of other women, "Did you write that yourself?"

"Yes." I wanted to look away from her raised eyebrows.

"How did you get it?" she asked.

Was I supposed to apologize? "I just wrote it." I wished I had never shared it aloud.

Her questions may have been innocent, but identity was a confusing word in the church.

In fact, being a woman wasn't as easy as putting on two-inch heels. Too often the woman I'd hoped I was becoming felt like the twelve year old with bruised knuckles and tearless eyes when her husband made love to her. He took the train ride to bliss alone, leaving me behind. I didn't know why. Talking didn't help. Books didn't help. Emotional pain was becoming a way of life. Like religion, it was something I lived with, believing that one day God would heal me.

Sometimes Gabe and I stood on the hill behind our house and looked out over the valley to the mountains that cradled it. He would tell me how happy he was that we made the move to Montana where I could be home with the kids. He liked being free from the pressure of having to own two new cars, a boat, and a house with a garage big enough to store them the way we would have if we'd stayed in California. Dear God, I wanted him to mean it. I wanted to believe him. When I looked into those eyes the color of light fudge, all I could think about was pleasing him, making him happy, doing anything it took to make him proud of his wife.

But Gabe's silence had the edge of a steel blade at times, and I was afraid I knew the reason. Did he resent me because his folks didn't approve of the choice he had made without them, moving to Montana? Maybe he blamed me for wanting to come.

With wildflowers coloring the open field behind us, neighbors waving from their pickups as they drove by, my kids living the kind of childhood that I'd missed—for reasons I didn't want to think about—and a God who loved me, I tried not to worry about the salary Gabe had given up to move to my Promised Land. I tried not to think about the pressure he was under to pay off the loan for the house since his brother had told his folks about it.

I'd applied for a part-time teaching position in a new reading program. But the woman who interviewed me said the school district where Gabe worked wasn't hiring couples any longer. I was glad. I wanted to start a private pre-school in my house, and add grades as soon as I could afford it. Why wouldn't I want to use my education to teach my own children? I didn't care if I had to buy my clothes at the thrift store if we could spend what we had on our dreams.

Maybe it was the low beat of the drum within, but I worried about how long Gabe would be satisfied with making sacrifices. He lived in his successful older brother's shadow. After his parents' visits he usually withdrew into silence. The antique bathtub and sink that the previous owner, a college professor, had scrounged from the old Broadwater Resort to renovate the farmhouse didn't impress them. A chipmunk ran out from under the tub when my mother-in-law was sitting on the toilet. Even though she said our kids were the healthiest, most well-adjusted she'd ever seen and that it was because I was home with them, Gabe still felt like he'd failed again by the time they left. I didn't understand him.

Again, a vehicle told our story. When the gravel road had loosened every screw possible on the Vista Cruiser, the fall we moved to Montana, we sold it and bought a used pickup. Sometimes Gabe hitchhiked with another teacher who lived up the road in the mornings so I could drive to town for groceries and get out of the house with the kids. We never told him how many times I nearly wrecked, trying to manage the icy or muddy country road in winter and spring, or loose gravel in summer and fall. If all of his vehicles had been able to talk, they would have had a story to tell, but that dingy forest-green pickup's tale would have been the wildest by far. Nevertheless, by Mom and Dad Gaynor's standards, we were moving down in the world. Moving over a thousand miles away from them hadn't given their son his freedom. For some reason, I thought my freedom hinged on his.

I felt like his folks were marking time until Gabe divorced me and came back home where he belonged. His upbringing might come back for him someday. He'd tell me he had enough and give me an ultimatum. Anxiety took its toll on me as I wondered how long we had before the apron strings and the conditional love that hung from them choked the life out of our marriage.

Christians said either Satan or sin was responsible for the bad things that happened in our lives. Where is my sin? I asked God.

I love you, DeeAnn. Grow through the hard things, He said.

Instead of feeling free as a bird, I was feeling as if I walked with a limp when a pigeon flew into our sliding-glass door one day. Like animal medics, Calli and Ryan ran to its aid. They said its wing was broken. Sure enough, the tip hung apart. Setting up their hospital, Ryan found a box and Calli got a twig for it to perch on when it was ready, food and water, and rags for a nest. For the next month, the bird lived in the box with the lid closed, two slits for windows, unless they were exercising it. One morning the kids put it on the carpet, and it flew from the floor to the couch. They took the bird outside where it flew to the branch of the great old tree that grew near the house.

I hoped I'd fly free in time.

It was spring when I took an unexpected trip to California by myself. My sister had been in a terrible car crash. Mom needed help. Gabe and the kids took me to the plane and sent me off with hugs. He held me in his arms and said he would have a surprise for me when I came home.

So I will be coming home again. I assured myself, trying to silence the terrible fear that I might die while I was gone.

Connie came with Mom to pick me up at the airport; her mouth was wired shut, and she had bad some scars on her face. Hard as it was to be away from my husband and kids, I was glad I'd come. My mother, sister, and I did things together we had never been able to do when we lived in the same house. Shopping, a trip to the beach, and laughing together when Connie sucked her food through a straw made the trip worthwhile.

If Dad hadn't invited me to come to his home to visit him and the vicious woman he'd married, I would have thought my family was going to become the healthy one I'd prayed for all those years. While I sat on the couch across from Dad's chair, he told me every-thing he hated about me: I was high and mighty, thought I was bet-ter than anybody else because I went to college, married a teacher. He hated both of us for who we were and what we had accomplished. There was more, but I couldn't remember it. I didn't cry. Sitting there, watching his mouth move and his eyes fire bullets into my heart, I felt like I was somewhere else that he couldn't reach, couldn't penetrate. I'd been there before.

The jet approached Bozeman airport through a bracelet of bil-lowy clouds that hung on the arm of the sun, strong and protective against the big sky. I felt like I'd barely escaped the presence of evil with my life. Safely at home, I walked up on the hill behind our cozy house, sat down in the alfalfa, and looked out over our neighbors' thriving fields. "This is who I am," I told myself. "This is where I belong, not to him." I tried to think about the wonderful job Gabe had done making the porch into a family room while I was gone.

I was in bed with my eyes closed, the first week after I got home, when the most beautiful flower I'd ever seen appeared. It was lavender and purple with a yellow center. I thought it was a gift from God. Other mornings He woke me with songs I loved. The world of the spirit was becoming more real than the one that kept pain alive. Mostly, I think God was teaching me how to tell the difference between my spirit, soul, and body.

When I heard that a woman who had a ministry devoted to love was coming to Bozeman, I wanted to hear her. A crowd gathered in a small room at Montana State University. From a seat in the back row, I watched a striking beauty with thick dark hair, a fair complexion, and a figure that made her plain suit sparkle walk away from the podium and face the crowd. "Okay," she said, "get all the looking over with because I'm here to talk about our Lord, Jesus Christ. He deserves your full attention."

She had been sick most of her adult life. Painful back problems had crippled her. She still suffered at times but traveled when she could. Before the woman had turned twelve, God told her that he would use her to heal people when she grew up.

"He wants to heal you," she said. "Whatever you need, he's here for you. Come now, and I'll pray for you."

As men and women went forward, she lifted one hand over them or touched them and prayed. One man fell to the floor. "Just leave him," she said. "This is God's business." Others fell, as if in a trance.

My spirit nudged me.

Not in front of all these people. Most of them were strangers.

I stood in front of her, waiting for a bolt of lightning to strike me like it had the others. Instead of a bolt, I felt as if I was melting like butter in the pan, softened by a love so warm and intense there was nothing I could do to stop myself from falling to the floor, not with a thud, but into unseen arms that let me down gently. Safer than I'd ever felt in my life, I cried, then sobbed. All the time, I was conscious that no one else cried or sobbed. They lay peacefully where they had fallen, with smiles on their faces. The tears wouldn't stop coming no matter how hard I tried to shut them off. Finally I was able to get up and go back to my seat where I stayed until I gathered enough strength to ask the woman why I cried and everyone else was smiling. What was wrong with me?

No sooner did I approach her than my knees went weak, my body light, and I fell to the floor again. As if pain was measuring itself in sobs, they bled from deep inside and wouldn't stop. I lost track of time. But when I stood up, I felt peace as if it was dripping through a tube from heaven, nonstop. Love could have been my name, I was so filled with it.

A friend drove me home from the meeting because she didn't think I had the strength to drive myself. Gabe met me at the door, stood back, looked at me, and asked what had happened to me. "You look different, more peaceful or something," he said.

The bird with a broken wing may have been transformed into a bird in flight right then.

Maybe I let the noise of the world get to me. Maybe the bud needed complete darkness to bloom.

30

Muffin and the Dead Horse

Before Calli went to sleep at night, she'd call Ryan and me to come look out the picture window just above her bed. In silence we watched the light that looked more like a star forever hanging over Story Mountain, an extension of the Bridger Mountains. Flashing against the night, it warned airplanes not to fly too low. I saw the beacon as a sign of hope.

Too late, I realized that it could have been a warning for me. Birds shouldn't fly too low. Eagles soar the high currents for a reason. An arrow can shoot off a wing if you're in range. But I didn't worry about the currents when I was a young mother. I worried about my family and keeping my children safe. Wherever they flew, I hovered. My wing touched my husband's so we wouldn't stray too far apart.

If there was a flame on Bridger Peak, I didn't see it. If Evening Star was telling God's warriors to bury the hatchet, I didn't hear her. A crisis of authority among pastors and their congregations and conflicts among denominations stirred a hurricane of emotions among Christians in Bozeman. Unlike the battle that raged among tribes in the legend of the Valley of the Flowers, when messengers came to tell us God wanted us to listen to his voice, there was no truce, no peace. Some said it was an evil attack on the holy revival, a spark from the blaze that raged on a larger scale all over the country. On Sunday mornings at church, the pastor preached on the truth that sets you free. But no one was free; not anyone I knew. I began to wonder if I understood what freedom meant.

I never heard of another murder like the one that happened not long after I moved to Bozeman. No mutilations either. Not that kind anyway. But I learned that there is another kind. Mutilations of the soul happened all the time.

———

Calli's Welsh pony, Apple, was dead in the pasture when the first real snow came that year. Bloodworms, the vet said. Muffin, our cocker, wouldn't leave the bloated animal's body, not even to come eat the food we set out for her. Rain or shine, night or day, the guardian angel stayed, barking and scolding if anyone or anything strange approached. It took Gabe a week to dig a hole big enough to bury the pony. Until Apple was covered up with dirt, Muffin didn't budge from her side.

Mushrooms began to grow in the dried piles of her manure, and I remembered what the Holy Spirit had said at my kitchen table, *Bloom where you're planted.*

Maybe the idealist got the better of me when it came to dead horses and manure piles. Like Muffin, I wouldn't give up on reviving a corpse no matter how bad it smelled. I remember thinking I was a mushroom in a manure pile about the time Stone Harmon came to town. Trusting his reputation as an author, healer, and teacher, the four pastors of the community church invited him to join their "fivefold ministry."

He wasn't dressed in a fur hide and didn't have grasshopper legs sticking out of his beard like John the Baptist, but when Reverend Stone Harmon showed up on the podium, I thought he might have been sent by the Lion of Judah himself. Claiming he'd been called, his message had a sting; foreboding, serious changes were about to happen in our lives. Running his thick hand through his silver mane, Reverend Harmon leaned toward the crowd and said, "We can establish the Kingdom of God on this earth if we're willing to pay the price. Dying to yourself is what it's all about."

I'd made some risky choices in my life, suffered for right and wrong alike, so I thought I knew what dying to self was about. Love lays down its life. I hoped God had sent this graduate of Princeton to work miracles. My family was going to be safe at last.

Within five months Stone Harmon had split the church. The head pastor accused the acclaimed healer of betrayal and said Stone had tried to take over leadership while he, the head pastor, was out of town. Appearing deeply wounded, claiming former congregations had also unjustly accused him, Stone denied the charge and stepped down. None of the other pastors publicly defended or condemned him. They just let the foundations of trust split naturally.

At the time, it seemed right to support the lion from Princeton. He had the vision for healing lives. Without healing, my child's prayer would never be answered.

Gabe and I had already committed ourselves to the mission when we found out that the lion was touchy. He had a temper that seethed through the cracks of his sermons, casting truth in an angry light. He didn't misquote Scripture, of course, not with his education, but through his mouth, dying to self had a sharp edge. God's love had a price. Eloquently, we were encouraged to turn the other cheek while the pastor bled us of impurities, one Scripture at a time.

Something didn't feel right to me when the young men Stone handpicked to take his orders called Gabe to a special meeting. After a couple of hours, my husband came home looking like he'd been shot through the heart, his face was so pale. "They want more money," he said. "They said that I'm not tithing enough." It was not the last time, nor was Gabe the last man in the congregation of professors, teachers, businessmen, musicians, young parents, and grandparents to face the inquisition. After all, Stone publicly called us "rejects" and "losers." No one met up to his expectations, whether he was asking for money, wisdom, prayer, or church maintenance. He had a lot of work to do if he was going to shine us up for God.

Women were called into Stone's office for private consultations. Pale faces and sad eyes told secrets, but I'd already heard them. Reverend Harmon had once told me in anger that I should keep quiet and let my husband do more of the talking. If the pastor had been wounded in the past, women had dealt the blows he hadn't forgotten. When my turn came to meet with him in his office, I talked first, hoping my enthusiasm for real healing and a loving church would ward off an ugly confrontation. By the time I left him, Stone was patting my shoulder and hugging me for supporting his vision. When I got home, I told Gabe that it was the last time I'd ever see the pastor alone. He had a way of making me feel we'd been intimate, even though we hadn't.

Like a savior, a pastor from out of town interrupted a Sunday night church service. Stone's tone had an unmistakably sharp edge when Reverend Tim Logan stood up to speak. Lean and short as Stone was thick and tall, the pastor was visiting his stepdaughter and her family, and they'd brought him to church.

"There's a problem here," Pastor Logan said, ignoring the challenge of authority in Stone's eyes. "You've all been wounded and need healing," he said, including Harmon in his gaze.

Stone looked like a stone: rigid, gray, hard and cold. Logan wasn't polished like Harmon was, yet he had the nerve to interrupt and interfere. If Tim Logan hadn't been a humble man with a smile that would tame the wildest temper, Stone might have asked him to leave.

It wasn't with open arms that Pastor Harmon and his wife Milly took Tim Logan into their confidence after that night, but it seemed like the beginning of trust, like the foundation for the mission of healing would start within the flock.

Our congregation visited Logan's church up north where the women could cook and the men could sing, the children happy, the adults content. Except for the uniform long dresses and scarves the women wore, the Levi's, boots and vests the men wore, the log houses and wheat grinders, it might have been like Garvanza at the turn of the century, the light of the West—for Christians, that is. Unlike the small community in East Los Angeles at the turn of the century, the imagination wasn't the frontier of possibilities in the church. Instead, it was the playground that the devil and God shared, and no one was beyond being seduced by their evil lusts for worldly pleasures. Passion for anything but prayer, repentance, and missions was under suspicion by Pastor Logan.

For reasons I still don't understand, he and Stone Harmon became friends.

Something didn't smell right in the corral of Christendom, but like Muffin, I wouldn't budge. God was my friend, the Church, his body on earth. If it smelled bad, I'd put up with the stink and hope it wouldn't stick to me. Being an idealist is a little like being a fool, isn't it?

Desperate for change, if living in a log home and grinding our own wheat would heal our pastor and his wife, Gabe and I decided we'd grind wheat and help Stone build a log church and home. If God wanted the foundation of our vision for healing to be built on community property, we'd do our part to support it. The vision Gabe and I shared seemed real: If we taught in a private school, our kids would benefit from our family bond. They'd have freedoms public schools didn't allow. Of course we wanted to have a say in every decision that concerned our children and ourselves. We let Stone know how we felt.

After all, we were mushrooms, and no one could tell us we weren't, could they?

Building like tremors before a massive earthquake, rumors shook Gabe and me. Friends told us that Stone and his chosen few had warned them to stay away from us. Behind our backs, our pastor warned the congregation that Gabriel and DeeAnn Gaynor were rebels.

Why? I didn't know for sure. We asked questions. We told Logan how controlling Stone was. If we didn't agree with our pastor, we said so. I probably "said so" more often than Gabe. Neither of us said anything when Harmon told a couple they shouldn't have any more than their three children. But we should have. I didn't think he should cuss at the men whether he was in the pulpit or not. He called prayer meetings but didn't want to hear what anyone thought God was saying unless they'd talked to him first.

In the distant corridors of my mind, I saw a shriveled figure with a smile on his lips. The Grand Inquisitor? What was he smiling about? What had I done but stick by my old pal after he died?

31

Locked in Stone

It didn't feel like my favorite time of year. A night chill was in the air when we got in the car to drive to church. Less than a year after we committed ourselves to Shalom Ministries, Stone's retirement plan, I made my stand for freedom. I publicly confronted our pastor. If everyone who felt threatened would have stood together, maybe he would have listened. But I stood alone: legs trembling, hands sweating, and my headscarf tied securely in place. Holding the Scriptures that God had given me, when I talked to him at the kitchen table a few mornings before, in my shaking hands, I stood quietly while Gabe asked permission for me to speak. In other words, we performed all outward signs of submission. Stone had to say yes; we had guest speakers from out of town.

Doing a poor job of keeping my voice from shaking, I faced the captive congregation and read the Scripture I had written down. "It was for freedom that Christ set us free; therefore keep standing firm and do not be subject again to a yoke of slavery . . . . You were running well; who hindered you from obeying the truth? This persuasion did not come from he who calls you. A little leaven leavens the whole lump of dough."

With Stone's eyes burning holes in my not-so-thick skin, I didn't have the nerve to say that in Galatians 5, Paul tells once strong free Christians that strangers have come to town in the name of God, using the law to mutilate them. Faith is the only way to enter the Kingdom, he said. If you're trying to please man and live by the law, you'll never make it. Maybe I was too afraid of the law, too bound to risk being mutilated by it. My soul had the scars of Dad's law, and Stone was man and god at the same time.

Swallowing hard, no spit to spare, I sat down.

Stone proceeded with his agenda as if I hadn't said a thing.

Afterward one of the visiting ministers came up to me and told me to guard my gift. I didn't know what he was talking about until a week or so later when the man who called himself Reverend, and his wife, came to our farmhouse. Leaning forward in the chair, Stone looked at me in a way he probably thought was pastorly, but was intimidating. He said, "The men in the congregation think you're hearing from Satan and influencing your family in an evil way. They're wondering why God would talk to a woman when he has them."

"They're losing respect for Gabe because you're so outspoken," Milly said, appropriately, as the minister's wife. She'd recently given me Corrie Ten Boon's tapes on love to listen to.

They mistook our patience for weakness. Clearly, hacking away at a sheep's heart wasn't new to them. The lion could be feral. If Stone hadn't been a bonafide pastor from Princeton and I hadn't been raised to honor God's ordained, I like to think I would have shown him the way to the door and slammed it behind him. They were wrong and I knew it. Regardless, their blows hit their mark. It wasn't hard, the open wound was already seeping.

Satisfied with their mission, Stone and Milly left soon after.

The ache was dull, from the inside out. Mutilated, that's how I felt. I couldn't hear God's voice at all that night. My kitchen table became a place to grieve for a while.

If Pastor Logan hadn't told us to trust God to change Stone and heal our church, we probably would have left. He talked like we'd be missing God's perfect will if we gave up on Harmon. This trial would build faith and prepare us for our "calling." Stone had convinced Tim Logan that he really wanted to be a good shepherd of the flock. Gabe began to take on responsibilities he hadn't taken before. He began to pray with the kids and me for direction. Happier than I'd ever seen him, my husband decided we should give our lives to God completely. We talked about teaching in the new school our church wanted to open, even if it meant giving up the dream home we were building in the mountains. He didn't seem to care that his parents thought he'd lost his mind: Their son was willing to give up financial security, a beautiful home, and the potential for advancement.

Gabe's folks said they were coming for a visit late spring. I was frantically trying to get ready for them—making sure toilet paper and paper towels were hanging right, fridge full, the least thread-bare sheets on their bed—when I thought how impressive a dust ruffle would be to his mom. I couldn't afford it, but rushed to K-Mart to buy one. If I hadn't broken my leg in three places when I tripped getting out of the Subaru in the K-Mart parking lot, only Gabe would have known what I was up to. He was used to the frenzy I got in before his folks came to visit.

Both Mom and Dad Gaynor cooked, cleaned, and taxied the kids and me while I got used to crutches and a cast up to my crotch. In two or three weeks they were gone, but they were back by fall.

The rookie contractor had drastically underestimated expenses, pushing us way over the limit of our construction loan. The Gaynors came to help us finish construction. They knew we loved our mountain home and probably thought we'd give up our plans to live like missionaries at some point in the near future. When friends moved us up the mountain, in the fall of 1980, I was still using crutches.

Instead of flying like the birds that visited the feeders on our deck, I was sinking into despair under the weight of pain and anger. I longed for God's voice and missed our talks at the kitchen table. Looking at myself in the mirror, sometimes, I felt like I was seeing a stranger: She wore a scarf most of the time, no makeup, no smile, not one that reached her heart anyway.

A few months after we moved into our new dream house, I was sitting in front of the fireplace, feeding the fire with pages from my journal. The Holy Spirit said, *He's not your shepherd,* but the words wafted up the chimney with the ashes, the proof that God had called my name. It didn't make sense to burn it, but I did, as if someone else inside was making choices for me now. I lost confidence in my ability to think for myself, and I knew it.

How could I not know that I'd changed? Christmas revealed who I was becoming, living under Stone's mutilating laws. All I had to hear was the Scripture that said men had made trees into gods and I felt guilty for every Christmas tree I'd ever decorated and loved in my life.

"You want to come find a Christmas tree with us?" Gabe and the kids asked before they took off to go look for one on our property. "Please," the kids begged.

"No, you guys go ahead," I said, feeling like we were all going to hell for worshiping a tree with decorations and lights and—oh, how I loved that tradition.

Looking at me like I wasn't much fun anymore, they all promised to bring back a big one.

An hour later the kids yelled from the yard for me to come out on the deck and see my surprise.

It was huge. Branches thick, green, and full as a dancing woman's skirt hid the kids while Gabe held it for me to see.

I gave my husband a look of frustration, then smiled for the kids and said, "It's beautiful. How are we going to get it up the stairs?" Our home was tri-level.

Gabe lifted it over the deck rail.

Looking back, the Illuminati was supposed to be the force behind the Antichrist, not some greedy preacher who was afraid he'd have to live on a modest income like the rest of us. The Church was supposed to be Christ's body on earth instead of one of those institutions that wore away at your ability to hear God, like Dr. Schweitzer warned us about. Church wasn't supposed to be one of those places that undermined your confidence in knowing truth when you heard it.

Why didn't other pastors hold Stone accountable? It wasn't because they didn't notice. They advised the suffering congregation to be loyal to him anyway.

I had heard it hundreds of times: there was nothing worse than leaving the Church, not even a Church shepherded by a pastor who mutilated the souls of his sheep in the name of Jesus, one by one. I couldn't help but wonder if those pastors were immune to the unholy sacrifice because they saw it all the time. Was Reverend Inquisitor a common name in Christendom, where forgiveness was the unholy excuse for letting a man get away with murder? Like Dad, Stone used others' forgiveness to stab a little deeper.

It shouldn't surprise me that the pastor penetrated my defenses. I came to feel as if nothing I had ever done or studied was good enough for the Church. With Milly, Tim, and Stone's encouragement, for the third time in my life I was baptized to make sure salvation took. The whole congregation couldn't have been victims of childhood rape, and Stone penetrated their defenses too. A Christian's supposed to be vulnerable, open, and humble, we were taught.

"Jesus didn't entrust himself to any man because he knew what was in a man." Stone never mentioned that Scripture, and I didn't find it myself until after I learned you can't revive a dead horse.

That winter and the next, I walked two miles down the dirt road to meet Gabe and the kids when they came home from school in the afternoons. Aspen stood out in the forest like the spine of a strong lean man. Lodgepole pine and blue spruce carried burdens of snow on their outstretched branches. Creeks were frozen over, and mallards flew in circles, looking for a place with running water. Curled up in the crooks of limbs, porcupines looked like nests, and I almost didn't recognize them. Repeatedly the thought came that I was in the winter of my life, but not to be afraid—deep in my roots the spirit was working and I'd bloom in season. Not in a manure pile, I hoped.

In the Bible, Jacob's youngest son, Joseph, had been imprisoned by other people's lies. Yet God used Joseph's time in bondage to strengthen his eternal identity and prepare the young man for his purpose on earth. Walking along, listening to the quiet, I thought I could feel my roots, hot with activity beneath the frozen earth. Sometimes I felt as if I were living my life and watching it at the same time. Like colors on a canvas, a painting in progress, it changed constantly.

Because I was often alone, I had time to think, time to listen. The fire was crackling in the wood stove when I heard God's voice. *Would you like to dance?*

Overwhelmed by His love, I started to cry. *I thought You were angry with me.*

No, DeeAnn, your hand dropped Mine.

My sobs made it hard to think. *I listened to man instead of You.*

He took my hand.

I didn't know how much shame and pain I had until He took it away.

Will you never give up on me? I asked Him on my walk the next day.

My memory fed me, "You were running well; who hindered you from obeying the truth? It was for freedom that Christ set us free. Keep standing firm. Do not be subject again to a yoke of slavery."

If I was going to bloom where I was planted, I had to put God before man's approval. But that didn't mean He wanted me to give up on His Church and the vision of healing. It was His body, His Kingdom on earth. I wanted my heavenly Father to be able to depend on me.

One day Ryan was home sick from school, stretched out in his rubber raft, when I started to read him Wilson Rawls' *Summer of the Monkeys*. For the next three days, we cried and laughed our way through the whole story.

Building within like a geyser about to erupt was the desire to write stories of my own. I began to check out books at the library by the armful. I wrote down a list of authors, Lewis Carroll and Carl Sandburg among them. Making a note to look up one of my favorites, Madeleine L'Engle, I got lists of all the Caldecotts and Newbery Award winners, from past to present. Some I remembered from Dr. Stallings' class, others I'd read to my students in California and when I substitute taught in Bozeman. Some of my most wonderful memories were reading Calli's and Ryan's favorites to them.

Except for Gabe and the kids, I didn't tell anyone what I was doing for a long time. Just the thought of someone as cruel as Stone telling me what God had meant for good I'd turned to evil made me ache inside.

Our church was in an organization of non-denominational churches. Stone had a pastor in another state that he was accountable to. Pastor Holland revived my hope for healing in the church when he came to visit. He didn't see it as a dead horse, so why should I? Gabe and I were both weary, but we weren't quitters. Pastor Holland was respected in the Northwest. He always came with a message for me. The lights were dimmed just right the night he spoke to the congregation. Reverend Harmon insisted lighting was important for a message to have the right effect, just as he insisted the best musicians perform or lead worship.

Standing under soft lights, Pastor Holland told a story about how God speaks to his people, then he concluded by saying, "Many of you have been hurt by your earthly fathers." Looking at Stone, he explained, "So it's hard for you to believe that God wants to speak to you in your hearts, but he does. He wants you to talk with him and trust him. He wants to be your heavenly Father."

Pastor Holland revived the disheartened idealist in me and my schoolgirl notion that love never fails.

Seeing Stone as a boy who had been hurt by his father made it impossible to give up on him as a man. What if God gave up on me? Or Dad? I asked myself. Imagine Stone if he were free. His sense of humor, his love for music, Montana, potlucks, and preaching. He really could have a ministry in healing. He'd had one before. So he'd said. So he'd written.

Hoping for a miracle—that God would raise the dead—Gabe looked for ways to help Stone with his chores. I let Milly advise me on being a mother and a wife and sold my microwave when she said I'd be a better example for Calli if I used the oven. Filled with anticipation, Gabe and I put our dream home up for sale so we could be ready to team up at the new school the church wanted to start. As much as we needed the money from the sale of our home ourselves, we gave the elders a hefty amount to help pay for the logs for the new church. Our family spent the summer building the mission.

We had moved into a rental at the east end of town when Stone asked Gabe to become an elder and to share in his ministry by counseling and teaching a group of members. Thinking our patience had reaped the healing that we'd been waiting for, Gabe accepted a role in leadership. He agreed to quit his teaching job and give up his tenure with the district to be a principal of the alternative school when it opened. He hoped Stone would learn to trust him and other new leaders enough to release his grip on the congregation.

Instead, Gabe felt like he was a judge at inquisitions as he listened to Stone verbally castrate men who'd been loyal to him for years when they confronted his decisions. Over the next year, we both became weary and began to pray God would show us another way to serve him while we still had the energy.

The summer before the school was to open, a pastor of a church in California asked us to take over the youth ministry. We met him when we were visiting Gabe's folks at their lake home in Northern California. Their church was as alive and free as ours was paralyzed under Harmon's control. At the time, living near them seemed healthier than trying to get water out of a stone. On the condition that the staff agreed to finance the ministry, we accepted.

At home in Bozeman, Gabe and I waited for the call that could change our lives. We told Stone that we might be moving, hoping he'd be happy for us, or at least happy to get rid of us.

"Aren't you too worn out to move?" he asked. "How can I disciple Gabe if he's in a state that far away?"

A month later, the guillotine fell. The church in California still didn't have an answer for us and didn't know when it would, so Gabe met with the elders to discuss his income and the cost of running the school. They offered him an income that not even our move into a cheap rental would afford us to live on. On previous advice from Pastor Holland, Gabe told them he needed more income; the school would need more money to operate. Stone called a couple of days later to tell him that only those who supported the leadership could be leaders themselves.

Sitting at the kitchen table of the rental we'd sold our dream home to move into, I had questions and no answers. God asked me to turn to Malachi: "For the lips of a priest ought to preserve knowledge, and from his mouth men should seek instruction . . . . But [the priests] have turned from my way and by [their] teaching have caused many to stumble . . . ."

If I was a cracked cup, I wouldn't know which leak to plug first. Now I knew for sure what my spirit was, because Stone had crushed it.

Gathering my pen and papers, I went back to work on the book I'd begun: Todd's story was fiction, but the love in it was true. Hopefully, writing about how a boy healed from blaming himself for a death he hadn't caused would help me heal from feeling helpless as I'd watched Christ's body mutilate itself.

32

Deadfall on Dark Alleys

Man's approval is a child's toy, DeeAnn. Adults must learn to live without it.

His voice is so clear as I walk home on the nature trail this spring morning. I wish I'd known how vulnerable I was to man's disapproval before I met Stone Harmon over twenty years ago. My need to please and my hatred of control confused me for most of my adult life. When I got trapped in Stone's church, the conflicts inside me seemed to explode. I couldn't stand myself anymore. Despite the healing I described toward the beginning of the story, and despite the emerging identity I celebrated with a rose on my desk, the root of my pain didn't surface until after Calli died.

This spring is the first I've noticed nature's pulse in the bark of trees along the trail. As I walk the narrow path, it's like watching blood vessels pump just beneath the surface of plump branches and lean trunks. Suddenly I can feel my heart beat in my arms and legs and chest, feel it pushing blood through my body. It's spring all right.

The pulse of life isn't hidden in the deadfall, yet a bulldozer or fire would help young saplings get more light and feel blue sky when clouds open, like drowsy lids after a night's sleep.

The spring Calli died, in 1991, the pulse of eternity rose to the surface of my soul. But I wasn't free from the past heartaches yet. I didn't know that if a person lives truth, laws of death are deadfall on the path to freedom. I didn't know that a song of identity lights a brush fire in the heart that burns long after our breathing stops. But I was about to learn.

At midnight in late August, I went crazy in the mall parking lot. I began to write my story, a story of healing, the next morning.

"I'm not a whore!" My desperate scream dissipated in the vacant mall parking lot. Collapsing on the hood of the car, the smooth cool surface of the Supra became my body's contact with reality. Nearby, Curt stood off to the side, seeming to me like an apparition, a blurred vision.

"Of course, you're not a whore," he said. The confusion in his voice matched the fear in his eyes.

But I couldn't respond because a voice inside me insisted that I was a whore, that Curt's comment to friends we'd just left at the bar was meant to expose me, strip me in front of them.

When the clock struck midnight, I'd run out the door.

Shadows created by last night's terrifying experience hovered over my soul as I wrote the opening paragraphs to the book I'd hoped would be a celebration of new beginnings in my life. Morning sun filtered through pine boughs where I sat in my wicker chair in the backyard of the home we rented when we moved from our condo.

Until last night, it hadn't seemed too late to leave a legacy to Ryan and Curt's three teenagers, and a memorial to Calli who died three months before. Now, my hands trembled as I exposed my insanity to fight my fear of it. I wrote to prove to myself that I could live dreams instead of bury them.

My grip on the pen weakened. What had happened to me? In my head, I could still hear that small voice crying, *Don't hurt me.* Words I actually screamed in the car as it raced down back streets toward home.

Home to hell, an evil voice taunted me as Curt accelerated the speed of the car to get me home faster. *Trapped. You'll get yours now,* it promised. Crying, I tripped out of the car and ran into the house.

Curt ran after me, grumbling. "Stop it, DeeAnn. What's wrong with you?"

Curt became the demon fulfilling its promise. I ran from room to room, put on my nightgown, tore it off, beat his chest, and screamed, "No, don't hurt me!"

"DeeAnn, what's wrong with you?" He held my wrists. I broke loose and started to fight him. Curt pushed me on the couch. I fell to the floor, writhed in pain, and screamed, "Don't rape me. Please, don't rape me."

"DeeAnn!" Curt slapped me. Then I was silent. The demon's promise was fulfilled.

Sitting under the ancient pine now, I covered my eyes in agony and tried to hide my shame over my insane behavior. *This isn't who I am. This isn't who I want to be. Will I ever be in control of my mind again?*

Dear God, I didn't think I could endure the memory of the police walking through the front door at an hour I was usually sound asleep. I felt like a child who had no place to hide, no one to protect me. Someone in our neighborhood of professionals probably called them, thinking Curt was beating me. All I'd wanted was to be held and safe, and yet I wouldn't let Curt come near me.

Two of the officers had followed me into the bedroom. The policewoman had stared, looking fascinated with my skimpy nightgown. The man hadn't tried to conceal his curiosity either.

"I can't bear this." I ran my bare foot over a dry patch of grass in front of my wicker chair, trying to wipe away those damning faces, feeling, feeling—*Oh, God, had I been dressed or naked?*

Curt had looked strangely relieved to see those suspicious faces, those nighttime intruders. I tried to explain to the officers that my husband hadn't beaten me; I might have been abused when I was young. They scowled and said, "If this happens again, you'll both be arrested."

Their insensitivity was like cold water on me. What right did the policewoman—whose lusty gaze undressed me—have to threaten she'd arrest me? What right did the wide-eyed rookies—who looked like they had to wear nametags to remember their own identities—have to threaten me?

Gathering strength from the morning sun, I refused to heap more condemnation on myself. Kicking the tree stump that held my coffee cup, I heard my wicker chair snap in several places.

Curt was listening to the radio in the house. He took a walk right after we woke up this morning. We needed to talk about what happened last night, but I wasn't ready. Not yet.

"Whether near or far, I'll be there; just think of me. . . ." There was that song again. It had played on Calli's birthday in July. Morning after morning, day after day, when I thought I'd die if she didn't walk through the front door and hug me, that song had come on the radio. A person who had died was singing to the one left on earth.

Oh, Cal. What am I going to do, sweetheart? I thought this nightmare was behind me.

At the top of my yellow legal pad, I wrote a phrase I remembered from my journal: "Bird with a broken wing." God had promised to heal me so I could fly.

Looking up at Montana's vast August sky, I thought how lucky the birds are that get to fly the way they are born to fly. Had I ever flown the way I was born to?

With my yellow legal pad and pen in my left hand and the coffee cup Calli had made in her college pottery class in my right, I managed to open the latch to the screen. Walking through the kitchen to the living room, I could see Curt was sitting in his big green velour chair, like I imagined he would be—his long legs stretched out in front of him on the mismatched ottoman.

"You okay?" he asked, but he didn't turn to look at me. We went to bed last night without discussing what happened. My stomach was tied in knots most of the night, like it usually is when Curt's anger or frustration turns to silent withdrawal. I knew he needed space and time to think as much as I needed him to tell me that he was proud of me for surviving my terrifying battle with insanity.

Testing the climate between us, I walked into the center of the living room where I could see his face, especially his eyes, because that's where his heart hid when he felt threatened. The trust we'd had the day before wasn't there. Yesterday, I'd watched the sun highlight silver streaks in his hair as we talked about how strong we'd become in spite of everything we'd been through in the past two years. The hope he'd tell me I could be whoever I wanted to be, the way he had twenty-four hours before, withered.

Until last night, I'd thought I was becoming who I wanted to be.

Please tell me we're a win-win team like you usually do after we've survived another crisis, I silently begged him.

Curt finally motioned me to sit near him. I chose to sit on the floor at his feet. "Was it me? Did I say something?" he asked.

I shook my head. Darkness had disappeared and taken the evil stranger with it, leaving me with the dust that coated the furniture, dust I stirred up last night, fighting ghosts in this house I thought was marked for good times and happiness. Now it, too, was filled with my loneliness, confusion, humiliation, defeat, and anger. The late August sun penetrated my bare skin through the window. Its light was all that was left of my hope for new beginnings. *I really need to dust today.*

"Was it what I said about making love, DeeAnn? Was it the alcohol?" Curt asked.

We weren't big drinkers. We didn't have alcohol in the house. I knew when I drank a couple of beers with pizza last night that alcohol didn't mix with my medication, but antidepressants hadn't cured anything in the four years doctors switched me from one prescription to another. My dosage was small now. If I hadn't thrown up for a week when I tried to get off the drug several months before, I'd be rid of it.

All I'd wanted was to feel free and happy last night. I needed to relax and have fun!

In Curt's silence, I thought I heard, "Why don't you stop yourself from freaking out?"

How could he have forgotten what I'd asked him after we made love the day before? "I asked you to never talk or joke about making love with me in front of anyone. It makes me feel like we're doing it in front of everybody." I felt undressed again.

"We don't have anything to be ashamed of, DeeAnn."

That's just it. That's why I don't want anyone watching, twisting—"I don't know why this happened, Curt." I felt exhausted. Why had I felt desperate, betrayed, and abandoned when my husband carelessly joked about our intimacy with another couple? Yesterday we were best friends all day, from the time we sat silently on the porch steps in the morning sun until we sat face-to-face talking in the living room, ignoring evening shadows that reflected off cool mint-green walls.

My stomach revolted now just as it did last night. *No. It wasn't funny—the image of me being screwed, me being exposed in front of everyone. I didn't say this was okay. Not okay.* I cried to myself and tried to reach for the ball of anguish that hid from the morning sun, just as it hid from the crowd last night.

I leaned away from Curt's long legs. I felt as if I'd been loved and abandoned a million times in my forty-six years, figures that didn't match with reason.

Curt's troubled eyes scanned the pastoral lithograph on the opposite wall. I couldn't ask him if he was sorry he married me. He might say yes.

Shocking-pink dried petals in the rainbow wreath hung next to the lithograph's quiet blues and muted browns. I remembered how bright, fresh, and fragrant the pink roses were when my friend Kathy gave them to me last May, just before Mother's Day—that empty-armed day.

How can I deal with all of this pain? I pull my knees close to my chest.

Curt stood up abruptly and took two tickets out of his shirt pocket. "We've had enough of this," he said, not touching me. "Let's walk up to the Bobcat scrimmage this afternoon. The sun's shining."

Yes, let's go to a game you understand, to your alma mater where logic, grit, and skill earned you the titles of winner, outstanding, excellent "pro" material.

I wasn't being fair. The scars around Curt's left eye and ear reminded me of the cost he'd paid for his mistakes. He walked like an Olympic athlete. But wasn't his own identity a question mark on his soul?

"I'd like that." I stood up by myself. Snuggling my bare feet into the sunny spot of the new plush carpet, I yearned for Curt to take me in his arms and give me something real to fight the nightmare with.

I kicked the hot carpet, trying to scatter ugly memories. Slipping on my Birkenstocks, I hurried to join Curt outside in the sun, hoping it would wrap me in the warmth that I desperately needed to feel.

———

The next evening, Curt and I drove up the Gallatin Canyon at dusk to have dinner at our favorite restaurant, the Corral Bar and Cafe, which was less than an hour from our home in Bozeman. I rolled down my car window so I could feel the cool air on my face. Curt maneuvered the Supra around mountain curves, and I began to relax the way I usually did when we drove Montana's uncluttered highways. The thick scent of pine and the lazy August flow of the Gallatin River wakened me to nature's order, its innate drive to create, replenish. Creation moves in cycles to cleanse itself of pestilence, I noticed.

Curt's face softened. "I don't know why you lose touch with reality and go crazy at times, DeeAnn. But I guess we both have many wounds that need to heal. Do you think this is part of grieving?"

He wanted to be there for me, but not too close. The emptiness was bigger than both of us.

"In spite of all that's happened to us, we get stronger all the time. We're going to make it," he said.

Earlier that afternoon he'd held me while we lay on the floor listening to tapes he'd recorded. Curt usually backs off when he's struggling with his feelings, but he always talks with me after he's had time to think, so I reminded myself I didn't need to fear his silence the way I had Gabriel's.

Evening shadows made dark shapes on the road. Jim Croce sang a sad song on the car stereo about a past relationship. Curt reached over to take my limp hand in his strong grip. "We're worth the trouble, DeeAnn." He smiled and squeezed life into my fingers.

Tears tumbled through my closed lids, and I exhaled to release the fear that he'd leave me before I could find out what was wrong and fix it. Love was fragile. A twenty-year marriage had broken to pieces. I wanted this one to work.

Ryan was spending more time with us, between work and rock climbing. He was talking about moving home. Chad was nesting in his big freshly painted room downstairs, with its new carpet. I brushed a kiss across the back of Curt's hand, then searched the sky for a sign of hope. Twilight settled over dense forest. I felt peaceful and let my mind rest. Again, what should have torn us apart was bonding us to each other.

"What were you like as a girl, DeeAnn?" Curt asked as we talked over loaded hamburgers and onion rings. Beyond the huge picture window, stars boldly winked timeless assurance of good tomorrows in an otherwise black sky. "Were you a child of contradictions, the same as the woman?" He smiled at me. "Were you anxious to please, yet afraid of being hurt? Have you ever stood up for yourself? Have you ever known your worth?" My husband probed, careless of hitting nerves, obviously hoping he would revive the fight in me.

Anger formed a knot in my stomach; my back stiffened, and I started to come back at him, then noticed he looked satisfied, as if I hadn't disappointed him.

"I didn't think so," he said.

33

Santa Ana's Return

The top of my neighbor's bald head glistened in the heat of September's afternoon sun. It appeared to be detached from his body as it bobbed along the high weathered redwood fence that separated our lots. I still thought the professor and his wife were the ones who had called the police that humiliating night I'd had over two weeks to think about. Maybe I was hoping they were the only ones who heard me screaming through our open windows.

"Forget it, DeeAnn," Curt said several days after we were threatened with arrest. When I told him I couldn't look at our neighbors, let alone speak to them after what I'd done, he said, "We know who we are. That's all that matters. You didn't do anything but have a bad time. Don't dwell on it. We're stronger for what we went through, and we're still going to become who we want to be. Right? Two whole people creating a home for our kids. Don't forget you have a computer arriving in a couple of months, so you can write your story."

Now I could hear my husband calling the professor's name, Tim, Jim, or something short like that. Tim or Jim looked over the fence and smiled at Curt, who was walking out of our small dark garage where he was trying to fix our lawn mower. Curt had met most of our immediate neighbors and said they were friendly. It wasn't unusual to see him talking with their kids on the sidewalk under the tall old tree that drooped with dead branches.

Stepping back further from the kitchen window, I leaned against the stove where I could listen to the relaxed dialogue between my husband and the professor at a comfortable distance.

"DeeAnn!" Curt shouted through the open kitchen window, totally ruining my peaceful protected cover.

I didn't answer.

"I thought she was in the kitchen, writing in her journal," he told Tim or Jim. "DeeAnn—"

"Curt?" I was standing within an inch of the meshed window screen.

"Finn just retired from being a professor of English here at Montana State University. I told him that you're a writer. Come on out."

Great. "Oh, okay." I felt as if my husband was tossing me butt naked into a rushing river so I'd have to learn to swim.

Finn greeted me with a smile and asked what kind of writing I did. "Non-fiction," I told him. In a stroke of defiance against my own shame, I explained I was starting a book that would be the true story of my life.

The professor raised his eyebrows with interest and said, "That should be good."

I thought he meant it.

———

"Grab your tennis shoes," Curt said the next morning. He put his hand on my hip and moved me toward the bedroom closet. "I'll get the racquets and balls."

"Oh, good!" I planted a quick kiss on his unshaven cheek and hurried to take off my sandals and put on my tennis shoes.

Since we had moved into our house, I'd asked Curt to walk to the nearby courts several times. I loved to play tennis. He insisted he wasn't very good at tennis, which made me suspicious. When we moved from our condo I found a box full of his trophies and medals. I had to dig to find a second place award among all the firsts and championships in a multitude of sports.

"I think we have a new can of those fluorescent lime-green balls someplace," I said. The vibrant color and texture of new tennis balls held promise. Even though I'd told Curt that I wasn't competitive and had never cared whether I won or lost in sports, I felt excited about this match. I was good at tennis.

I couldn't stop smiling as I tied my shoelaces. Curt seemed to revive a world of feelings that I'd either forgotten or never known I had. The past couple of weeks I began to remember myself as a child, a girl, and young woman, how I loved to laugh and have fun. With Curt I could be ornery, not mean, but ornery. An independent, determined, stubborn streak was emerging that reminded me of Annie.

Curt waited for me in the alley behind our house. We walked together, but I was in my own world. I shook off the feeling I'd run into Calli any minute and made myself stop looking for her in the distance. Instead, I kicked at dry leaves that had fallen early and let myself feel the crisp day and warm breeze. It promised a night cold enough to put all the blankets back on that we took off for the summer. Looking up, I thought the sun was brighter than when we left the house.

"We both forgot to bring sunglasses," I said.

Curt opened the gate and motioned me to go ahead of him into the courts. He smiled and walked to the far side of our court with his racquet, leaving me with the full can of traffic-stopping lime-green balls. The sun was in his eyes.

Flint struck rock somewhere within, and I felt sparks of nervous excitement. The sun penetrated my shirt and loosened the muscles in my back. I knew I had the edge. Confidence felt as good as the fuzzy ball I held in my hand. I visualized a serve Curt would miss.

On the other side of the court, Curt wore a big smile that dared me to beat him. Deliberately, I lifted my racquet above my head, cocked it to serve, and said, "I'd love to."

Curt volleyed to my right back corner. Returning the ball to his left, I barely missed the net. Time was the only loser as we reached deuce in the first set. Until that moment, I never thought he lied.

The disadvantage I had was not the sun or his skill, but my mind. Curt knew what it felt like to win. I couldn't remember anything but losing. Not in tennis, but in life. Swamp-green cement suddenly loomed like prison walls. White lines locked me in with labels and the behaviors that had earned them. I was sick of feeling like a victim!

"Ad out," I called. No, not Ad out! Suddenly, desperation flew at me like lime-green darts. Please, not Curt's advantage. Sometime in the game I had become the survivor instead of a competitor. No, he can't win! My stomach churned with unreasonable fear. The racquet became my weapon. My defense. I wanted to cry, to scream, to hurt him so he couldn't hurt me first, so no one could hurt me first.

Panic began to rise, cutting the air off in my chest, making it hard for me to breathe. Could he see I was afraid? Could he see this wasn't a game anymore? That I needed to win? Blast it, I was tired of losing!

Tears clouded my vision, but I still had to hit the ball. No one else was going to hit it for me. No one else was going to win for me. Even if I broke my leg, or my wing, this was my game.

"Ad in," I called, wondering how I'd won the last two points.

Curt was smiling and squinting on the far side of the net. He was behind, and he was smiling!

A cool breeze cleared my senses. "You're behind, Curt." I tested curiously, wondering when he'd lose the edge, the psychological edge I thought he often had on me. "You're losing." Sounding more play-ful than I felt, I hit hard fuzz where I hoped he couldn't reach it.

He missed. "Yes!" I yelled. "Curt, I did it!" My joy was sincere, vulnerable, capable of being shattered.

"Don't get too excited. It was just over the service line." His blue eyes twinkled in the flickering sunlight, and I could see that his pride was in me. But he wasn't giving me the game. "Show me a good loser, and I'll show you a loser."

"Ad in," I called, feeling like a winner.

I watched a veteran athlete straighten his back, move into re-ceiving position, focus his attention, and split air with the force of his return.

His point. So that's how he does it. Losing is not a threat to Curt. It's the rush before victory.

The next two points were mine, and so was the game. That was only one game, and the sun had been in Curt's eyes.

We switched sides, and my undaunted opponent burned cement just outside the back line with his first serve.

"Long," I called.

Not a word from my husband as he straightened, focused, formed his body in the shape of victory again and again, playing to win, but not afraid of losing. Not to me anyway.

"Thirty–forty," he called his score first. Looking as if he was gathering energy from forces in the universe, Curt brought his racquet back to serve, then seemed to move with the speed of light as he cracked the ball . . . .

His racquet split like a fractured bone, immediately folding in half. Curt stood still for a moment and stared at his broken racquet. Then he rolled his head back and let out a belly laugh, reminding me of a kid who'd just lit a firecracker and watched it explode.

Not defeated, only resting. My laughter shattered tension as I ran to hug my husband.

I mounted Curt's broken racquet over my desk to remind me that losing is an attitude just as winning is a condition of the heart. It was time for me to let myself win, but I wasn't sure how.

A gust of wind blew against my hot skin through the open window of my office. I thought of my old friend and antagonist, Santa Ana.

So you're back, I said.

34

Bird with a Broken Wing

So Jacob named the place, Peniel—The face of God.
Genesis 32:30

There would be no illusions that Christmas; 1991 would be a year I'd never forget. Any hopes I ever had of being a woman I'd want to know vanished overnight.

It was early November, that indecent month before December when I woke up to a memory of the sheep barn. The barn was not a word. It was a place, real with smells and a door; the door was shut, and he was there. He was safe. But I wasn't safe. I didn't know who he was.

Two hours later I was sitting in Gene Dover's office, telling him what I'd seen. Gene was the therapist Lars referred me to when he left town after my incident in the hospital. At our first appointment, Gene said the most amazing thing I'd heard from a therapist in the two years I'd been seeing one or another. "Have confidence in your own thinking." Later, I cried as I wrote it in bold red letters in my journal.

"DeeAnn, I want you to pretend you're looking through the lens of a camera," he told me now. I couldn't remember anymore about the barn. I felt like vomiting. "Your emotions are strong, and this will give you distance, as if you're directing a play, even though you're in it."

"A man is holding my hand and taking me into a room in the barn," I said.

"What's he doing?"

"He's laying me on the floor."

"What else?"

"I don't know." I felt like I was suffocating and gasped for air.

"Can you tell me about the room," Gene said. "Sometimes it helps to remember the objects, the clothes."

"There is a window. The door is closed." I was so glad to get away from the man and what he was doing. *God, don't let me have a dirty mind.* I begged, trying to keep myself clean in the manure of my thoughts—a habit I'd had since I'd known what a thought was.

"What is the man doing?" Gene asked.

"He's opening his pants." I whispered. I was a little girl who was ashamed and embarrassed. Shamed and exposed not only by the man, but also in front of Gene, I bent my head and folded myself over my knees, which were shaking. Sitting across from the thera-pist, I felt like I had to go to the bathroom—the memory of the cold air on that part of my body. I couldn't get up or get away. *God, I was so little, am so little—not supposed to see what the man is showing me, feel what he's making me do, let him touch me there.*

"Who is it, DeeAnn?"

"It can't be Dad." I sobbed. I was the "apple of his eye." He called me Pumpkin. Gripping the name "Daddy" as if my next heart-beat depended on the safe love of him, I felt the overwhelming trust that this little girl was feeling for the person who was? *My God.* I thought I heard the bones snap as he broke my baby wing. Dying was easier than believing my dad's strong hands were teaching me what trust was all about. Pain.

"No, Gene, it can't be Dad," I said.

Before our hour was up, Gene looked directly into my eyes and said, "You may eventually see who the man was, DeeAnn. I want you to remember three things. I'm sorry for what happened to you, but it wasn't your fault. You didn't do anything wrong. And I'm glad you survived. There may be more memories. If there are, just handle them the way we have this morning."

He was right. When I got home, I sat on my bed alone, clutch-ing my journal like it was my last thread of sanity. Waiting for what I could feel was coming, I braced myself for a hurricane of memories that could tear my soul from my body. A Scripture came to mind, Psalm 13. I swallowed it word by word. As if in bold print, this sentence stood out: "Give light to my eyes, or I will sleep in death."

Oh, God. I see Annie.

It had started. She was stretched out on a cot with her panties off, maybe as young as four. One man she recognized held her arms and her mouth while her dad raped her, then her dad held her the same way while the other man did the same. Taking their time, their rough shirts brushed my face, my naked stomach, while I tried to close my legs and protect my "self" from the penetrating force that didn't belong in me. They talked to me, to each other, and the bright light seemed to sway above their heads as they moved over me and taught me what love is all about—Dying. "I can't breathe," I wrote in my journal. "Pressure on head. . . . IT HURTS. Gene hasn't called back."

Panic took over. "Curt," I called, trying to control my fear, holding back vomit, trying to take deep breaths. "Curt." I cried, believing I was about to give my husband the reason he needed to divorce me.

"What's wrong, DeeAnn?" Curt said. Tenderly, he pulled me onto his lap so he could help me hold my body still. I had to make myself look at him or else I'd run and hide from Dad's strong arms—his raping, breaking love.

"I can't reach Gene." I was whispering. "I've seen some things. Most people who see these kinds of things have help. They need help!" Desperately, I looked into Curt's eyes and tried to pull understanding from them.

"That's good you're seeing some things, DeeAnn," he said. "Gene may not be able to see you long enough to do you any good." Appointments were limited to one hour and had to be made in advance. "We'll do this together." Curt pulled me close to his chest when I twisted to get off his lap. "I'll be here. I won't leave you."

"No. It's too bad. You will leave." I was the one who was leaving as I felt myself, the child, being held down, couldn't breathe.

"What's happening?" Curt said.

I cried and told him all I'd experienced, all I was remembering.

"Trust what you see," he said. "Good job. You're finally getting free." He hugged me close.

The phone rang. I told Gene about the memories.

"It finally makes sense. You aren't crazy," he said. "You've come through the valley of the shadow of death." He knew the truth. "Curt's doing fine with you, DeeAnn." We made an appointment for the following week.

In the days that followed past and present melted together in pain's heat. I wanted to see everything Dad had done, the way you want to vomit until there's not a drop of poison left in your body. There were time lapses in my memories, yet vivid scenes moved in sequence. The barn was not the last crime scene. The rapes didn't stop when Dad moved us from Colorado.

In my memories of California, I smelled rooms, felt hot colored lights in the studio-warehouse, feared both men and women as I fought the positions they put me in. I closed my eyes to their faces as they fondled and raped me. I heard conversations as if they were recordings. There was a man in a suit who saved me from all of them. I didn't know who he was, couldn't remember.

Finally the depression I remembered suffering when I was thirteen years old made sense. Suffocating fears, crippling feelings and thoughts that I'd had throughout my life finally made sense. The lies had made me crazy, but there were days I thought the painful truth would kill me.

Curt held me while I vomited into the toilet. He listened when I begged him to take me to Warm Springs, the mental institution, rather than believe what I was learning about Dad, about Annie's world, about the family of man I'd come from.

At the same time I learned that God would crash the doors of hell to be with me. I was never alone. When a figure opened the bedroom door, I thought it was real. By the smell, I knew it was Dad. There was nowhere to run from the power of live memories but into my Father's arms.

Darkness is as light to Me, He said. Night was like day to God. In my spirit, I saw angels moving around in the house. Others walked around our yard, talking as though there was no difference between heaven and earth to them.

"Are you awake?" Curt asked.

"Yes. Dad was here, but so are the angels."

"Come here, woman," he said, and kissed me like I was the lady I'd wanted to become.

The next day friends called to ask Curt to work for them in Helena, Montana, for a couple of days. "Go ahead," I told him, believing he might not come back. I wasn't living in a world where love keeps its word.

We were both sitting on the couch in the living room when he made me look directly into his eyes. "DeeAnn, I want you to re-member these things. I'll never leave you. I'm proud you're my wife. None of this was your fault. I love your breasts. You are beautiful." He gently massaged my breast through my cotton turtleneck. His hands felt healing after the painful touching I'd remembered. "And we're going to win. Six things. Say them with me." He was crying. "DeeAnn, I won't ever let anyone hurt you again. I'll protect you at all costs. I promise." He held my face in his hands. "You've been hurt enough. No more."

Curt left early in the morning for Helena. He promised to call during the day and come home that night rather than stay over. But I was not alone in the house. My husband wasn't alone either. I saw angels with him as he drove away.

Overwhelmed by the presence of the spiritual realm, both good and evil, I sat on the couch. Had it only been a few days since the memories surfaced? I'd seen faces and felt touches of everyone who had penetrated or violated the boundaries of my identity, whether brutally or innocently, since early childhood to the present. Though fragile as a bird with a broken wing, I felt protected in my living room that morning.

Calli appeared. I felt the peace that always came with her pres-ence. Graced in colorful garments, she was vibrant. Living light, moving particles, she was my Cal just the same. The indescribable force of her gave me joy and felt more real than my heartbeat. She sat on the edge of the couch and put her arm around my shoulder.

There were other spirits or angels moving near the kitchen. Their voices were safe, although they spoke in another language. Eternity was not foreign to me, nor was the dark cloud of evil that gathered above it, moving like swamp slime, as if waiting, waiting for what?

A memory came to mind, not violently, but clearly. Dad made me drink something. His chest was spattered with blood.

I didn't want to understand. I wanted to be someone else and began to cry. An angel showed me the bundle she held in her arms. I thought it was a baby. A burden was released from me.

The experience was healing and freeing. I just let it happen.

As if He'd walked out of the stained-glass window stories I'd loved when I was a girl, the Man appeared. I called him Truth now. I'd seen people cripple the already crippled in His name. Christians had used Him to lie. They'd slathered Him in spiritual feces.

DeeAnn. Moving toward me, He said, *Annie is wounded, but she is your strength. She's suffered and won.*

Sitting down next to me, He put my head on His chest. *You've had a long fight, little warrior. Now let out the pain.*

It was finally over. *Oh, Jesus.* I sobbed until I ran out of strength. He called me "warrior."

That evening, Ryan was upstairs in his room and Chad was downstairs talking on the telephone with his mother when Curt came home from Helena. I had told Ryan that Dad had raped me so he'd know why his mother had let him down when she should have been strong. But I didn't describe the terrifying images. I hadn't told Curt's kids anything because I was afraid of what their mother would do to their dad, using my shame as ammunition.

My husband had no sooner walked in the door than he said his youngest daughter, Gina, wanted to come visit us for the weekend. Almost pleading, he said, "You have to tell my kids what's happened to you so they'll understand why you've been emotional."

My daughter's death isn't enough of an explanation? I panicked. *What about his promise, I'll protect you at all costs?* Suddenly gripped by terror, I was sucked back into the hell I'd been reliving for days. Locking myself in the bathroom, I took the scissors out of the medicine cabinet and began to etch trails of pain on my breasts for the first time since Gabe had left years before. Under my breath, I said, "You whore. You are evil," repeating words Dad had spoken to me in memories. I heard Curt trying to pick the lock.

Finally, my son's voice broke the spell of darkness. "Mom, open the door." Concealing my shame with my clothes, I opened the door, wondering who would abandon me for being a bad girl.

"You alright?" Ryan said, a familiar look of concern in his eyes.

Torn between a father's responsibility to his kids and a husband's promises to his wife, Curt looked at me, then walked into the kitchen. When we went to bed later, he lay far away from me, in silence.

Don't be afraid, Calli said as the darkness closed in.

Two days later the truth finally penetrated what was left of my wall of resistance. I hurried out of the grocery store while the boxboy rushed and bumped behind me with the basket of groceries. I needed to be alone. *You did it! You really did this to me!* was shoving its way past *Not Dad, No, not Dad.* He set me up for destruction. *And I was your daughter!*

I slammed the car door and locked it with a woman's fury. The steering wheel bruised my fists as I beat it hard and yelled, "Liar! You bastard! You son of a bitch!" Curses carried the weight of my pain as I shouted them at deaf car windows. Somehow, I drove home, my eyes blinded with tears.

Once home, I made sure that Gina and her friend weren't around and then faced my wide-eyed husband. Tears of rage and pain poured down my cheeks, I spit Dad's betrayal all over kitchen walls. "Curt, he did it. He really did this to me. I loved him. I was his daughter. My God!"

Curt nodded like he was expecting this. "Gina and her friend are at the Swim Center. Go in the living room and get it out."

Using the couch as an anchor to reality, I sobbed into my hands. "You're not my dad. You don't deserve me. You never did." Mentally, I wiped flesh and blood from my severing sword and let cleansing anger go along with it. "You'll never use my love to destroy me again."

No one will.

For the first time in my life, I knew how "quiet" sounded.

If I'd run a marathon, a break would have been in order. Rest would have been my reward. But the fight for sanity wasn't going on just within me, it was always going on in the angry world around me at the same time. The next night, Chad and Curt had a heated argument over ground rules; a teenager was testing the limits of authority. Angrily, he called his mother. As if this was the opportunity she'd been waiting for, Vera asked to speak to me over the phone. "You've come between Curt and Chad," she said. "They were fine until you came along." Sucking her vulnerable kids into her scheme, Vera sent her oldest daughter to Bozeman to get her brother, "because we didn't want him." By midnight Chad had left home.

The next morning, after Curt left for work, the phone rang. "The kids want to talk with their dad alone," Vera said. "They will meet him halfway." "He's not here" didn't mean anything to her.

She called repeatedly until I took the phone off the hook to meet an appointment I'd made with Gene, between Vera's calls. I needed help.

The answering machine's light was flashing when Curt and I returned home after eating a light dinner out. Neither of us were hungry. He'd already talked with his kids earlier and didn't like what he was hearing. Now he flipped the switch on the machine and heard his ex-wife say, "Get rid of DeeAnn, Curt. She's the problem."

35

The Eternal Struggle

Too stunned to speak, we looked at each other.

As if trying to separate lies from truth, Curt disconnected the phone and then wrapped me in his arms. "I can't believe this is happening to us."

Feeling devastated, we promised, "We're going to win," though our dreams for a big happy family were crumbling before our eyes.

Before the week was over we knew that Chad would not be home for a long time. His mother drove him back to Bozeman to pack up everything he owned.

We were starting our new life together on the front lines of a war we didn't know how to fight. Curt and I took walks daily and worked out at the gym to deal with stress. We decided to start playing racquetball.

It seemed like more than a week had passed when we both met with Gene Dover. He told us we were doing a great job together of dealing with everything. "Your healing has an unusual spiritual dimension to it, DeeAnn," Gene said. "Sometimes it takes a victim years to recover memories." Then he handed me a list of symptoms for incest survivors and apologized for himself, Lars Mitchell, and the medical profession that had missed them.

He was suspicious of the appendicitis attack I'd suffered as a five year old. My appendix was shoved so far up inside me, the surgeon had to lengthen the incision to find it. Gene had questions about the surgery when I was ten. The muscles in my lower abdomen were weak and falling. Mom said I might not be able to get pregnant and carry a baby if the doctor didn't operate.

"Should I investigate my memories?" I asked Gene. "There were faces I recognized, places I didn't." The man in the suit didn't have a face yet. I'd seen a woman in uniform, and much more.

"Do you feel that you need to prove what you've seen?" he asked.

"No. My brother has memories of Dad trying to sexually molest him when he was little. A counselor told him that when a father sexually abuses a daughter, it's not uncommon for him to physically abuse the son. Rod's remembered enough to advise me to get on with my life, for the sake of healing."

"I agree. Get on with your healing. Bury these memories in the sea of forgetfulness. You should be able to find them if you want to, but not be controlled by them."

Before we left his office, Gene asked if I'd like to join a support group for rape victims. I didn't want to relive my pain or anyone else's. I wanted to move on. He said to call if Curt or I had questions. He thought the flashbacks would ease up now that the memories had surfaced.

They did ease up. But a night in the hospital a few summers before reminded me that even one flashback could be fatal. I didn't know how to stop them completely. Christmas lights wouldn't be hung in town for two more weeks when I ended seven hours of insanity under my desk, the one where I normally sat to write. The three feet of space in which I had to move was the only place I felt safe from uncontrollable terror, safe from myself, the woman who lost track of tangibles, like tables and chairs. Living in timeless outposts of truth and lies, I hungered to hear a human voice that might give me meaning to latch on to. I was Annie hiding from Dad. I was DeeAnn hiding from everyone.

"Give me your hand, honey," Curt said, when he found me later. We'd had an argument that had triggered flashbacks for both of us, but he wasn't the one hiding under the desk.

The little girl shook her head rapidly side to side without speaking.

Curt stretched out on the floor in front of the desk where he could see me better. "What are you doing, DeeAnn?" He spoke softly.

"I'm hiding." I looked around to see where Dad was and listened for the metal sound of his belt buckle.

"He's not here. You're safe." Curt reached for my hand.

I shook my head determinedly. I definitely didn't feel safe.

"It's okay, DeeAnn. Give me your hand. Let's go into the living room." Curt was gentle. He watched for his wife to respond.

Truth broke the bonds of darkness, and dignity replied, "No, it's okay. You go to the matinee and take a break. I'll be fine." It felt good to take care of myself, even if I was under the long desk that I usually wrote on.

Curt's smile strengthened me to calm the furies. He laughed. "I took a break. I worked on the car for a while. Now I'm back. Give me your hand, Annie. We're going to do this together."

"Okay." I sighed with relief that I could touch reality instead of whirl around its outer edges.

We hugged each other, then walked into the living room. Curt sat me in his lap. "You did good. I lost track of truth myself for a while and had to get away, but you made it." He brushed my short hair away from my face as if he were dusting off a diamond.

"Curt, I have to talk to someone who knows about flashbacks, about what they can do to a person, and who understands the insanity they create. Does Dr. D have any experience like that?" I did not intend to rely on my husband for sanity the rest of my life. I'd rather be dead than be a dependent wife. My first psychotherapist said I was dependent. I'd hated the term then, and I hated it more now. Now that I was remembering who I was. Now that I knew who I was not.

"Dr. D told me he worked in a mental institution for fifteen years." Curt dialed the psychologist that his insurance company had sent him to for evaluations on his head injury from the motorcycle accident. My husband told the doctor what we were dealing with, then wrote down a date and time and hung up.

"What did he say, Curt? Does he understand?"

"He said he's worked with people who have had serious flashbacks. He said they can make a person insane."

I wiped away the tears with a stubborn jerk of my hand. "That's what I've been trying to tell people for how many years? And this man acts as if it's common knowledge! Now I'm going to heal, Curt. I'm going to get on with the rest of my life. I hope you're ready to meet the woman you married."

"I already have." He pulled my body close to his.

I felt a rumble in his chest. "What are you laughing about?" I was thankful for my even breaths and relaxed muscles.

"Guess I'll always know where I can find you," he said.

"Under the desk you mean?" We laughed at the outrageous image, and I felt deeply grateful I could tell the difference.

Spring 1992, ranchers are seeding the fields when Curt and I take one of our favorite drives up the Gallatin Canyon and back through Ennis.

He pulls over to the side of the road above the Madison River. We both get out of the car. It's a warm day. Clouds float high and lazy in the blue sky, but there's thunder rolling between the banks below us. The turbulent deluge of late spring runoff cracks and crushes splintered debris as it roars by. A cow moose approaches the bulging banks on the opposite side. Fearlessly, she enters the violent river and begins to forge the heaving liquid mass toward the small green meadow pasture that spreads up from the bank between the river and us. Battered by the current that's forcing the river to swell above her belly and splash over her back, she stands undaunted, then moves steadily onward to the other side, as if using the conflicting forces within the river to gain strength and momentum. My strength is spent just watching the drama, the struggle of beast against the force of nature. Finally she steps up on the bank and sniffs the grass that stretches lush and green, the banquet she risked her life for.

Curt and I don't notice the young calf that waits on the other side of the cauldron until the mother looks at him and signals for him to cross the river. He's willing until his front legs head down river before his back ones have even gotten wet. Pacing back and forth along the river, he keeps his eyes on the mother. The cow paces and waits until her young finally retreats into the protection of a stand of aspen in the distance.

Curt nods and watches the drama in silence.

This is a world I understand. I know the contest of the river. The Madison churns and boils. The river isn't safe, but it makes us strong if we know that we're made to cross it. We live and die in these genesis waters. My struggle to overcome the dark side's language—thoughts, words, behaviors—make me more aware of the current's pull on the cow and timid calf.

In the few appointments we'd had since last December, Dr. D said the more I resisted the dark side, the stronger I'd get. By exposing myself to triggers, such as feelings of abandonment and rejection, I'd get stronger. I made myself watch violence on television, including rapes. I made myself face Vera and Curt's friends and relatives who had listened to her lies about me.

If the emotional pain was beyond bearing sometimes, I tried to catch myself before I headed for the medicine cabinet or lifted my fist to beat my own body. Ninety percent of the time I was successful. The empty page was my battlefield, and I wrote my story of healing to expose the lies as well as to find the truth. God's voice reminded me who I was, who I belonged to, and where I was going: *You're okay*, he'd say when I was hurting. *The wound is bleeding, but you aren't sick.* Other times He'd say, *It's fear. It's a lie.*

A person could be well and still hurt sometimes, I realized. Strong people bear pain. My confidence grew. I was going to the other side of the river. Vision moved me beyond the battering debris. To cross the river without vision makes no more sense than a bird without a song.

Like the cow moose, the struggle makes me strong. Curt, Ryan, Dr. D, and my family and friends are amazed at my progress.

Curt strains to see where the calf has gone. I think our vision keeps him strong when the loss of the kids seems beyond bearing. We've talked about dreams since we met, but the first time we talked about a vision for our lives was on the trip we took to Southern California, for the holidays, a few months ago. Rather than celebrate the New Year without our kids (Ryan was with Gabe, visiting the Gaynors in Northern California), we drove south to see my family. My brother and his wife had invited us to stay with them.

Snow flurries were making it hard to see out of the car windows. I looked at my husband and traced the worry lines under his eyes with my fingers. Bitter winds were piling desert sand around scrawny bushes outside Saint George when he said, "There's a reason for all we're going through. My kids will see the truth someday, although they may be married and raising their own children when it happens. Meanwhile, you and I will continue to heal and get free of the past. I'll become who I want to be. You need to write the story of your healing."

At the moment, the river's boiling and Curt's pacing like the cow moose. My husband paces, then waits and watches the stand of aspen on the other side of the Madison River.

It's been five months since the trip to California. We've grown closer and stronger through the heartache. It's not over, and probably won't be for years. We've driven to Helena regularly to see his kids and watch them play sports. Like calves caught in turbulent waters, they have no way out. Meanwhile, I've had poems accepted for publication. A couple of magazines are looking at my articles. But my only work of fiction waits for revisions, while I write my story to heal.

Curt looks my way. "I can't go back and carry my kids across."

We didn't know until years later that Vera had promised Chad a new truck if he'd leave his dad for a few months. She made other promises to her son, but the only one she kept was to get even with his father. Instead of his son coming home, Curt had to go to court last month. As a late Christmas present, Vera served him papers for more child support.

We walk back to the car. Before Curt opens his door, he looks back at the scene of struggle. "No one survives unless we learn the way to freedom on our own. With freedom comes responsibility." He looks across the river for the calf one more time.

The cow grazes peacefully in the lush meadows as we drive away.

36

Blue Sky

By the summer of 1992, the break I'd been yearning for finally came, bittersweet. When Mom called on the phone one day in early June, I thought it might be Curt's attorney delivering good news about the judge's decision regarding child support. At the April hearing, the judge told Curt he had a lot of money coming to him for paying child support to Vera that he legally hadn't had to pay over the years since the divorce.

"Darling, I have a buyer for the cabin," Mom said.

Uselessly, I tried to ease the ache of not having the cabin to go to by focusing on the woodpecker where it attached itself to the sunny spot on the thick trunk of the tall pine tree out the kitchen window.

"I know, sweetheart. It's hard for me, too." Mom's laugh was gentle with memories. "But we have a buyer. I can't afford to keep it. Could you and Curt get our things out? The closing isn't until August 1."

At least Curt and I had the summer.

"Sure, we'll take care of it, Mom," I said. "Curt's never seen the cabin." Last time I was there, Calli and Ryan were too. I didn't say it. Mom knew. Calli's death had shaken her to the core.

For several weekends in a row, Curt and I stayed at the cabin on Four-Mile Creek. I relived wonderful memories and created new ones with my husband. Finally it was time to say goodbye to the place I called my Montana Eden. The trip this weekend would be our last.

We bumped up seventeen miles of gravel road along the Boulder River toward the cabin, in Betsy, Curt's 1975 Ford pickup truck. I read an article in the *Bozeman Chronicle* about a painter whose exhibit I'd recently seen at The Hole in the Wall Gallery, in Ennis.

"Curt, this article doesn't begin to describe this painter's work."
I quoted excerpts.

"Write one of your own." His confidence in me made me think
I could.

I wanted to. I wanted to tell Rocky Hawkins that his paintings
released colors to laugh and cry on canvas. His vital shades set colors free to be afraid and hide, to walk through the wilderness of
emotions, barefoot in the dark. His primitive figures honored the
Native Americans and redeemed the dignity of their eternal origins. I wanted to tell him thank you because Hawkins' colors exploded with "Now" and whispered secrets that I wondered if even
he was aware of.

"Write to him yourself, DeeAnn. Write the article the way you
want to."

I didn't have anything to lose. Some things needed to be said,
and I didn't count on tomorrow anymore.

Late afternoon sun filtered like bright memories through pine
boughs when Curt and I drove up the long driveway to the cabin,
the tires crushing tall grass and wildflowers. He parked near the
front porch. I jumped out of the truck and ran to the tree swing,
pumping myself high enough to hear Calli's and Ryan's laughter
everywhere around me. How can I give this place up? Curt unlocked
cabin doors, pulled back curtains, and began to unload groceries
and luggage from the truck. He cast glances my way as he worked.
Familiar purple wildflowers that smelled like carnations caught my
eye, and I ran to gather a bouquet for our table, the way Calli and I
had always done.

Curt smiled when he saw the bouquet. "You okay with this?" He
was lighting the kerosene lanterns and oil lamps. Chinked walls
were already shimmering in fire glow.

I nodded. "Look, I found some. I wish I knew what these flowers
are called. They're more fragrant than carnations. How are the lamps
coming?" The last time we'd come to the cabin, Curt had accidentally started a fire on the table. We would be taking it home this
trip, and the burn mark would bring back memories in years to come.

"See for yourself." He had one lamp to go.

I pulled a cotton print tablecloth out of the drawer.

Curt said since we had been coming to the cabin, I was healing and changing. He called me Annie when I played like a child in the river. He laughed when I joined him in the cold outdoor shower and cooled my hot cheeks with his hands when I cooked huge meals on the wood stove.

Immersed in emotions, I shoved the screen door wide open, grabbed a can of pop out of the cooler, and hurried to the swing. I was lost in the forest sounds—the birds, the breeze, and rustling trees—when the back screen door creaked. Curt carried the stereo. A tape of James Taylor was playing. I slowed my swing and anticipated his next move. He set the stereo on the crude bench between the trees, walked toward me, opened his arms, and said, "Let's dance."

Fading sunlight streamed through shadows while we danced under the scarce boughs of lodgepole pine. Twilight pink, coral, and blue reflected off fluffy clouds.

The music stopped, and we automatically turned toward the dirt driveway that was bordered by tall, wispy grass and wild daisies all the way to the rocky road. Curt lay his arm on my shoulder. Mine hung loosely over his opposite hip. We headed down the road to the bridge that crossed Four-Mile Creek where it flowed to the Boulder River.

"Do you see any trout?" I asked him. We both leaned against the thick rough wood railing and looked down into clear water where it flowed over a bed of large rocks.

"No." He reached over with his hand and gently rubbed my cheek, saying no more, not needing to.

Curt rested his elbows on the rail. I don't know how long we looked for trout in the river before he said, "Do you want to cross the bridge or go back to the cabin?"

Either direction we chose held nothing but pleasure for us. I felt a rush of joy, to be able to make such an easy decision. "Let's go back to the cabin now and cross the bridge tomorrow." I wrapped my arm around Curt's neck and nuzzled his warm cheek.

He leaned toward me, then stood, and we took our time walking back to our log cabin in the wilderness. Two deer grazed in a neighbor's yard near a little creek that ran through this property.

The sun had heated river water in the outdoor drum all day, so we stayed awhile in our tepid shower. Wrapped in one of Curt's big shirts, I hurried to our sleeping bags where they were zipped together and spread on the hide-a-bed. We played cribbage and listened to music from the sixties. Oil lamplight danced from walls to ceiling. The flannel interior of our sleeping bags felt good on bare skin later when we sank into them. This is how I dreamed our life together would be when Curt asked me to marry him, not one crisis after another. I wanted to remember every moment. We traveled familiar paths on each other's bodies with hands, fingers, lips. Unfolding arms and legs, murmuring, laughing softly, we made love until stars twinkled through skylights and feelings consumed thoughts. Silent in the language of trust, Curt and I slept while the river rushed by just on the other side of log cabin walls.

The next morning I woke early to birds chirping. Thinking I'd go back to sleep, I snuggled close to Curt. Instead of snuggling with me, he complained about the springs in the hide-a-bed. Before I went outside to take my shower, he shoved the crude wooden chair that was in his way. The water in the outdoor drum was stinging cold from being in the drum all night, but it felt better to me than the mood my husband was in.

I dried off quickly and wrapped my wet hair in a towel, then walked back into the cabin. Curt was making coffee on the blazing stove. He looked ruggedly handsome standing under the skylight—unshaven, wearing cutoffs and his old ragged football jersey—Number 10, I noticed. My husband's imperfections were what I loved about him.

As much as I wanted to wrap my arms around him, I dried my hair at a distance, instead, to give him space. Curt's losses often hit him first thing in the morning. He'd told the truth when we went to court in April, but it didn't set the kids free. Or us. A few days ago we found out that the court sided with Vera, forcing Curt to continue paying her for hurting his kids and turning them against him. The law had locked us all in the stone-cold reality of pain and past mistakes.

He reached out and pulled me into the security of his arms. "Sorry, I'm angry, but I'm dealing with it."

"I know. And your anger is just pain with nowhere to go. Wish I could remember that and not feel rejected." I hugged him hard, pulled his face down to mine and nuzzled his beard.

He laughed and nuzzled back. "You think of more ways to touch than anyone I've ever known."

"That's why we're so good for each other." We laughed. Curt kissed my neck and moved way beyond his anger.

The sound of coffee perking got our attention. In the cupboard, I found two antique mugs I liked and set them on the table. I turned on the stereo and slipped in an old Lionel Richey tape "Stuck On You." And I was: Today I was stuck on Curt, life, and living dreams in log cabins. Alive with good feelings, listening to my own laughter, I heard Annie: *The rest of the world can love me or leave me, but this is who I am. The strong streetwise kid is the best part of all I want to be.*

I was going to write Rocky Hawkins and tell him what I thought of his paintings so he'd know someone had really *seen* them.

———

"You write like I paint—in pictures," Mr. Hawkins said when I met him at his exhibit in Bozeman. A pair of eyes looked right through me from the painting that hung on the wall of the restaurant where the art show was being held. It was early December 1992. He'd called a month before to tell me that he loved the article I'd sent him, and asked if he could use it at his exhibit.

On the walls of the restaurant and standing at easels were paintings some critics called abstract, figurative. To me, they were the dark alleys I'd walked through and the green pastures I'd found refuge in. Most of them only Daughter of Fire would understand. If I'd never walked barefoot with God through the night side where dayside is never seen, the soul of man would still be a mystery to me. Rocky's primitive scenes spoke the language of the soul, and I heard it in colors.

Before Curt and I left the exhibit, the artist asked me if I'd write about his paintings and work on a book with him about his art and life. Holding back a shout of joy, I told him we could start and see how it went. I had a story of healing to finish.

Right in front of the restaurant that lit up the block on Main Street, I jumped into Curt's arms and wrapped my legs around his waist. My long skirt must have looked like it was on him instead of me as we hugged, laughed, and kissed while traffic streamed by, a parade of headlights.

37

When Love Walks Away

"What more could you want?" I said under my breath as Curt slammed the back door one Saturday morning, early October 1993. "I've healed in record time!" I growled, not wanting to draw attention from the neighbors by yelling. He got in the truck and slammed the door, scraping my head with his arm.

Curt put the keys in the ignition. He'd had it. I'd lost control, he said, but he was wrong. I'd lost my temper when he snapped at me this morning. Since I'd finished my story of healing a month before, the only fuse of dynamite left had his ex on the other end. And I'd told him so.

"This is not about me," I yelled. Curt backed down the driveway. "This is not about us!" I shouted as he drove away in his Ford pickup.

I felt empty watching his bumper in the distance. I was already anticipating his homecoming by the time I walked through the back door, into the kitchen. He likes white cake. I took a Betty Crocker mix out of the cupboard. He'll like chicken. Smiling, I pulled frozen parts out of the fridge.

At suppertime I wasn't hungry. Feelings of abandonment worked on my emotions, and I tried to keep in mind what Dr. D had said when I'd called him earlier.

"He's just taking a break from healing," he said. "Just ask Curt if he wants a sandwich when he gets home."

I tried to sleep, but listened for the truck, instead, until late that night.

"Do you want a sandwich?" I asked when he walked in after midnight. The question seemed appropriate. We'd worked hard. We both needed space. It had been two years since Chad had left. Weary of riding the emotional roller coaster in Helena, he and Gina had told us last spring they were moving to Bozeman this fall. Curt's tears fell on my cheek when he hugged me. "They're coming home. They're coming home." But the kids' mother sent them out of state for the summer and scheduled their return right before school started. Either the kids didn't want to risk her reaction or it was too late to make the move. Whatever the reason, Curt was missing everything he'd looked forward to when his children were born. Instead of standing on the sidelines at his son's football practices every day, he continued to drive three hours round trip to Helena for home games, for every sport. We had seldom missed the kids' activities since Chad had left. It broke my heart to see Curt sitting in the bleachers like a stranger while Vera wore her son's number. A sandwich question was fine with me.

"No, thanks." He looked stunned when I didn't ask questions. Relieved, stunned, and sad. Very sad. I had the feeling Curt wasn't back yet, and might not be for some time. His wounds were fresh and bleeding. His war went on and on.

Gentle goes it, I thought the next morning, hugging him before I got out of bed.

What will I do if he walks away for good?

Sitting at the computer later, I wrote from my heart. It was the only language I could count on.

> What remains unshaken in the heart
>> when the earth has parted,
>> the sky's exploded,
>> towers have fallen,
>> and love has walked away?

> What remains when blue joins red in violent upheaval
>> green cries tears of somber hues,
>> and fire sinks into darkness,
>> yielding to black night, not a twinkle in the sky?

> What remains is the mystery of life,
>> the soul of existence,
>> the dawn of knowledge,
>> answers that bleed from the heart.

When riches are peeled from a woman's exterior,
>her Core finally speaks,
>and It says, "Welcome,
>I've been waiting for you for a long time.

"Now that you're naked,
>You can begin to know the friend you've been seeking
>in all the wrong places.
>You can embrace the soul you've hovered near
>but never touched.

"Meet yourself, your link with Eternity,
>the Master's touch on His canvas of life.
>Meet Unshaken.
>She's risen from the ashes
>to smile at you in the mirror of acceptance.
>She says, 'Welcome.' "

The loss I felt when my love walked away was still fresh in my heart a few days later when Curt asked me to come into the living room. He was stretched out on the couch. I sat on the floor next to him and relaxed when he smiled.

"Remember that older couple I told you about, the clients I had before the accident?" he asked.

"Sort of. Why?"

"The way they looked at each other across the table, I could see how much they loved each other and envied them. I wanted to experience a love like that. When you and I met, I knew it was possible for the first time in my life. Remember now?"

I nodded, wanting to cry with relief. "You said when we get old, we'll have two rocking chairs on our porch where we'll sit and talk about all the wonderful memories we've made together."

"I'm still looking forward to that day, DeeAnnie." He pulled me up close and hugged me hard.

I'm back at the computer after my morning walk on the nature trail. Curt's broken tennis racquet is propped on my file cabinet. I can still see him laughing when it cracked in two, nine years ago.

I hear him in the living room now.

Standing at a distance in the doorway, I watch him water the plants.

"I fertilized the geranium; it'll really take off now." He pulls off a few dead leaves.

If I'm standing in our yard looking through the glass, the geranium already takes up half the picture window, which forms the wall of our house. It was less than a foot tall when I bought it at Osco's summer closeout sale, hoping Curt could revive it. My thumb has never been green, but Curt can look at a withered, dead thing and it starts to grow. He looked at me when I was a wound wanting to heal.

Curt's drive to win is focused on cribbage and racquetball now. He says the game of life is measured by endurance. Even though holidays still feel like a wool blanket on bare skin some years, my husband and I cherish the memories we make with our kids, who are all adults now. They're scattered from Montana to New York, but we're a family, and as close as a phone call or e-mail. The message Chad wrote in the book he gave me this past Christmas makes me grateful for the struggle: "DeeAnn, I see in you the strength and courage that is found in these characters. Thank you for that. I love you, Chad."

Sometimes Curt and I have to remind each other that the hard years are behind us; blue sky is here to stay. Sometimes we have to remind each other that we have a date on the porch in thirty years. Yet beneath all the reminders is the unshakable truth: Against all odds, we choose love.

38

Queen of the Night

The sun is setting on the Valley of the Flowers. Days are longer than they were almost five months ago when my journey following Annie's prayer began. Standing in my studio, I'm looking at a new painting, where oils are telling me to let go of what I think I see in order to discover what is.

Two rooms are emerging on canvas, but they're not your usual rooms with four walls, windows, and doors. The floor of one becomes liquid and flows like a waterfall into the other. A figure approaches in the distance through the only door. If the figure is me and the painting is my mind, there's something missing. Hell is missing. Hell on earth.

The two rooms become clearer now. The walls of one room shimmer with color. They reflect the vibrant heavenly realm its floor flows toward. In the other room, or realm, a river of light cascades down a distant canyon, through narrow mountain gulches, and over eternal stones to form pure pools linked by waterfalls, clear to the bottom where the two rooms, which may be heaven and earth, flow together.

It's been seven years ago, but it seems like yesterday that I was visiting with friends over coffee at the Western Cafe. A flower was the link between heaven and earth.

"Wait," I said to my friend's sister, who was visiting from Arizona. Reaching for the photograph she held in her hands, I studied the enormous white flower. It was created to be touched. Velvet petals draped elegantly. Strikingly highlighted with yellow, the bloom could have been mistaken for an ethereal fairy sitting on a stem. I wished that I could inhale its fragrance, sensually know everything about it.

My friends continued to chatter over coffee and rolls as we

crowded in a large booth. But my mind was on majesty where it grew on a thick vine-like cactus plant.

"Please tell me about this flower." The delightful woman who sat next to me was the owner of the photo, the one who had experienced the touch and smell of the radiant floral cloud.

"That is a night blooming cereus, or Queen of the Night. It blooms in the dark." We all looked at the photo for a minute.

"It blooms in the dark?" I was intrigued by nature's ability to use darkness as its stage to bloom, its environment of revelation and beauty. Night temperatures were perfect for bidding delicate petals to unfold, the heavy dew perfect for their velvet skin, whose fiber exuded strength. "I understand." I handed the photograph to my friend.

I had bloomed in the dark.

Most mysteries are best explained by creation itself.

39

Nina

Her body was made of rags, and her hair, yellow yarn. She was small enough to hold in my arms. Rod was my hero, but my rag doll Nina was my best friend while I lived on the farm. She was there when thunder shook the windows and lightning split the sky. Nina was always "my Nina" when I wasn't sure who I was.

"Jesus Loves Me" was a song I learned in Sunday school. The words put to music made me feel special. As a child I knew the meaning of transformation: Love made me want to be good. But I didn't know that love can raise the dead until I was an adult.

Vibrant fall colors had nothing on me in mid-October 1993. On fire with freedom, I was crimson, flaming orange, and sunburst-yellow with joy. An arrow spinning toward her target, there wasn't anything that could distract me from sharing the love I felt. The past was a file in my cabinet that I could find when I wanted to. The present was a Voice that spoke to my heart. The future was what happened when I listened. Yet when I least expected it, a feeling would snatch me from myself, like a kidnapper of souls. Was I like Cinderella? Could I be reduced to rags at midnight if I didn't live the truth I'd found? Thoughts were the drug that could wipe me out.

During the winter semester of 1994, I took an independent study course at the university to keep my teaching credential current. I had hoped to use the time to work on my next book. But Dr. Folsom had other plans for me after he read my story of healing.

The professor was sitting behind his massive oak desk, looking warm and toasty, when I met him at his office. Snowflakes were melting where they fell from my wool coat on the polished hardwood floor. There was respect in his eyes when he stood and reached out to shake my hand. We talked about the frosted windows and long winter ahead for a while, then he picked a thick book from the wall of shelves behind his desk and handed it to me. On the cover was a beautiful woman: dark hair, slim, with angles and curves that made her look like one of Tenny's sculptures.

"This is Anne Sexton. She was a Pulitzer Prize-winning poet who committed suicide in the early seventies." He spoke of her in the same tone I'd heard pastors talk about martyred apostles. I shut off his voice and read his lips. "Mental illness. Addicted to drugs and alcohol."

My heart sank. *I'm not going back there. Don't you understand? Don't you see where I've been and what I've come out of? Had I asked to hear about every poet who deserved to be recognized for the price they paid to stay alive?*

Unaware of my feelings, the professor continued. "I've focused my academic research on Sylvia Plath, a Fulbright scholar who was thirty when she committed suicide in the early sixties. She suffered from depression."

I wanted to skip this conversation. I didn't think I was afraid of anything anymore, but if my mind was going to take a walk, I checked the ground for land mines ahead of time.

Dr. Folsom didn't wait for me to respond before he started rummaging through his files. He didn't say how the women killed themselves. I imagined blood spurting from a pale wrist, an empty bottle of pills, taillights flashing over a dead body. I felt sick to my stomach.

"I have more information on them right here," he said, rummaging.

I wanted to crawl under his desk and hide, wanted to give in to a little madness and giggle. Outside, snow blanketed the trees and colored the world gray. The sky might as well have been exploding with thunder, shattered with lightning; I felt like a little girl again. It wasn't a flashback, just a feeling: I was ready to have some fun. The work to stay strong in my identity would never end. Never. If I didn't know it before, I knew it now.

I took the article and sheet of paper he handed me. "Here is a list of their works. You can choose what you want to read."

Struggling with feelings of defiance, I said, "I'm not going to kill myself." I tried to smile and act like I was in control of my wild emotions. "I've made my choice, but thank you. I'll check these out at the library."

He raised his eyebrows and smiled.

My shoes sank to the ankles in snow, on the way to my car. From a dark corner in my mind, I heard thunder shake the windows and saw lightning split the sky. I needed a rag doll and a song. When had I felt so alone?

At home, later, I studied the image in a photograph. It wasn't Nina, but a work of transformation that made me feel strong inside. Massive as the Rocky Mountains, a man's torso was sculpted out of clay. Rippled with valleys and cut like a jutting cliff, the head lay like a boulder on the shoulder of *The Dying Centaur*. I called it "The Wounded Warrior." The French sculptor Emile-Antoine Bourdelle made suffering noble and gave death dignity. Over a hundred years before, society still believed artists were divinely inspired. How sad that during Ms. Plath's and Ms. Sexton's lives, creativity was linked with mental illness, addictions, and suicide.

Bourdelle's monument reminded me of a quote by another sculptor, a Romanian, whose life, like the French artist, also spanned the turn of the century. I looked for it on the white board that hung on my office wall: "Constantin Brancusi: 'It is not the outward form which is real: it is impossible for anyone to express anything real by imitating surface appearances . . . A man can do anything so long as he enters the Kingdom of heaven.' " His sculpture *Bird In Flight* looks like a flame reaching toward the One whose Breath keeps it alive.

Fortified, I put a tape in the stereo. It wasn't "Jesus Loves Me" but a work of the Bohemian composer of Jewish descent, Gustav Mahler's *Titan*. I listened to what I thought was the tormented composer's eternal struggle for identity, tears running down my cheeks. *Oh, God, please keep the flame burning within me.*

Finally I picked up the book that had Anne Sexton's picture on the cover. Inside I met a woman searching for answers, for meaning to her life and identity. She couldn't get past the corpses, spiritual corpses. They were all around her, she said.

Emotional pain, the scream that never ends.

It was Dr. D's educated opinion that I was infused with evil at an early age. Infused—a hopeless word. But if he meant thunder shook the windows and lightning split the sky, I knew what he was talking about. Nina was made of rags. She couldn't feel the shaking and splitting, but I did.

It could have been me who died. I was thinking to myself and talking to Ms. Sexton at the same time, like she was listening. Sometimes I take long drives in the country to separate from the sleeping crowd.

I imagine taking a trip to Costa Rica with my husband, away from all the problems. Like honeymooners, we would swim and dance and laugh until our sides hurt. Instead, I work on the new book I hoped the professor would let me write for credit. Heading every page is this sentence: "A woman is what she thinks." It isn't the title, but a reminder of the choice I make every day of my life. Not all warriors survive their addiction to the dark side. Some thoughts work like poison.

I wasn't complaining. When I woke up each morning, the Spirit said, *You are my likeness.* I'd look out the window and see the naked trees and blue sky and hear birds chirping in the bushes by the bedroom window. I'd think of how much I loved my husband and our children. I didn't look in the mirror to see His likeness, but in my heart and Creation.

Out of respect for Dr. Folsom, I read poems, scanned books, and reviewed articles about the two brilliant tormented women who became famous reaping a harvest from the cracks in their souls. Ms. Plath gassed herself with a cooking stove. Ms. Sexton parked her car in the garage, closed the door, and left the motor running. Their explosive poetic images blew in a storm that shook me, uprooted me, then planted me in ground I grew from. But writing didn't keep them from committing suicide. Neither did psychotherapy, drugs, and shock treatment (for Ms. Plath). Shrouded in darkness, shards catch light. Were they prophets of their times, or a needless sacrifice, trying to survive in culture torn from its roots, a river cut from its source—the same culture I grew up in?

Some people said America didn't listen to her poets any more and hadn't for a long time. Maybe Dr. D was right, an addiction that is put on you is harder to break than one you choose. Would I have survived if I hadn't heard a voice in the night when I was suffering: *Daughter of Fire, will you follow me through the dark side where the day side is never seen . . . through dark alleys . . . to the grave, and love me just the same?*

More. I love You more, Dear One.

Suffering with purpose and identity made the difference between life and death for me.

Now I understood why Dr. Folsom wanted me to meet the two women. It helped me know myself better, and I was stronger than I thought. The professor wouldn't edit my story, but not because it didn't need revisions and polishing. He said he didn't want to touch my language, like it was sacred. "Those few who walk the dark alleys see things differently than the rest of us," he said. When the book was accepted for publication, an editor could decide the necessary changes.

He was helping me format the manuscript of my finished book so I could begin marketing it when he asked me to meet Josie, a student of his. She was also a writer.

A few days later I met Josie at a local café. There were no tears or self pity when the young woman told me she was gang raped in a pig pen as a teenager. Still a natural beauty, she modeled and went to college after high school. At a Christian college she met an energetic handsome young man who was studying to be a minister. They married and had three children together. He preached on Sundays and beat her the rest of the week until she divorced him several years before, to save her own life. Josie said she was being treated for multiple personality disorder (MPS). She heard voices but thought her memories had frozen where they shattered, and was putting the pieces together, one at a time.

If Josie had multiple personalities, two of them were like Nina and "The Wounded Warrior." Another was like the Queen of the Night, the flower that blooms in the dark. She didn't know that after I left her at the restaurant I drove to the gym, dressed, and went into the racquetball court by myself, where I beat that blue ball against all four walls with my racquet until I didn't have the energy to hit it again. Then I sat down on the floor in the corner and sobbed.

Josie and I lost touch over the summer. But I thought of her a few years later when the head of a major hospital announced over television that MPS was a fad. He apologized to all the victims who had been irreparably damaged by their therapists' diagnoses and treatments.

I imagine the therapists wandering with their patients up one dark alley and down another, calling out names and labels: Anybody home? They probably did the best they could, just like Lars, Gene, Dr. Reed, Dr. D, and the others. A woman has to learn to trust her own thinking, even if she makes mistakes sometimes.

My brave friend Josie said something I haven't forgotten: "If it's freezing outside and the only blanket you have to wrap up in is denial, then wrap up tight." You do what you must to survive.

I listen to the Voice that tells me the truth. I get too spread out, otherwise. As long as I have a rag doll and know "Jesus Loves Me," I'll survive.

40

Filling the Cracks

Not far from my house, there's a huge crack that runs the full block of the sidewalk. A crop of the healing plant chamomile is growing in the dirt between the concrete, the entire distance. There's dirt in the cracks of a broken soul. Some of it is fertile. With water and a tender touch, it will not only flourish, but take over.

The wind must have been blowing my way and dropped seeds in the fertile cracks of my soul in early summer 1995. My friend Kathy invited me out to see the crab apple tree that had been a memorial gift from Calli's trainer, Tammy. I couldn't wait to see and smell the blossoms. Curt and I didn't want to plant that special tree in the small yard of our rental. We tried keeping it in a huge pot for a winter, but when it didn't bloom in the spring, we were afraid it had died. I hadn't seen the rather sick-looking tree for a couple of years.

It wasn't sick now. Remembering the fragrance of my daughter's skin and hair, I smelled each blossom of the small harvest, one by one, until I didn't have an excuse to smell one more.

Kathy was crying. I was crying. And Curt was getting in the car to leave when I promised myself that if I couldn't have the tree at our new rental, I'd paint it on canvas—but I didn't know how to paint.

The next morning I called my friend Tenny. "I have a picture I need to paint. Will you get me started?"

He laughed. "Now why doesn't this surprise me? Of course, I will."

After I painted Calli's tree in oils, I would paint Nina. She was just a rag doll, but she was there when I needed her the most.

At home the setting sun sheds twilight shadows on my painting of two worlds that meet in the imagination. I realize I've never actually painted Calli's tree, yet it seems every time I apply a brush loaded with color to canvas, I'm the one who blossoms. Maybe applying love works the same way in an angry world.

41

Betsy

"Let's take a drive," Curt says. It's one of those warm spells in mid-spring that breaks up the long cold season Montana's known for.

Above the sheer stream of clouds, Montana's rugged Rockies dominate the sapphire-blue horizon around Bozeman. It's a spectacular day, almost six months into the millennium, perfect for taking a drive to Three Forks with my husband, who's let me in on a secret. We're going to look at the shortbox a farmer is going to give him to renovate the '75 Ford pickup he calls Betsy. Now that I know a truck has two parts to the body: a cab and a box—which is either short or long—I've decided I like the short one with a stepside the best.

I want to see this day that will never come again, not with sunlight, but with the light that transforms all it touches. It transforms me. And taking drives in this beautiful country helps me remember. Below the massive mountain bastions, I see family farms and ranches that stretch and roll in pastoral harmony as far as the eye can see, giving the impression that America's agricultural foundation will never be shaken. It seems as though the families will never be separated from the land that has defined them and the country they've fed for over a century. Today my roots in this earth appear to be secure. But then, before the pioneers, the Indians thought they'd never be separated from their sacred roots in the land they loved.

For a moment I want to reclaim my lost innocence and have Curt stop the truck so I can dig my hands into the rich damp soil. But this is not the kind of day night crawlers (those earthworms that are as big as baby snakes) poke through the surface of the soft ground. It's still too cold to take my shoes off and dig my toes into dark brown velvet, watching it crumble like chocolate cake. As I look out the truck window at the tranquil illusion of permanence and security, I can almost smell the fields that will be harvested in a few months. I can almost smell the budding lilac bushes that hedge farmhouses. Their scent alone makes me glad that I live in Montana.

I remember another spring day a few years ago that was not so brilliant as today, but wildly temperamental. Curt navigated Betsy through the coulees on the high plateau above the chalk-white cliffs of Missouri Breaks while the rancher, a potential real estate client, admired the beauty of his land. When Curt stopped the truck, the rancher looked around like it was the first time he had seen his own property. He said ever since he quit law school to work the 15,000–acre family ranch, he'd been too busy to enjoy the scenery. Many ranchers had degrees in engineering, computer science, and other professions they left to be true to their hearts and conscience.

Bone lean and agile, the rancher got out of the truck and hurried toward the knoll, a few feet away, that overlooked the Missouri Breaks. My husband joined him, but I stayed inside with the windows rolled up. While the wind howled outside, I absorbed the wonder of the Breaks and the river that runs below them. In the silence, I heard unearthly chimes and bells ringing. It was as if an angelic symphony played for me.

Ten minutes passed before Curt and the rancher got back in the truck and shut the doors that the wind was trying to blow off.

"Have you ever heard anything unusual when you've come up on this plateau before?" I asked the man who had said he seldom took time to appreciate nature's beauty.

"It sounds like angels, doesn't it?" He had paid more attention to both heaven and earth than he thought. The man had poetry in his blood, after all. "It may be the radio antenna though."

We were sitting in the truck on the mountain while the wind whipped up white caps on the Missouri River down below: Curt, the rancher, and me, all listening to angels.

You don't always know when heaven's right beside you. Like right now. I notice my husband is happier than a kid with a new bike. He's driving his favorite truck, with his special lady sitting next to him. The new tie rod he put on today, to replace the worn-out original, is working great on these winding, gravel country roads.

I try to remember whether a shortbox has room for one of those cute little nooks, a storage compartment. Where could Curt put it on this sweet old Ford he named in memory of the cocker spaniel he lost as a boy? My husband is absolutely content with his vision of Betsy all fixed up. It's as if he's already completed the job. Maybe better.

42

When the Train Whistle Blows

Imagine your favorite place to ponder and you'll know how the hill that overlooks the nature trail feels to me. Benches are scattered along the dirt path that extends from one end of the ridge to the other. I'm heading for the bench on the knoll with an uninterrupted view of the entire valley and all the ranges it leads to. Today the distant Spanish Peaks and Tobacco Root ranges look like shadows hanging in mid-air. Wildflowers are abundant for mid-June.

Look Calli, they're everywhere. We're never more than a thought away.

A bumblebee zips from one flower to another.

Do you remember how Ryan used to catch them with his fingers and put them in a jar when he was little?

The bench is vacant, so I sit in the middle. Out of habit I slip off my sandals, put my feet on the varnished wood, and wrap my arms around my legs and hug them close to my body.

Below me a sea of green—pine green, aspen green, cottonwood—is broken by a red roof here and there. Apple blossoms, chokecherry blossoms and varieties of flowering bushes I don't recognize look like bubbles in the sea's current from here. At a distance, Bozeman looks like the sea below the little village that sits on the plateau in my painting.

Questions I asked months ago at the beginning of this book come back to me: "What if I paint this mysterious place in words . . . . If I listen to my heart, will I find Paradise on this angry earth where man has learned how to lie, has come to love it . . . ?

The Valley of Flowers could be Paradise in oils. But it could also be a spiritual Wilderness. Like words of a song, endearing phrases that the Spirit spoke to the prophet Hosea come to me, "I will allure her, bring her into the wilderness, speak tenderly to her . . . . And make the [valley of bitterness] a door of hope . . . she will sing there, as in the days of her youth."

Your love overwhelms me, Father. You have made the valley of bitterness a door of hope for me. What is Paradise but Your presence in the wilderness.

I have so many memories buried in the green sea of trees and fields below. It's good to let them go with the current now—Stone Harmon and all the rest. I don't want harm to come to any of those who have taught me hard lessons. Mom used to say that if I would just listen to her, I wouldn't have to learn the hard way. Yet I don't feel guilty for the path I've taken, like I did as an angry teenager looking back at a shorter path. A woman's identity isn't worth much if it comes without a struggle.

Tonight this valley will be a black sea, and the lights in houses and town will be moonshine on the water. If I live in the present, new truths change me and how I look at life. One painting or one book is not enough to tap the truths I hunger to learn.

This afternoon the small lake I've already gone swimming in this summer looks like glass beneath the Bridger Mountains. Distance is like Spirit: it gives a different perspective than looking at something up close.

Behind me lies the past. I can't see the renovated farmhouse Gabe, the kids, and I lived in, but I can see the hill it's snuggled up to. I can't see the dream we built in the mountains, but I see the gulch that leads to it. Beneath Frog Rock is the last home we built together. Above Story Hills, the beacon looks like a lightning rod buried in a dense cloud. It's in view from two of our homes, symbolizing that I was never alone in the dark, never without a Guide to safety.

The past gives meaning to my life. I hope it gives meaning to my son and his bride-to-be in the album I'm making for their wedding, which is a couple of weeks away. With the help of Curt and the other parents, I made them a photograph album of their lives, starting the day each was born. I can't promise them heaven on earth. That promise is not mine to give. The album is a legacy of love Ryan and Jennifer can look at, and perhaps show their children someday.

A train whistle blows in the distance, and I feel a pull I can't explain. It blows again. Not so loudly now, it blows. And again. It's the whistle of a freight train; that's all. I close my eyes and feel it pulling me toward the unknown, the wonderful and terrifying unknown. I want to cry.

Is it calling me home? Is it weeping for me? The whistle blows far away now. Sometimes God seems far away, like the whistle of the train. Yet when the shaking comes—and it always comes—faith is all I have to hold on to.

There's a cloud in the sky that's a thin veil compared to all the puffy ones. All my understanding is like that cloud when the shaking comes. I'm out there in the vast blue sky, the laws of gravity working against me. But there is another law working in me: Spirit. I know who I am now. Faith is my wings. I can hang suspended on a Word for as long as I need to—if only I wouldn't look down.

The cool breeze caresses my skin and massages my heart and mind.

Be still.

The valley of green below conceals secrets I want to know, but His Spirit says, *Be still; know that I Am.*

A tiny bird flies from brush to sky. Within me is a place called Unknown, and it feels safe. God is here, like a warm blanket on a cold night. An ocean of gratitude spills from my heart. *Thank you. Thank you. Thank you.*

Acknowledgments

There are people I want to thank for helping me get this book into print. Kenneth and Talita Paolini, veteran book producers, led me through the complex process of publishing. From the first three-hour phone call, months before I became their client, Kenneth made my book a personal matter. He and Talita shared their expertise generously from beginning to end (contact information on page two).

I appreciate Jeanie Olson's contribution. Linda Grosskopf did me a favor and gave her best when she didn't have to. S.W. offered a gem of advice that made a difference. Dennis Schweitzer shared valuable insights about the manuscript and generously shared his heavenly "cabin" in the wilderness. The great staff at the Western Cafe let me pick any table as my office away from home over the years.

A special thanks to my best friend, my husband Curt, for going the distance and telling me what I wanted to hear when I needed to hear it.

Western Cafe

In this book, the names of several people have been changed to protect their privacy; however, you'll find the Western Cafe is exactly where I said it is, just off the corner of Church and Main in Bozeman, Montana. Photo by Curt Brandon.

Author's Note

Thank you for reading my story. I welcome your comments and hope you will share this book with friends and loved ones. And I invite you to visit my website at www.wordsonwings.net, where you can stay in touch and share your own story of healing.

If you feel this book has been of value to you, please take a few moments to post a review online at Amazon.com or Barnes & Noble (bn.com). Your help spreading the word is appreciated.

Currently I am working on the sequel to my story, *Riding Wild Horses, No Hands*. I also do book signings and presentations at stores and for organizations. Please contact me for details.

May your spirit soar on wings of courage.

DeeAnn Brandon
P.O. Box 1604
Bozeman, MT 59771
E-mail: dab@wordsonwings.net

Order Form

- **Fax orders:** (734) 633-6839
- **Telephone orders:** (406) 586-3808
- **Online orders:** www.wordsonwings.net,
  E-mail: dab@wordsonwings.net
- **Postal orders:** Words on Wings, P.O. Box 1604, Bozeman, Montana, 59771, U.S.A.

✣ *The Bird with a Broken Wing:* $15.95

Name:_____

Address: _____

City: _____

State or Province: _____

Zip or Postal Code_____ Country: _____

Phone: _____

Payment:
Check or Money Order enclosed ____
Make your check or money order payable to Words on Wings, Ltd.

Credit Card:
Visa ____ MasterCard ____ Discover ____ American Express ____
Card Number: _____
Expiration Date: _____
Name on the Card: _____
Signature: _____

US Shipping:
Price includes US Postal Service Media Mail shipping.

International, US Territories, APO, FPO orders, and Shipping:
International orders must be paid by credit card, International Bank Draft, or Postal Money Order. International Bank Drafts or Postal Money Orders must be in US dollars. International Bank Drafts must be drawn on a bank with an office in the US. Contact us for shipping rates, or indicate here your authorization to process your credit card order and ship by Airmail now. ☐

Printed in the United States
6189